LACAN

MALCOLM BOWIE is Professor of French in
the University of London and Director of
the Institute of Romance Studies. Born in
Aldeburgh in 1943, he took his MA degree
at the University of Edinburgh and his
D.Phil. at the University of Sussex. From
1969 until 1976 he was lecturer in the
University of Cambridge and a Fellow,
Tutor, and Director of Studies at Clare
College, and then Head of the Department
of French at Queen Mary College, London.
He has been a Visiting Professor at the
University of California, Berkeley and
Visiting Distinguished Professor at the
CUNY Graduate Center in New York. In
addition to his numerous guest lectures at
universities in Britain and abroad, he has
addressed analytic audiences – including
the British Psycho-Analytical Society and
the Tavistock Clinic – on matters
discussed in this book. He has been
general editor of *French Studies*, and is the
founding editor of the monograph series
Cambridge Studies in French. His
publications include *Henri Michaux: a
Study of his Literary Works* (Clarendon
Press, 1973), *Mallarmé and the Art of
Being Difficult* (CUP, 1978), *Freud, Proust
and Lacan: Theory as Fiction* (CUP, 1987)
and *Psychoanalysis and the Future of
Theory* (Blackwell, 1991).

Modern Masters

Lacan

Malcolm Bowie

FontanaPress
An Imprint of HarperCollins*Publishers*

First published in Great Britain in 1991 by Fontana Press,
an imprint of the HarperCollins Publishers
77–85 Fulham Palace Road,
Hammersmith, London W6 8JB

9 8 7 6 5 4 3 2

BRITISH LIBRARY CATALOGUING IN
PUBLICATION DATA

Bowie, Malcolm
Lacan, – (Fontana Modern Masters)
1. Psychoanalysis. Lacan, Jacques, 1901–81
I. Title
150.1952092

ISBN 0 00 686076 1

Printed and bound in Great Britain by
HarperCollins Manufacturing, Glasgow

Contents

Acknowledgements

My warm thanks go to all those friends, university colleagues, psychoanalysts and graduate students who have educated, advised, corrected, encouraged and cajoled me during the writing of this work. Although it does not seem appropriate to place a long list of acknowledgements at the start of a short book, my individual debts are numerous and each of them is keenly felt. I am especially grateful to the staff and students of the CUNY Graduate Center in New York for the hospitality and stimulus they provided during the final stages of composition, and to Alison Finch, Philip Gwyn Jones, Frank Kermode, Dinora Pines, Stuart Proffitt and Lindsay Waters, who by many acts of kindness smoothed my lengthy passage from rough draft to printed volume.

1 Freud and Lacan

'It is precisely because desire is articulated that it is not articulable' (804; 302).[1] Lacan is a theorist of the human passions who maintains a steady hostility to the language of 'theory'. Desire is the subject-matter of psychoanalysis, but something is always left out when the analyst writes about it. A shadow has fallen across his page and will not go away. However hard he tries to 'articulate desire' – by constructing a theory of it, say – desire will always spill out from his sentences, diagrams or equations. But theories should not be silent on that which eludes them, Lacan insists.

What follows is an outline of Lacan's theory, but it is also an account of his elaborate quarrel with conventional theoretical writing. In order to perform this double operation intelligibly within the confines of a short book, I shall be obliged to leave a number of major topics out. One omission causes me particular sadness. This is the 'Lacan legend'. Lacan's relationship with Freud will be prominent in the following pages, but his relationship with the general public and with his professional associates will figure scarcely at all. This is a matter for regret because Lacan is a writer about whom stories are told, and these could provide the basis for a fascinating case-study of the power that rumour and folklore still possess in an 'advanced' electronic culture. Before I turn to my main business, I shall, however, say a few words about one feature of the legend, for this may serve as a useful pointer if not to the content of his theory

1

then at least to a characteristic indecision that is visible within it. Where the scandal of Freud's doctrine as first formulated by him in the early years of the present century found, and can still find, expression in such questions as 'how can he, how dare he, mean *that* (about the structure of the mind, about sexuality, about family life)?', the scandal of Lacan is well caught by the questions 'what does he mean?' or 'how, writing like that, can he *mean* at all?' Where Freud's detractors often think of him as intelligible but wrong, Lacan's often think of Lacan as unintelligible and for that reason worse than wrong – dangerous and perverse.

Much of Lacan's writing is indeed exceptionally difficult at first reading and may remain so during later readings even for those who are well equipped to negotiate the polysemous textures of much modern imaginative litera-ture. And Lacan often writes about this feature of his reputation in a tone of defiant self-congratulation. Introduc-ing the relatively accessible spoken manner of his paper 'The agency of the letter in the unconscious or reason since Freud' (1957), for example, he warns his reader of what not to expect:

> Writing is distinguished indeed by a prevalence of the *text*, in the sense that this factor of discourse will assume here – a factor that makes possible the kind of tightening up that I like in order to leave the reader no other way out than the way in, which I prefer to be difficult. In that sense, then, this will not be writing. (493; 146)

The difficult writing which seeks to be at once an emanci-patory 'way out' from the structure of the unconscious and a constricted 'way in' to that same structure is exceptional within the psychoanalytic tradition. Many other analysts have of course written unclearly, and a few – D.W. Winnicott, for instance, or W.R. Bion – have had recourse to an adventurous poetic diction at moments when the plain international style of psychoanalysis seemed unable to handle their insights and self-questionings. But Lacan is quite alone in placing a continuous positive valuation upon ambiguity, and in suggesting that students of the unconscious mind, when they become writers, are somehow morally obliged to be difficult.

One element of Lacan's writing, however, is notably absent both from his characterization of himself as an impenitent and embattled baroque stylist, and from the indignant talk to which the dense verbal texture of his *Ecrits* has given rise. This is his capacity to be memorably simple. Lacan may hold that writing originating in and concerning itself with the unconscious cannot be other than heterogeneous and plural, but the writing that is called upon to enforce this doctrine often breaks the doctrinal rule:

The unconscious is structured like a language.
The unconscious is the discourse of the Other.
A letter always arrives at its destination.
The most corrupting of comforts is intellectual comfort.
There is no such thing as a sexual relationship.

Sentences like these have been used as publicity slogans for Lacan's works and as passwords among Lacanian initiates, and in neither role are they being seriously betrayed. They will make their fullest sense, of course, only when read or spoken in the context of Lacan's elaborately self-aware theory as a whole. But even when removed from this context they retain a special sort of efficacy: they are glimpses of what a fully intelligible and transmissible psychoanalytic theory might be like, and their being passed readily from hand to hand in literate human society is a rehearsal for the moment when a fully-fledged logic of intersubjective communication might become possible. When psychoanalysis has achieved this status, no refinements or opacities of literary style – indeed no style at all – will be required by it in the performance of its theoretical tasks. It will have become, in Freud's words, 'an impartial instrument, like the infinitesimal calculus' (XXI, 36).[2]

The construction of sample axioms for such a future logic goes on continuously in Lacan's works in a rough-hewn, semi-conversational way, but it goes on in much more studious and formal ways too. Lacan's fascination with model-building devices borrowed from mathematics and symbolic logic is often thought of as a sign of amateurism. This is exactly how, it is suggested, an intellectual over-reacher might be expected to disguise his dubious credentials. Yet judgements of this kind seem to me to miss the entire atmosphere of Lacan's theoretical project. For Lacan dreams, on the one hand, of merely possible psychologies in a language of overflowing semantic multiplicity and, on the other, of *one* psychology, the only one that would be right, in a language that aspires to simplicity and self-evidence.

The writing and publishing careers of Freud and Lacan overlapped for a dozen years from the late twenties onwards, and in 1938 reached an extraordinary moment of convergence. In this year Freud wrote his last book, *An Outline of Psycho-Analysis*, which was at once an epilogue to his theoretical work and a dogmatic restatement of the views to which he still adhered (XXIII, 144–207). Lacan, in the same year, published a long encyclopaedia article on 'The Family' (now reprinted as *Family Complexes in the Formation of the Individual*),[3] which not only restated a number of fundamental psychoanalytic tenets in their classical Freudian form but provided an elaborate preliminary sketch of the themes that were to preoccupy him for decades to come. Freud in his leave-taking and Lacan in his call to arms, while placing a common emphasis on the family as the essential force-field, arena and laboratory in which the structure of the human mind is created, disagree in the plainest fashion on what the theoretical articulation of mental structure involves.

Freud's book is still haunted by biology. Biology was important to him not simply because it reminded students of the psychical apparatus that such 'apparatus' was more than contingently related to the world of organisms, but because it provided a lesson in strictness, and a persuasive model of scientific rationality, for those who sought to bring mental states, acts and dispositions within the purview of science. However independent from the biological sciences psychoanalysis was to become in its theoretical and clinical procedures, it could not be allowed to forget that an eventual unified science of humanity would encompass both disciplines in active partnership. From the first paragraphs of Lacan's work, on the other hand, a strong anti-biological note is sounded. Biology not only provides unreliable models for the mental scientist but invites him to misperceive the very objects of his enquiry. If his intention is to explore that which is distinctively human in the human mind, he will attend to cultural rather than to 'natural' determining forces; he will consider complexes rather than instincts,[4] structures rather than appetites, and will have the anthropologist and the sociologist rather than the biologist among his closest co-workers.

The first of the 'family complexes' to be considered by Lacan in this work is the 'weaning complex', and this is given a logical as well as a temporal priority in his account of the developing human individual: 'weaning leaves in the human psyche a permanent trace of the biological relationship that it interrupts. This life crisis is indeed reduplicated in a crisis of the psyche – the first, no doubt, whose solution has a dialectical structure' *(Family Complexes*, 27). For

5

Freud, this interruption of the creaturely relationship between mother and child was similarly momentous: 'however long it is fed at its mother's breast, it will always be left with a conviction after it has been weaned that its feeding was too short and too little' (XXIII, 189). Weaning gave a backward drift, a helpless retrospective tenor, to all passion. Lacan, however, dramatizes the moment quite differently: the acceptance or rejection of weaning gives the nascent human mind its first serious piece of prospective work to do and launches it upon an unceasing internal dialectic. Passing from the biological to the mental sphere marks a definitive break within the life of the individual and is reversible only in phantasy. The later complexes that Lacan isolates for discussion – the 'intrusion'[5] and Oedipus complexes – can only make the situation worse. They bar the individual's return route to the lost world of his nursling self and turn him into a mental site where ambivalences and conflicting passions endlessly play themselves out.

Lacan acknowledges as readily as Freud that retrospective longings and phantasized returns to Eden cannot simply be uprooted from the human mind, but he expects the psychoanalyst, when acting in a professional capacity, to resist their subtly varying pull. Biologizing explanations of the mind are themselves the products of such phantasy: they postulate a primal oneness that it is somehow possible and desirable to restore or to emulate. Such explanations are to be resisted as soon as they arise. Lacan's vigorous 'culturalist' polemic in this short early work was to be amplified and diversified throughout his later career. For not only was it necessary for theorists of the human mind to be weaned from their infantile habits of explanation, but elaborate precautions had to be taken to prevent them from relapsing into dependence.

A complete pattern of dissenting assent to the ideas of Freud is already visible in *Family Complexes*. Freud was right but not right enough, or not right in quite the right way. Lacan's argument is conducted on Freud's behalf and, at the same time, against him. It is all the more surprising to find Lacan writing in this confident vein when we notice just how insecurely based his account of culture is at this stage. In later years two notions that appear in subordinate roles in this work – 'language' and 'the unconscious' – were to be essential to his thinking, and to provide his discussion of cultural topics with firm anchorage in the realm of human behaviour and speech. But in 1938, Lacan's 'culture', his 'human order', were susceptible to 'infinite variations' (*Family Complexes*, 23) without having a fully specified medium in which those variations could be observed. Language and the unconscious were eventually to supply that medium and in Lacan's continuing campaign constant reference was to be made to their interaction. Indeed in certain of his later formulations, the unconscious, and language which its structure resembled, *were* the human order – the whole of it.

Already in *Family Complexes*, Lacan is a disciple who races ahead of his master, and an independent-minded thinker who makes large claims before he is able to support them. But his loyalty to Freud is intense, and the originality he seeks is that of an inspired and devoted reader, one who can think fruitfully only from inside someone else's text. In the chapters that follow, I shall be examining a series of psychoanalytic topics in roughly the order of their first appearance in Lacan's writings. And at each stage, I shall refer to the Freudian texts from which Lacan takes his cue, and sketch certain sections of the continuous dialogue with Freud that underlies even the most idiosyncratic and self-opinionated of Lacan's theoretical statements. My reason for doing this is a practical one: readers who have little or no knowledge of Freud will find much of Lacan's work unintelligible. But before I embark on the detailed examination of this singularly complex relationship, I shall set down a few general guidelines. For although the successive phases of Lacan's career each bring different Freud texts to the centre of the stage, certain points of agreement and disagreement between the two writers recur often enough to be worth glancing at in advance.

I shall begin this brief survey by considering a little-known paper by Freud entitled 'On Transience', which was written and published during the First World War as part of a collective volume celebrating Goethe. Freud's essay contains an anecdote and a fragment of theoretical conjecture. The anecdote tells how Freud, walking in the countryside before the war with a friend and a young poet, found the poet unable to share his own rapture at the beauty of the scene: 'he was disturbed by the thought that all this beauty was fated to extinction ... All that he would otherwise have loved and admired seemed to him to be shorn of its worth by the transience which was its doom' (XIV, 305). There are two unsatisfactory responses to the fugitive spectacle of nature, Freud claims: to become despondent in the manner of his young companion, or to persuade oneself that fragile-seeming beauty is, in some dimly intuited alternative dimension, imperishable. A third response, greatly to be preferred to either of these, is then offered. The evanescence of the beautiful object, Freud suggests, does not reduce and may enhance its charm: 'a flower that blossoms only for a single night does not seem to us on that account less lovely' (XIV, 306). Those who are made despondent by the spectacle of the plant are anticipating its death and casting themselves prematurely into a state of mourning. The fragment of theory that Freud appends to this tale is based upon the essay 'Mourning and Melancholia' (XIV, 243–58), which he had just completed but was not to publish for another two years: when a desired person or object dies or disappears, the libido that had been attached to the object is rediverted to the ego. And for reasons that neither essay goes far towards explaining, this process of reabsorption is a painful one. The ego resists this return flow of libido and seeks helplessly to maintain its former attachments.

What is characteristic of Freud in this account, and not at all to be echoed by Lacan, is the clarity, wholeness and structural integrity that he attributes to the object in the moments before its decay begins. 'On Transience' contains one of those visions of universal cataclysm to which Freud, like Leonardo whom he so much admired, was periodically drawn. But before he presses ahead in imagination to the worst, to the ending of the days, the objects of the world are perfectly still and available for inspection. For Freud, as for Leonardo, the individual bloom could be described both in the multitude of its separable parts and in its power of cohesion; described in either way, it bore no prophetic sign of its imminent passing. There it was – complete, self-contained, in equilibrium, a stronghold against disaster. And for Freud those *mental* objects that comprise the subject-matter of psychoanalysis were the more useful as explanatory tools the more they resembled simple whole things from the physical world. Theories themselves, in so far as they sought to explain the causal structure of mental processes, were expected to possess separable parts and cohesive power in the manner of material objects: theories were of course acknowledged as transient conventions, powerless to resist the catastrophic upheavals of nature, but, for the brief spell in which they held together and worked, they were splendid timeless fixities. Indeed they were useful in psychoanalytic practice only in so far as they represented a stable supra-individual causality in the light of which individual passions, drives and appetites could be understood.

Lacan's style of theorizing can be seen as an attempt to

write transience back into the psychoanalytic account of the human mind. The world of sense-perception, in which the one-night bloom achieves its loveliness, is for Lacan a world of illusion; it is the realm of the Imaginary,[6] in which the human being seeks to provide himself or herself with consolation by identifying with chosen fragments of the world, by finding an imagined wholeness of the ego reflected in the seeming wholeness of the perceived thing. For Lacan there is no point in daydreaming of a future cataclysm, in reminding the physical object or the psychological theory of its coming disintegration, for the disastrous separation of desire from its objects has already occurred. Such is the price that human beings unwittingly pay for their admission to language and to culture. All productions of the human mind are already marked with their death's head: fading, failing, falling short, falling apart, lapsing and expiring are their native domain. A wish can be fulfilled; desire cannot: it is insatiable, and its objects are perpetually in flight. Lacan addresses the human sciences at large when he says all this. How wrong we have all been until now, and how deluded; what a lesson we all need on the vanity of our wholeness-talk, our selfhood-talk and our integrity-talk. How mortifying is the spectacle of human desire . . .

When we move from the metaphysical atmosphere of psychoanalytic theory to its conceptual content, the comparison between Freud and Lacan becomes much less straightforward. The new Freud scholarship often depicts the founder of psychoanalysis as a theorist in whose writing the larger intellectual tensions of his age found dramatic expression. Freud is at once the creator of bio-energetic models of the human mind and a student of human discourse: he attempts to characterize the mind as a wordless interplay of pressures and intensities and, concurrently, to understand the hidden meanings of each patient's speech. In an uncertain middle-region between hydraulics and semantics, psychoanalysis begins to find its voice. Even when Freud simply studies discourse, he may be seen moving in two directions: he is both a comparative philologist in the grand Victorian manner and a proto-structuralist linguistician. And when he seeks to position his new discipline in the wider field of the humanities, a further uncertainty is revealed. On the one hand, psychoanalysis must be attentive to the liberal arts at large, for without doing so it will be unable to pick up the cultural resonances of an individual patient's speech and will lose therapeutic opportunities in the process. On the other hand, knowledge of the unconscious has made psychoanalysis into an interpretative art *sui generis* and, in order that it shall remain so, its theoretical and practical procedures must be protected. The combined listening and speaking that psychoanalytic therapy always is cannot, for Freud, be 'cultural studies' pure and simple.

Looking at Lacan's contribution in a simplifying preliminary way, one could say that he is more certain than Freud both about the subject-matter of their science and about its position among neighbouring intellectual disciplines. For Lacan, psychoanalysis concerns itself above all else with the understanding of human speech, and linguistics, rhetoric and poetics are its indispensable allies. Where Freud hesitates between the natural and the human sciences, Lacan does not. He dislikes the phrase 'human sciences' and proposes 'conjectural sciences' as a more accurate description,[7] but it is to those disciplines, however they are named, that psychoanalysis must begin looking if it is eventually to find its conceptual coherence. Linguistics seemed to Lacan in the 1950s particularly well equipped to organize and control the observational materials that psychoanalysis had amassed, and at other times he followed different technical paths towards the same goal. But this is not the whole story. For even while Lacan sets about freeing Freudian thinking from some of the major uncertainties that haunted Freud himself, a new uncertainty begins to invade his own work.

What Lacan confronts as a theorist is an oceanic surge of cultural products, born of language and borne along in language, and what he then seeks is a logic with which that indefinite flow might eventually be arrested. In the meantime, his theoretical pronouncements are pulled in two directions at once: towards the promised logic, and back into the signifying welter of human speech, towards the formal language of mathematics and back into the unstoppable flim-flam of the desiring unconscious. For Lacan, psychoanalysis cannot be other than 'cultural studies', but in accepting that designation on its behalf he creates a problem. If he has the uncircumscribed provinces of 'speech' and 'culture' as his field of enquiry, how can he ever know when and where to stop theorizing?

Lacan came to the view, in the early fifties, that his own theoretical language had to sound like the unconscious of which it spoke, or at the very least to bear a prominent trace of the uncanny company that his clinical practice obliged him to keep. Like any other form of discourse, 'theory' for Lacan is a chain, a skein, a stave, a weave of interconnected meaning-producing elements; it is born by hybridization; it inhabits time; it is perpetually in process. Wit, irony and ambiguity are immanent in it. The analyst who tries to jump clear of his own language as he uses it – or tries to build within that language a permanent conceptual home – is a charlatan or a fool. And Lacan's attempts to teach by example in this area, to be the knowing non-fool among psychoanalytic theorists, make his whole project seem remote from the Freudian ideas to which he repeatedly declares himself loyal. Among the many notable differences between the two writers as writers none is more extraordinary than this: that where Freud cultivates clarity in the presentation of his ideas, Lacan cultivates obscurity. But where Freud employs an elaborate rhetoric of self-doubt in order not to seem too clear too quickly, Lacan, who runs the risk of not seeming clear at all, often contrives to suggest that a supreme obviousness is at work beneath the busy textures of his writing. If these truths are worth knowing, he seems often to be saying, they must in some sense already be known; and if I am to be their spokesman, I must find ways of making them sound ordinary as well as recondite. In the traditional manner of an oracle, his confusing speech is offered as plain speech for those who know how to listen.

A further feature of Lacan's rhetoric may be mentioned here, for it will be of help to anyone who wants to follow the development of his ideas over several decades. I have in mind his very un-Freudian liking for hyperbole, and his search for the extreme form of his own ideas. Let us look briefly at some examples. The 'name of the father', when first introduced in the early fifties, was an emblem of human speech and desire as law-bound: the father's name was that which had to be invoked in order to maintain the incest taboo and which sent forbidden desires, in disguise, on their circuitous journeys through language.[8] But by the mid-sixties the notion had become far prouder: it was now the 'Name-of-the-Father', an imperious metaphysical force that could no longer be described simply in terms of family, society and sexual conduct and that was not so much an observable feature of speech as the origin and ubiquitous condition of human language. In the same way the unconscious, from being pictured as a mental region or territory that *had* structure, in the later thinking *was* structure, boundless and quite unpicturable in topographical terms; and *la langue*, from being the underlying system of a language considered independently of all individual acts of speech became *lalangue* – the complex, interfused and unmasterable sum of all possible language effects. But if the history of Lacan's major concepts is reconstructed simply as a series of gradual or sudden shifts in scale, as the exposure of what were originally fairly modest notions to a process of hyperbolic amplification, a major dimension of that history is likely to be lost. And if Lacan's search for extremity takes him far away from Freud's characteristic style of theory-making, the other dimension to which I refer brings him very close to Freud again.

Lacan's theory recapitulates and restructures itself as it develops over time. For Freud, as we shall see, mental causality seemed to have one peculiarity that set it apart from the rest of nature: in the mind, the present could alter the past.[9] A later event could release new memories of an earlier event; a new desire or intention could cause the mind to rewrite its own prehistory; and the dispositions of the individual upon reaching a new configuration – during therapy, say – could entirely transform the individual's sense of the life he had previously led. Retroactive causality of this kind, which Lacan was the first commentator to draw attention to as a distinctively Freudian theme, may be seen at work in the building of his own theory. Few of his early concepts or *aperçus* are merely discarded as bolder and more encompassing ones appear: they are retained, and transformed by the new theoretical work they are called upon to perform. Although self-consistency is not a virtue that Lacan particularly prizes, he is so skilled in the reinte-gration of early views into late that his writings can easily seem all of a piece, a progressive revelation that has the force of a single creative event. Freud himself was proficient in the same way, and a common feature of his many essays in intellectual autobiography is their suggestion that the present state of a theory is no more than the definitive ordering of its past states and that there have been corre-spondingly few errors, blind alleys or volte-faces on the way. In both writers this integrative action of the theoretical imagination performs remarkable feats. Freud's second model of the mental apparatus – comprising id, ego and superego – is almost able to subsume the first, seemingly quite separate, model in which the preconscious-conscious and the unconscious were two opposing systems, each with a logic of its own. Lacan's theory of the unconscious as a signifying chain is presented as the necessary outgrowth of an earlier phase of his thinking in which the unconscious had scarcely existed.[10]

What I have said so far about the rhetoric of Lacan's theoretical works and about their general conceptual style might suggest that he has taken psychoanalysis into a thin upper atmosphere where, beyond the terrestrial riches of human culture and beyond the lives of real people, minds model minds and theories reflect upon theories. This impression is a wrong one, although it is certainly the case that Lacan addresses himself less often and less directly than Freud did to the fabric of daily experience. In Freud the central corpus of observable and linguistically manipulable *stuff* upon which psychoanalysis works is an agglomerate of dreams, fantasies, bungled actions, neurotic symptoms and behavioural oddities of all kinds: under the scrutiny of his theory such lowly, earth-bound material could be revealed as the bearer of complex meanings. Moreover, for Freud, the human being even as he or she dreamed or theorized was still unmistakably a bag of guts, with motor devices and pleasure-pursuing organs attached. Lacan, while not seeking to compete with Freud on these terms, has his own powerful view of terrestrial humankind. In his account, which insists upon speech at every turn, the essential day-to-day facts about human beings are these: they address each other and affect each other by what they say; they say what they mean and what they don't mean simultaneously; whatever they get they always want more, or something different; and at any one moment they are consciously aware of only some of what they want. Psychoanalysis is thus a science of common things – of speech as the vehicle for desire, of the connections between those desires that are directly speakable and those that are not, and of the reciprocal pressures that speakers exert on each other.[11] Far from being a cult of 'theory', Lacan would claim, psychoanalysis studies that which is most distinctively human in human beings, which is the constitution of the speaking subject in relation to others: 'If one has to define the moment at which man becomes human, we can say that it is the moment when, however little it be, he enters into the symbolic relation' (I, 178; 155).[12]

These, then, are some of the recurrent differences and similarities between Lacan's approach to mental science and Freud's. But Lacan's career as a reader and reinventor of Freud lasted for fifty years, and was uncommonly full of incident. I have divided that career into five main phases, and to the first of these I shall now turn.

2 Inventing the 'I'

At three forty on the afternoon of 3 August 1936, Lacan began to deliver his paper on 'The Looking-Glass Phase' to the fourteenth International Psychoanalytical Congress, which was being held in Marienbad. The bibliographical guide placed at the end of the first edition of *Ecrits* piously records the details of time and date and in so doing suggests that the paper was an event of unusual historical significance.[1] In certain respects its significance cannot be doubted. For on this occasion Lacan made his formal entry into the psychoanalytic movement, propounding a notion of human selfhood that was to be discussed in professional circles for many years to come and that was, in a variety of new and inflected forms, to remain active in his own thinking for the rest of his career. But if too much emphasis is placed on this inaugural moment the characteristic complexity of Lacan's early psychoanalytic writings is likely to be lost. The papers of 1936–49 show Lacan engaged in numerous intellectual debates and subject to a variety of fertilizing influences.[2] And they show him as the precocious creator of a complete metaphysical system, much of which he was later to discard.

The papers in which Lacan's new picture of ego formation is drawn are: 'Beyond the "reality principle"' (1936), *Family Complexes in the Formation of the Individual* (1938), 'Remarks on psychical causality' (1946), 'Aggressivity in psychoanalysis' (1948) and 'The mirror stage as formative of the function of the I' (1949). In these works Lacan's tone is

17

already confident and grand: the day of reckoning has arrived not only for clinical psychiatry, associationist psychology, the Cartesian tradition in European philosophy, and a number of revisionist movements within psychoanalysis, but for Freud himself in so far as the founder of the psychoanalytic movement may be seen to have shrunk away from the scandalizing power of his own early insights. This sequence of papers contains an extensive catalogue of other people's errors. Sometimes an error is recent, local, and subject to rapid correction; sometimes it is ancient, and so intricately woven into European thinking that it comes to resemble an immovable propensity of the human mind. Error of this second kind can easily occur in the psychological sciences, and it is therefore all the more urgent that any new theory of mental process should seek to explain it. Freud himself went wrong in a special way. He attributed powers and responsibilities to the ego that the ego was ill-equipped to exercise, and in doing so repeated and re-endorsed a classic European overvaluation of the individual conscious mind. Freud's error was exceptional in that he alone possessed a theory that could have corrected it.

Lacan gives special prominence during this period to *The Ego and the Id* (1923), for it is here, in Lacan's account, that the later Freud offers a seductive false solution to an enigma that the early Freud had proposed. In *The Interpretation of Dreams* (1900) and its companion studies of slips and jokes, in the *Three Essays on the Theory of Sexuality* (1905) and the major case-histories, Freud had proclaimed the division of the human subject. Faced with the ineradicable fault-line that separated the conscious and unconscious portions of the mind, he had challenged a deeply implanted view by which the description 'mental' was identified with the description 'conscious' and by which the consciousness of the self-willing individual was held to provide the humanity of man with its official residence and its letters of credence.

Where, within the vastly extended field of 'the mental' that psychoanalysis proposed, was consciousness to be housed? And where, within the separate zones, systems or agencies into which psychoanalysis divided the mind, could the human self be held, singularly and rightfully, to reside? For Lacan, Freud's answers to these questions in *The Ego and the Id* are dangerously simple: 'It is known indeed that Freud identifies the Ego with the "perception-consciousness system", constituted by the sum of those apparatuses by which the organism is adapted to the "reality principle"' (178).[3] Freud is the grateful inheritor of this view from classical psychology, and systematically ignores or misrepresents everything that is ignorance or misrepresentation in the ego's response to the real (116; 21–22). But these reiterated charges against Freud's book themselves misrepresent its dubitative manner and the range of alternative mental models that it proposes. In the tangled conceptual texture of *The Ego and the Id*, the ego emerges as being in part – 'and Heaven knows how important a part', Freud says – unconscious (XIX, 18). And even as Freud's new ego-id antithesis gathers strength, it gathers uncertainty and a disputed middle territory too: 'The ego is not sharply separated from the id; its lower portion merges into it' (XIX, 24).

The most extraordinary simplification to which Lacan submits Freud's argument is the removal from it of any temporal dimension. For Freud it was possible to suppose not only that the ego was a 'precipitate' of the individual's abandoned attachments – to other people and to the world of objects – but that the process of precipitation could be reversed, and the history of those attachments thereby become legible, in analytic treatment (XIX, 28–39). Freud's imagery hastens the reader from the instantaneous world of chemical reaction to the time-bound worlds of history and archaeology: the ego is both point and process; it is a self-contained structure in the here and now but one that endlessly recapitulates its own past. But this double description of the ego is not designed as a simple tribute to its integrative power or to the centrality of the 'perception-consciousness' system in the mental life. For the id and the super-ego are precipitates too; they too are instantaneous structures that may be traced back through time. And they are all the more insidious in the pressures they exert upon the ego for being compounded of the ego's lost or disguised pre-existences: 'in the id, which is capable of being inherited, are harboured residues of the existences of countless egos; and, when the ego forms its super-ego out of the id, it may perhaps only be reviving shapes of former egos and be bringing them to resurrection' (XIX, 38). At this moment in Freud's theoretical reverie on the possible global structures of the mind, 'ego' has become the elementary building block of the mental universe: the agencies with which the ego competes in continuous, truceless struggle are themselves the compacted vestiges of egos that once were.

Lacan's charge against Freud is coherent and well-founded in so far as it is addressed to the aspirations that Freud expresses on the ego's behalf. 'Psycho-analysis is an instrument to enable the ego to achieve a progressive conquest of the id', Freud had said at the end of the book, summarizing the moral content of his argument (XIX, 56). Such instruments are necessary because the ego, left to itself, is fragile and besieged. And it seems reasonable to connect Freud's fervour as a moral visionary in *The Ego and the Id* with the sense of calamity that his ingenious theoretical modelling had produced. Far from adopting a unified view of selfhood from classical psychology, Freud found the human mind to be all too plainly self-divided and disputatious. His mental models, far from being clear-contoured experimental hypotheses, easily came apart into riddles and paradoxes. The notion of an integrated ego, buoyantly pursuing its goals and deflecting its antagonists, has the force not of an observable fact or of a logical necessity but of a wish, a hope, a recommendation.

Lacan reduces *The Ego and the Id* to a caricature of this recommendation and pays no attention to the detail of Freud's arguments. He does this not because he disapproves of psychoanalysts who declare a moral position or seek to give their theorizing an air of uplift but because he has, as we shall see, his own very different moral position to declare and wishes to base it, as far as possible, on premises laid down by an earlier and more provocative Freud. A hint that Lacan's 'ego' (*moi*) is to be a schismatic and not a stabilizing notion is detectable in the very title of his best-known early paper. The mirror stage (*stade du miroir*) is not a mere epoch in the history of the individual but a stadium (*stade*) in which the battle of the human subject is permanently being waged. Lacan's pun and the metaphorical jest on which it launches him (97–8; 5) seem at first to be the momentary effects of a prose style that is already playful and self-aware. But the pun has large ambitions behind it: to find an early moment in the human life-cycle when the individual's humanity is already fully at stake, and to find a new beginning for the moral drama of psychoanalysis. Lacan's account of the 'specular' moment provides the ego with its creation myth and its Fall.

The empirical observation from which Lacan appears to depart in refashioning the psychoanalytic account of the ego involves the young child, of between six and eighteen months, as it beholds its mirror image, or sees its behaviour reflected in the imitative gestures of an adult or another child. This is the moment at which the child seems suddenly to have a discovery to celebrate, and to be able to formulate, however roughly, the propositions 'I am that' and 'That is me'. Lacan remarks upon the child's air of jubilation, its fascination with the image and the playfulness of its reaction. In all these respects, it behaves differently from a chimpanzee of the same age:

> This act, far from exhausting itself, as in the case of the monkey, once the image has been mastered and found empty, immediately rebounds in the case of the child in a series of gestures in which he experiences in play the relation between the movements assumed in the image and the reflected environment, and between this virtual complex and the reality it reduplicates – the child's own body, and the persons, and even the things, around him. (93;1)

But jubilation and play have in fact a minor role in Lacan's narrative, which contains little by way of good news. At the mirror moment something glimmers in the world for the first time. The child is still entirely dependent upon adults for food, security and comfort, and still has limited control over its own bodily movements, but here, before the mirror, are the would-be autonomy and mastery of the individual in their earliest draft forms. The mirror image is a minimal paraphrase of the nascent ego. It would have been possible, on the basis of this very limited fund of observational data, to look forward in hope to the ego's later career and to perceive in outline upon a still distant horizon the 'mature' self, the self-made man and the social success. The child's delighted antics could themselves have seemed to promise a playful and wondering adult intelligence. But encouraging prospects of this kind are so much *not* a part of Lacan's business in these early papers that one is led to question his wisdom in allowing most of his ideas on ego formation to circulate by hearsay rather than in print during the thirteen years that followed the Marienbad congress.[4] Even after the publication in full of these ideas, it was possible for powerful readers to get them wrong: the mirror phase as it appears in, say, D.W. Winnicott's *Playing and Reality* (1971) or in Lionel Trilling's *Sincerity and Authenticity* (1972) is Lacan without Lacan.[5]

What has often been filtered out of Lacan's account, during the countless retellings to which it has been subject, is the sense that something derisory is going on in front of the mirror. Where the chimpanzee is able to recognise that the mirror-image is an epistemological void, and to turn his attention elsewhere, the child has a perverse will to remain deluded. The child's attention is seized (*capté*) by the firm spatial relationships between its real body and its specular body and between body and setting within the specular image; he or she is captivated (*captivé*). But the term that Lacan prefers to either of these, and which harnesses and outstrips their combined expressive power, is the moral and legal *captation*: the complex geometry of body, setting and mirror works upon the individual as a ruse, a deception, an inveiglement. The mirror, seemingly so consoling and advantageous to the infant, is a trap and a decoy (*leurre*). The idea that, even in the absence from the scene of anyone who could be thought of as a responsible agent, falsehood and underhandedness are somehow ingrained into the ego during its first, formative moments runs as a refrain through Lacan's early papers. The tone is one of gleeful exhortation: earlier psychoanalysts have 'thought the ego honest that but seemed to be so', and the moment for its exposure has now come. Man must break the charm of his reflected image by accepting the reality of its unreality. If he is to make progress towards truth, he must pass beyond the 'mirror without radiance which offers him a surface where nothing is reflected' (188).

The reader who attends closely to the rhetorical surface of Lacan's writings in the period 1936–49 is likely to be puzzled by the claim they clearly make to be contributions to psychoanalysis rather than to a much more general philosophy of mind-in-society. Any reader who thinks of the unconscious and repression as essential Freudian terms will be surprised to find that for the most part they appear only marginally in Lacan's arguments, while prominence is given to a term that had previously had no particular psychoanalytic force – *alienation*. The term allows precarious bridges to be built between clinical psychiatry, popular notions of madness, Hegelian metaphysics and the Marxist tradition in social theory. The mirror-bemused infant, setting forth on his career of delusional ego-building, is condemned to the madness of the madhouse (*aliénation*): Lacan does not spare the child these rigours. But the *Entfremdung* of Hegel and Marx, familiarly translated into French as *aliénation*, provides the infant's wretchedness with a certain philosophical dignity, just as alienation in its legal sense (as used of rights or property) gives it a faint air of juridical procedure. If I continue to speak of 'rhetorical surface' rather than of conceptual substance in discussing Lacan's handling of this term and its cognates, I do so because that surface is quite exceptionally elaborate and volatile even at this early stage. The various meanings of *aliénation* are played off against each other in such a way as to suggest that there is simply no exit from the condition it names, no recipe for de-alienation. But the usefulness of the term is more likely to be judged by the range of material facts that it helps to organise than by its susceptibility to semantic variation.

Lacan's usage contrasts sharply with, say, Marx's in the *Economic and Philosophical Manuscripts* or in the *Grundrisse*. For Marx the alienation of the individual from his labour, and from the products of his labour, not only acts as a prototype for all other alienated relationships (between man and nature, between the individual and society, between the individual and his own body) but gives a clear indication of where the route towards reintegration lies. The migration of the term from level to level helps him to produce both an extremely broad map of human society and a cogent political message. For Lacan, on the other hand, the prototypical alienation that occurs at the mirror stage is seen weaving its way haphazardly through society. He starves his hypothesis of the clinical data that could test its organizing power, and produces neither map nor message:

> Thus, this *Gestalt* – whose pregnancy should be regarded as bound up with the species, though its motor style remains scarcely recognizable – by these two aspects of its appearance, symbolizes the mental permanence of the *I*, at the same time as it prefigures its alienating destination; it is still pregnant with the correspondences that unite the *I* with the statue in which man projects himself, with the phantoms that dominate him, or with the automaton in which, in an ambiguous relation, the world of his own fabrication tends to find completion. (95; 2–3)

All human beings, Lacan reminds us, are born prematurely. It takes them a long time to acquire full motor control and to become capable of successful volitional acts. The mirror-image is a mirage of the 'I' and promises that the individual's latent powers of co-ordination will eventually be realised; indeed it has a role in triggering the development of these. So far so good. But the 'alienating destination' of the 'I' is such that the individual is permanently in discord with himself: the 'I' is tirelessly intent upon freezing a subjective process that cannot be frozen, introducing stagnation into the mobile field of human desire.

The inalienable alienation of the human species is, however, recounted not just in a hybrid philosophical language but in tones reminiscent of the Gothic tale. *Prégnance* (force, potentiality, weight of significance or implication) has, by contagion perhaps from the English pregnancy, become a matter of childbearing. The child, itself so recently born, gives birth to a monster: a statue, an automaton, a fabricated thing. Freudian theory had already talked at length about the 'constructedness' of the ego, about the field of conflicting forces in which it was assembled and the defensive apparatus that was necessary for its preservation, but here such talk is recast in terms that Dr Frankenstein would have found familiar. From spare parts, an armoured mechanical creature is being produced within the human subject, and developing unwholesome habits and destructive appetites of its own. The self-division of the subject, first revealed to Freud by dreams, is here being re-imagined by Lacan as nightmare.

An even more resolute departure from the formal language of psychoanalysis is to be found in Lacan's handling of the notion of the 'fragmented body' (*corps morcelé*). This phantasy has a clear structural relationship to the 'alienating identity' (97; 4) of the ego, for it is the means by which the individual retains an active memory of his earliest sense of physical disarray. The body once seemed dismembered, all over the place, and the anxiety associated with this memory fuels the individual's desire to be the possessor and the resident of a secure bodily 'I'. These projections towards the ego are constantly threatened by a retrospective pull towards fragmentation; and the very rigidity of the ego's armour can act as a violence upon the individual and scatter again his *disjecta membra*. Lacan insists that what is involved here is a Janus-faced phantasy structure rather than a simple set of memories associated with real bodily parts. Whether the subject looks forwards to the ego or backwards to the *corps morcelé* he is contemplating a construction – the same one in alternative states. Yet even in describing this structural interdependence,

Lacan calls upon imagery to do most of the work. What comes apart when the body is *morcelé* is not so much a physical organism as a 'heterogeneous mannequin, a baroque doll, a trophy of limbs' (*Family Complexes*, 60). Dr Frankenstein has been joined by Professor Spalanzani, the maniacal toy-maker of E.T.A. Hoffmann's *The Sandman*.[6] And the three bizarre verbal assemblages that Lacan here collects bring an air of perverse *jouissance* into his text: a mere theoretical notion has revealed itself as an obscure object of desire.

For Lacan, the 'fragmented body' has nowhere been more memorably represented than in the paintings of Hieronymus Bosch, and his own verbal accounts of the bodily catastrophes by which the human imagination is haunted – 'images of castration, emasculation, mutilation, dismemberment, dislocation, evisceration, devouring, bursting open of the body' (104; 11) – self-consciously echo Bosch's pictorial designs:

This fragmented body – which term I have also introduced into our system of theoretical references – usually manifests itself in dreams when the movement of the analysis encounters a certain level of aggressive disintegration in the individual. It then appears in the form of disjointed limbs, or of those organs represented in exoscopy, growing wings and taking up arms for intestinal persecutions – the very same that the visionary Hieronymus Bosch has fixed, for all time, in painting, in their ascent from the fifteenth century to the imaginary zenith of modern man. But this form is even tangibly revealed at the organic level, in the lines of 'fragilization' that define the anatomy of phantasy, as exhibited in the schizoid and spasmodic symptoms of hysteria. (97; 4–5)

Hell, for Bosch, has a cellular structure: individual scenes of torture and torment are brought together in a mosaic, and these are integrated not by an overriding narrative but by the studied interplay of painterly motifs. When Lacan devotes an entire paper to aggression, the fragmented body is his central emblem of human destructiveness, and it is simply re-imagined in a variety of contexts. The phantasmatic body of the hysteric, the symbolism of children's games, primitive rituals such as tattooing, circumcision and incision, together with the 'Procrustean arbitrariness' of fashion, are all to be understood by reference to this troubling and deep-rooted phantasy (105; 11). But there is no argument in the presentation of these clinical and social facts. No countervailing evidence is considered and no alternative methods of explanation: the fundamental psychical dialectic of wholeness and disintegration supports a cellular fabric of images that reactivate in the reader the very phantasies that Lacan discusses. This fabric is his own *Garden of Earthly Delights*. Caught between delusional wholeness and infernal disintegration, the ego leads a doomed life. Whatever it is that gives the ego its normal buoyancy, and allows the individual to do such straightforward things as formulate and then execute a plan, has been moved to the margins of the theoretical picture.

Lacan's poetic imagery in these papers has a broad philosophical sweep, and moves beyond the clinic and beyond society itself towards a vision of universal Discord. Freud and Lacan both present their theories as having been foreshadowed in the cosmological speculations of the Presocratics. Where Freud, in 'Analysis Terminable and Interminable' (1937), cites Empedocles, and allows that his own primal forces of Eros and the death instinct had already been recognised in the Empedoclean warring principles of Love (φιλία) and Strife (νεῖκος) (XXIII, 246), Lacan cites

Heraclitus as having proclaimed the primacy of Strife (116; 21).[7] Looking for prophetic evidence from antiquity to support his own ideas, Lacan would have been served quite as well, perhaps even better, by Empedocles. For in the Empedoclean physical system, the first stage of evolution through which creatures passed was one of *morcellement*, strikingly akin in its imagery to the world of Bosch: 'Here sprang up many faces without necks, arms wandered without shoulders, unattached, and eyes strayed alone, in need of foreheads.'[8] The presence of such images in the writings of the ancient world would tend to confirm what can scarcely be doubted: that phantasies of dismemberment are a burden that all self-aware membered creatures bear and that 'lines of fragilization' are drawn within the human body by all those who inhabit one.

This flight towards universality in Lacan's writing is propelled, moreover, not simply by his references to painting, literature and philosophy but by his use of the 'hard' terminology of science. He speaks, for example, of 'a vital dehiscence that is constitutive of man' (116; 21) and of 'a certain dehiscence at the heart of the organism, a primordial Discord' (96; 4). This is the Strife of the Presocratics no longer at work ubiquitously in the cosmos but localized in the human species. Yet 'dehiscence' – in botany, the opening up of seed-vessels – takes us away from humanity even as the specific character of *homo sapiens* is being described: the self-alienation of the subject is as 'natural', as unavoidable, as the self-propagation of plants. A similar harnessing of metaphorical power from the language of natural science, but on a larger scale, is to be seen in the early Lacan's special fondness for the term *imago*. This was already an accredited item in the psychoanalytic lexicon by the time Lacan first used it, and had lost most of its original biological meaning.[9] An 'imago' was a mental object, an unconscious prototype based upon the infant's earliest experiences, and referred only dimly to the culminating phase of insect development. Lacan plays upon this entomological meaning even as he forcibly rejects the biologizing tendency of Freud's own thought. The concept of the imago is given a central role in 'Remarks on psychical causality': 'We think it possible therefore to designate in the *imago* the proper object of psychology, exactly to the same extent that Galileo's notion of the inert material point formed the basis of physics' (188). Redefined in these terms, the psychoanalytic project has acquired an extraordinary power of levitation. It metaphorizes the language of biology, competes with physics in the simplicity and completeness of its explanations and seems equipped to produce an all-inclusive portrait of Nature. From its humble beginnings as a science of neurotic disorder, psychoanalysis is reaching outwards and upwards towards a new cosmology.

The central stabilizing thread of discussion that runs through Lacan's early papers is devoted to the concept of *identification*, and much of what Lacan says on the matter is phrased modestly enough and offered as an uncontroversial elaboration of Freud's own account. But verbal restraint does not, as we shall see, go hand in hand with limited philosophical ambition. Lacan's theoretical explorations in this area are as complex and as far-reaching as anything to be found in the post-1950 papers for which he is still best known outside psychoanalytic circles.

Although 'identification' (*Identifizierung*) is one of a number of terms that Freudian diction shares both with ordinary parlance and with philosophy, its specifically psychoanalytic role is for the most part clear. If the ego can be thought of as having components, as capable of 'coming apart' into building materials that are smaller and simpler than itself, then the infant's earliest identifications are those components. The identification of oneself with another being is the very process by which a continuing sense of selfhood becomes possible, and it is from successive assimilations of other people's attributes that what is familiarly called the ego or the personality is constructed. Freud, summarizing his own views on identification in *Group Psychology and the Analysis of the Ego* (1921), insisted on the primacy of this process:

> First, identification is the original form of the emotional tie with an object; secondly, in a regressive way it becomes a substitute for a libidinal object-tie, as it were by means of introjection of the object into the ego; and thirdly, it may arise with any new perception of a common quality shared with some other person who is not an object of the sexual instinct. (XVIII, 107–8)

Freud had already characterized in non-technical language the difference between an identification and a 'libidinal object-tie'. Using the example of an infant's feelings towards its father, he had offered the formula: 'in the first case one's father is what one would like to *be*, and in the second he is what one would like to *have*' (XVIII, 106). The contrast between having and being sounds straightforward enough, and plentiful clinical evidence seemed to lend support to the hypothesis that identificatory 'being' indeed comes first in the history of the individual's desires, and that 'identification is the earliest and original form of emotional tie' (XVIII, 107).

But the mapping of those desires became a complicated and arduous business as soon as the investigator reached the Oedipal phase. For even in the apparently simple case of the male infant – who desires the mother and identifies with the father – a number of interrelated factors could produce an enigmatic series of alternative maps: all human beings were bisexually constituted; the triangularity of the Oedipal situation allowed for all manner of dialectical reversals; and in the thick of the child's passions the desire to 'be' and the desire to 'have' could not always be kept clearly separate (XIX, 31, 176). In the case of girls the picture was even more complicated. The first object of desire for boys and girls alike is the mother. Where boys retain that object, girls abandon it, wholly or in part, in favour of the father. How and why? (XIX, 251) It is at this point that Lacan intervenes. Freud's answer to his own question about the Oedipus complex in girls involved, as is well known, the notion of penis envy and a specialized female version of castration anxiety. Lacan's objection to Freud's account is not a feminist one: he rebels not against a portrait of girls as secondary, subservient and over-impressed by the spectacle of the male organ, but against the over-elaborate machinery of causes and effects that Freud's model required (*Family Complexes*, 59).

For Lacan, as for Freud, identification is the mainspring of the psychical apparatus – the source of its dynamism and the trigger for the ceaseless dramatic interplay between the individual and others – but he differs from Freud in maintaining that this mechanism needs to be observed in its earliest prototypical form if it is to have compelling explanatory force. By the onset of the Oedipus complex, the infant is already too old, and the range of his or her possible identificatory manoeuvres too wide, for explanations based solely upon the principle of identification to be other than cumbersome or obscure. Lacan invites us to look back beyond the play of rivalries and aliases that the Oedipal phase initiates, and to behold an anterior world in which the individual has only one object of desire and only one alias – himself.

The pattern of Lacan's disagreement with Freud here is one that Freud himself had made familiar. For both of them, ego-theory is a quest for the primordial in human experience, the moment of origin, the irreducible principle in accordance with which the human subject comes into being and is transformed. Lacan's 'corrections' of Freud are attempts to redramatize this sense of primordiality and to postulate new points of departure for human subjectivity. Where Freud had largely been content to see the Oedipal identifications as primary – and fraught with potentially disastrous consequences for the individual as he or she grew towards adulthood – Lacan presents them as secondary and having a pacifying and normalizing role (116–17; 22–23).[10] His own primary identification, which is scandalous and disruptive, takes place at the mirror phase.

A similar reordering of priorities is to be seen in Lacan's handling of the term that Freud had borrowed from Paul Näcke and Havelock Ellis and given a special psycho-analytic sense: narcissism. Indeed 'identification' and 'narcissism' are remodelled together by Lacan and often merge. Freud had provided two quite separate two-phase histories of narcissistic passion within the developing erotic life of human beings, and in each of them he spoke of the earlier phase as that of 'primary narcissism'. In 'On Narcissism: an Introduction' (1914), the first phase was one of infant self-love, which existed in parallel with the child's love for the woman who nursed him. These two early varieties of passion formed the basis for later object-choices of the 'narcissistic' type on the one hand, and of the 'attachment' or 'anaclitic' type on the other (XIV, 87–90). But in later works, the primary narcissistic state was one of objectless self-absorption and self-sufficiency, held to pre-cede the child's discovery of the external world. Lacan's preference, here as in so many other matters, is for the earlier rather than the later Freud.[11] Where Freud's first primary narcissism, paired with a different kind of love, was a properly structural idea, and a key to the subject's later pattern of choices and identifications, the second was a blissful undifferentiation that led nowhere – it was simply grown out of and abandoned.

Lacan's return to the early Freud is not, of course, excessively loyal or literal-minded. He disturbs the symmetry that Freud had proposed between the young child's self-love and its attachment to the mother figure, and places upon the Narcissus myth itself two stress-marks that are entirely his own. For Lacan, the tragic story of Narcissus does not speak of delusional self-admiration alone, for the hero is held in thrall by the peculiar potency of a reflecting surface, and is infatuated with his reflected image to the point of self-destruction. Lacan's retelling of the myth at the level of theory sometimes respects its original chronology, and has a separate opening tableau: 'It is in this erotic relation, in which the human individual fixes himself upon an image that alienates him from himself, that are to be found the energy and the form in which this organization of the passions that he will call his ego has its origin' (113; 19). The ego thus constituted pursues its passion towards an eventual moment of suicidal sacrifice.

But elsewhere this two-phase history is dramatically foreshortened, and a link established between 'the primordial Ego regarded as essentially alienated' and 'the primitive sacrifice regarded as essentially suicidal' (187). Lacan's search for the inaugural and the irreducible in the mental life leads him to construct a single explosive moment and a single knot of interconnected theoretical motifs: 'narcissistic suicidal aggression' (187). The original act of identification is the original narcissistic declaration too; into the very constitution of the ego its destruction is already woven; the only escape from alienation is an aggravation of the alienated state. If the later destinies of the subject are to be understood at all, they may be grasped only as the untying and retying in time of that original timeless knot. Repeatedly in these early papers, Lacan's vision of the ego's remotest past is a savage vision of its future too, for his 'primary' narcissism is an inescapable structural imperative in the operation of all human desire: 'In this there appears that fundamental illusion to which man is subservient – much more than he is to all the "passions of the body" in the Cartesian sense – this passion for being a man, which is the supreme passion of the soul, narcissism, which imposes its structure on all desires, even the most elevated' (188).

It could be said of Lacan's prophetic tone in passages like this, and of his unusual skill as a dramatist of ideas, that they become irrelevant as soon as his strict and sober theoretical lessons have been absorbed. Those who hold this view could point to the very different skills that are evident in, say, *Family Complexes* – which contains much clear exposition and summary of existing doctrine, and shows Lacan to possess a laudable sense of scale in measuring his own contribution to a collective theoretical enterprise. They could also point to such works of synthesis as Jean Laplanche and J.-B. Pontalis's *The Language of Psycho-Analysis* (1967), in which Lacan's new concepts, and refashionings of existing concepts, are judiciously situated within the broad field of Freudian debate. And of course they would be right: Lacan the 'contributor' to psychoanalysis certainly exists. But my own view is that his theory has a more serious claim on our attention if his impetuosity and grandeur are retained. One of Lacan's recurrent purposes as a writer is to amplify theories to the point where they become deranged, to supercharge them with meaning in such a way that they no longer have uses or applications. It is as if he is prepared to ask the question 'how useful is all this?' only when the theory in question has owned up to its madness.

Even at the level of its local detail, his writing pulls against the reins of professional prudence in its search for the grand effect. By means of etymological word-play, as we have already seen, a stage may become a stadium: the double meaning of *stade* turns time into space, a reflection into a struggle, a chance encounter into a ritualized competition. A similar process empties the mirror itself of optical content: the *miroir* produces *mirages* rather than mere sensory *images* (95; 2). And again, without apology or explanation, Lacan may enlarge his *spéculaire* into a *spectaculaire* (112–14; 18–20). Suddenly a mirror has been punned into a spectacle, a specialized moment of seeing into seeing at large. We could say that in all these cases etymology is on Lacan's side, and that Latin knew in advance about the connections he is seeking to make. But the problem is that Lacan's puns run ahead of his arguments and make argument itself seem slow-witted and prosaic. There is, it eventually becomes clear, a fairly straightforward Lacanian route from *speculum* to *spectaculum*. At the mirror stage an identificatory mechanism is set going within the subject that will henceforth affect his every act of visual perception. The original impulse to self-identification is brought to bear indefinitely upon the world beyond the mirror: 'the specular image would seem to be the threshold of the visible world' (95; 3). 'Mirror' and 'spectacle' are the twin boundary posts of what Lacan was later to call the Imaginary order, but the route that connects them in these early papers has, for the most part, to be inferred.

This sense of precocity is still more marked in the claims that Lacan makes on behalf of Freudian theory as a whole. In particular the reformulated concept of identification is presented as the key to a new critical understanding of science and epistemology. 'Beyond the "reality principle"' (1936), for example, confronts associationism – the most respectable and 'academic' of contemporary psychological doctrines – with the error of its ways. This paper, which is a wide-ranging companion-piece to the 'The mirror stage', begins with a critique of associationism that is comparable, in its acerbity and its fondness for frontal assault, to the overview of clinical psychiatry with which Lacan began his doctoral dissertation on paranoia (1932). These two assured polemical performances have, moreover, a number of targets in common: disregard for the subject's report on experience; the denial of meaning to the subject's speech; the arbitrary removal of wide swathes of mental activity from the terrain of mental science.

The vice of associationist psychology is that it works constantly with the idea of *similarity*, uses it indeed as an all-purpose guarantee of coherence in building its mental models, but has no serious notion of what the idea entails (75–76). Such thinking, even when it proclaims its empiricist credentials, is inveterately idealist in character: it sanctifies the act of identification, but without knowing why. Psychoanalysis, on the other hand, does know why, and its knowledge is now freely available: identification in all its forms is the repetition of an infantile narcissistic rite. But where the infant has at least the virtue, as Lacan sees it, of provoking a schism that he cannot control, adult knowledge-seekers – psychologists, say – mechanically re-apply identificatory procedures that seek to disguise their delusional origins. Science and epistemology are not strictly speaking on Lacan's agenda, he reminds us, but they might as well be told that to assume a structure is to assume a developmental route as well (88–89). In the history of a scientific epoch, as in the history of an individual subject, early identifications are a destiny in embryo, a blueprint for the future. They are the unacknowledged source of an unacknowledged madness. Psychoanalysis is mad too but should at least know better than to submit naively to the seductions of similarity. It must constitute itself as a relational, relativistic science – one that takes place between communicating humans – and make knowledge of its own madness into a procedural watchword.

The madness inherent in human thinking provides Lacan

with his grandest prophetic theme. Beyond the admonitions that he directs at his fellow mental scientists, and beyond Freud's own pessimism as a cultural critic, he conjures up a vision of catastrophe for the human mind. And that catastrophe, which is endemic to it, has an exact-sounding clinical name: paranoia.[12] The ego has a paranoiac structure (114; 20); the switch from the specular *I* to the social *I* brings with it a paranoiac alienation (98; 5); psychoanalysis, as a therapeutic method, induces controlled paranoia into the human subject (109; 15); and knowledge itself is incurably paranoiac in all its modes (94; 2. 96; 3. 111; 17. 180).

The choice of any one chronic psychosis to symbolize a permanent disposition of the human mind might at first seem a strangely self-defeating move on Lacan's part. One of his main aims in his dissertation on paranoia had been to demystify this vastly influential psychiatric category and to show how a premature recourse to such notions could restrict and impoverish the clinical picture. In particular, he had set out to show not only that the onset and development of paranoia could be coherently related to the personality of the individual patient, but that the term paranoia became a meaningless descriptive tag if it was severed from that personality. Is he not remystifying the language of psychiatry by allowing a single clinical term to reappear from all points of the compass in his discussion of mental process? In the decade or so before Lacan's entry into the psychoanalytic movement, the term had in fact already begun to acquire a less specialized sense. Freud in his paper 'Some Neurotic Mechanisms in Jealousy, Paranoia and Homosexuality' (1922) had made it possible to think of paranoia as one of those pathological disorders that helped to reveal the infrastructure of ordinary mental activity (XVIII, 223–32), and Lacan in his dissertation had followed this lead: the problem lay not with the term itself but with the uses to which psychiatry put it. The patient, once liberated from the grip of paranoia in its narrowest technical sense, was to rediscover the condition – but on equal terms with his or her fellow human beings.

Although one would usually hesitate before enlisting Salvador Dalí as a historian of ideas, his *Unspeakable Confessions* (1973) may be consulted with profit at this point:

> Lacan threw a scientific light on a phenomenon that is obscure to most of our contemporaries – the expression: paranoia – and gave it its true significance. Psychiatry, before Lacan, committed a vulgar error on this account by claiming that the systematization of paranoiac delirium developed 'after the fact' and that this phenomenon was to be considered as a case of 'reasoning madness'. Lacan showed the contrary to be true: the delirium itself is a systematization. It is born systematic, an active element determined to orient reality around its line of force. It is the contrary of a dream or an automatism which remains passive in relation to the movingness of life. Paranoiac delirium asserts itself and conquers.[13]

It seems likely that Dalí and Lacan influenced each other at this time and on this matter. The 'paranoia-critical' method that Dalí began to proclaim in the late 1920s had two broad phases: first of all, it involved submitting the delirious system of one's unconscious associations to critical interpretation. But such interpretation led, in a second phase, to a much more challenging goal. From the superimposition of 'criticism' upon 'paranoia' the artist arrived not – as might be expected – at a constant vacillatory play between alternative mental registers but at a knowledge of the world that was complete and unanswerable: 'I believe my paranoia is an expression of the absolute structure, the proof of its immanence. My genius consists of being in direct contact with the cosmic soul.'[14] In comparison with these claims, Lacan's vision of knowledge as inherently paranoiac seems modest; the quest for such knowledge certainly has no triumphal conclusion. But Lacan like Dalí talks about an immanent structure of the human world. Human knowledge begins from an illusion – a misapprehension, a deceit, a seduction, an inveiglement – and constructs an inescapable autonomous system in its wake. Psychoanalysis is a 'critical' interpretative system that seeks to reduplicate and modulate the subject's original delirium. Unlike Dalí's paranoia-criticism, it vacillates interminably between mental registers, but its play of system upon system and delusion upon delusion is the closest approximation to truth that human beings can expect to achieve.

Lacan's recourse to the vocabulary of 'madness' in describing the formative stages of the human personality is not new within psychoanalysis. Freud had often spoken of the lover – child or adult – as being in the grip of 'insanity' and of his over-valuation of the loved object as being in a strict sense delusional. Melanie Klein had already begun to construct her revised Freudian model of ego-formation in infants, using terms that were not just metaphorical borrowings from psychiatry but formed a basis for the explanation of psychosis in adults. Her 'paranoid-schizoid position' was a developmental phase belonging to the infant's first four months, but it was also a mode of object-relations that could be expected to recur under certain circumstances throughout later life. The splitting and persecutory anxiety to which the young child was subject from birth were exacerbated by the maternal breast – experienced as the original 'good' object in so far as it satisfied his or her desires, and as the original 'bad' object in so far as it frustrated them. But although Klein's paranoid-schizoid position, and the depressive position with which she contrasts it, have potentially a very long explanatory reach, she and her followers are for the most part reluctant to move outside the clinical domain.[15] They certainly show little interest in constructing a new epistemology or a new science of mankind on the basis of their remodelled Freudian account of ego-formation.

Lacan, on the other hand, expects his conceptual innovations to have immediate large-scale repercussions beyond the psychoanalytic field. These paragraphs from 'Aggressivity in psychoanalysis' characteristically interweave workshop psychological discussion and an Olympian view of *homo sapiens*:

> Janet, who demonstrated so admirably the meaning of feelings of persecution as phenomenological moments in social behaviour, did not explore their common character, which is precisely that they are constituted by a stagnation of one of these moments, similar in their strangeness to the faces of actors when a film is suddenly stopped in mid-action.
>
> Now, this formal stagnation is akin to the most general structure of human knowledge: that which constitutes the ego and its objects with attributes of permanence, identity, and substantiality, in short, with entities or 'things' that are very different from the *Gestalten* that experience enables us to isolate in the shifting field, stretched in accordance with the lines of animal desire.
>
> In fact, this formal fixation, which introduces a certain rupture of level, a certain discord between man's organization and his *Umwelt*, is the very condition that extends indefinitely his world and his power, by giving his objects their instrumental polyvalence and symbolic polyphony, and also their potential as defensive armour.

What I have called paranoiac knowledge is shown, therefore, to correspond in its more or less archaic forms to certain critical moments that mark the history of man's mental genesis, each representing a stage in objectifying identification. (111; 17)

The relationship between ego-structure and 'the most general structure of human knowledge' is subject to variation as the passage proceeds. Where 'permanence' and 'stagnation', for example, represent in the domain of the ego a simple retreat from the flux of experience, a wilful refusal of desire-in-movement, they reappear elsewhere as necessary instruments of thought: if you are not prepared to stagnate, at least a little, you will not have access to the 'symbolic polyphony' that is your rightful world of meaning. But in general the parallelism is strict and scandalous: the structure of the ego and the structure of knowledge are both typified by a will to alienation, a sought-after madness, that seems on the face of it unanswerable and untreatable. In writing of this kind, a starkly pessimistic echo passes between psychoanalysis and its neighbouring 'conjectural sciences'.

What is especially remarkable, given the scale of Lacan's ambition at this stage, is the exiguousness of his rewriting of Freud, and the subdued role played in his account by two concepts that he was later to refer to as 'fundamental' to psychoanalysis: the unconscious and the transference.[16] The communicative and transactional character of psychoanalytic therapy had been described briefly earlier in the essay (102; 9) and at some length in 'Beyond the "reality principle"' (82–83), but the intersubjective speech that such therapy comprises has as yet no larger epistemological resonance. And the unconscious, which for Freud himself and for the later Lacan is the structural notion *par excellence*, and a perpetual trigger to theoretical speculation, is at this stage still 'inert and unthinkable' (182): psycho-analysis belongs to the ego and to the Imaginary order.

Lacan, one might at first suppose, is simply revising certain parts of the Freud corpus in these papers and leaving intact those parts that are doctrinal cornerstones for the psychoanalytic movement. But what is going on is in fact far from being prudent and respectful in this way. The factitious and delusional ego that Lacan places at the centre of his world-picture is portrayed with such single-minded vehemence that the entire psychoanalytic style of thinking is, for the time being, transformed. The clinical, moral and epistemological discourses that psychoanalysis brings together are all refashioned and redramatized, but from a single standpoint. This early Lacan is Wallace Stevens's 'lunatic of one idea', and that idea, under a variety of semi-technical disguises, is lunacy. He resembles a baroque ceiling painter who has laboured hard upon the *trompe-l'œil* porticoes, pilasters and cornices that surround his central vault, and upon the cerulean wash that covers it, but who then has no energy of mind and brush with which to populate his sky. The overall effect is one of brilliance, grandeur and vacancy.

The blank surface that teases him out of thought is not a transcendent abstraction but the 'unthinkable innateness' of human desire (114; 20). For Lacan, no language yet exists in which to re-express and make his own the already thinkable desire-realm that is the Freudian unconscious. But things are soon to change. The once empty sky is soon to overflow with elaborately interacting forms, and the human order is to be seen pressing towards an apotheosis of sorts – in Lacan's account of language and the unconscious.

3 Language and the Unconscious

'T.t.y.m.u.p.t.': these letters appear as a cryptic signature at the end of Lacan's paper on 'The agency of the letter in the unconscious or reason since Freud' (1957). When he eventually divulged their meaning they proved to belong to a confiding conversational register far removed from the exalted language of the final paragraph itself: *'Tu t'y es mis un peu tard'* (You got down to it rather late).[1] Where the final words of the paper had spoken of the lateness of the providential Lacanian message in the history of human thought, this last self-addressed remark speaks of a lateness internal to Lacan's own biography. *The Interpretation of Dreams* had been the work of a forty-four year old, but Lacan was fifty-two before he began publishing papers that for him possessed an inaugural force in any way comparable to that of Freud's book. He had come late to the task of recreating psychoanalysis, and now, it may be assumed, felt an urgent obligation to complete the task before his time ran out.

The two late-coming papers in which Lacan's 'system' is first fully articulated are 'The agency of the letter' and 'The function and field of speech and language in psychoanalysis', which had preceded it by four years. Both papers are complex and allusive. They are by turns elliptical and profuse, oracular and colloquial, serious-minded and facetious, caustic and cajoling. And beneath the playfulness of Lacan's text, and the unnerving fluctuations of his tone, a crucial indecision traces its endlessly deviating path. This

44

has to do with the kinds and degrees of adherence to the monumental theoretical achievement of Freud that Lacan could permit himself. He could be a grateful disciple, annotating and elucidating the Freudian texts, but not seeking to make an original contribution of his own; or a defender of Freud against misrepresentation and attack coming from outside the profession of psychoanalysis; or an apologist for the earlier against the later Freud; or the proponent of a 'pure' Freudian message in the face of those colleagues who have tamed and institutionalized his teaching; or a continuator of Freud who brings the whole doctrine to its point of consummation. Lacan adopts each of these roles in turn, and seldom pauses to announce or explain his switches of position. And occasionally a new master appears: Freud may become the mere harbinger of the Lacanian word, or the originator of a theory now eclipsed and made obsolete by Lacan's own.

A number of circumstantial factors help to explain Lacan's mobile aims and motives at this juncture. He had reached an impasse in his rewriting of the Freudian account of the ego, having created a new theoretical edifice that was often only fortuitously connected to psychoanalysis as a therapeutic method. On those matters of training and technique that many of Lacan's contemporaries thought of as the essential subject-matter of theoretical reflection after the death of Freud, Lacan's early papers seemed able to offer only general warnings and guidelines. And it was largely on a matter of technique – his use of short sessions – that Lacan found himself, in 1953, expelled from the International Psychoanalytical Association.[2] He needed a new theoretical position that could be linked robustly to the clinical work of psychoanalysis and that would explain and justify his own methods as a clinician. It was in Rome that Lacan delivered his address on 'The function and field of speech', and 'The Rome Discourse' is still widely used as an alternative title for the paper. He chose his venue well, for Rome had acquired in the works of Freud a special emblematic status. It was a city in which phantasies of knowledge and power – of omniscience and omnipotence, indeed – could be freely entertained, and one in which an archaic order of things was inexhaustibly topical. The process of burial and excavation that alters the Roman cityscape from day to day offered the psychoanalytic observer a flattering three-dimensional allegory of his professional task. Freud had imagined himself a new Hannibal as he entered the Eternal City, and Lacan in turn often speaks in triumphalist tones in his Roman address. But the object of his admiration and envy, and his target as a would-be conqueror, is a city not of stones but of words: at this time when the threat of exile and ostracism is in the air, it is the works of Freud that he seeks to disinter, rescue, restore and possess.

Yet the external circumstances in which the paper was composed do not take us far either in understanding Lacan's new conceptual construction or in working out the polyphonic principles that govern the organization of his text. Lacan, in his preface, begins to explain these by giving a specifically verbal twist to the Roman imagery of Freud:

> Indeed, I recalled that well before the glory of the world's most elevated throne had been established, Aulus Gellius, in his *Noctes Atticae* gave to the place called *Mons Vaticanus* the etymology *vagire*, which designates the first stammerings of speech.
>
> If, then, my speech was to be nothing more than a *vagitus*, an infantile cry, at least it would be an auspicious moment to renovate the foundations that this discipline of speech derives from language.
>
> Moreover, this renovation derived too much meaning from history for me to avoid breaking with the traditional style that places a 'report' somewhere between

a compilation and a synthesis, and not give it the
ironical style of a radical questioning of the foundations
of that discipline. (238; 31)

Rome is the place where new powers of speech are to be
discovered and where, under the protection of those powers,
psychoanalysis is to be refounded. Lacan announces the
infantile cry of his new science in a fashion that foreshad-
ows its firmest adult pronouncements. His reference to the
Vatican suggests something of the phantasmatic power-play
that is involved here. Just as the papacy incorporates and
transmutes the pagan culture of Rome, so the new speech
of psychoanalysis can be expected to refashion the spoken
forms which the discipline has had to make do with until
now. If this really is babble it already has a high opinion of
itself. Continuing to etymologize for a moment longer in
the vein of Aulus Gellius, we could say that Lacan's *vagitus*
is already beginning to sound like *vaticinatio*: psychoanalysis is aspiring once again from modest beginnings towards
grandiose prophetic utterance.

Later in the preface, however, Lacan enumerates patiently
the many reasons that analysis has for taking its own
verbalism and talkativeness seriously. As a therapy, it
inhabits the dimension of the spoken word; as a theory, it
has the task of explaining how fortunate and unfortunate
therapeutic effects come to be produced within the verbal
medium; and as an organized, rule-observing profession, it
monitors and refines the techniques by which those effects
may be produced or avoided. The theoretical statements
made by analysts are no less the products of linguistic
mediation and interlocution than the statements which
pass to and fro in the force-field of the clinical encounter,
and theoretical diction needs appropriate safeguards: 'I consider it to be an urgent task to disengage from concepts that
are being deadened by routine use the meaning that they

regain both from a re-examination of their history and from a reflexion on their subjective foundations' (240; 33). Above all, and in all contexts, the practitioner needs to be reminded that the unconscious is available to him only in the form of language. It is, of course, tempting to disguise this fact, and to think of the unconscious as a place, a force, a system, a collection of wordless drives or as-yet-unworded thoughts or ideas. And it is still more tempting for analysts to take a relaxed view of the whole matter, and think of the unconscious as a fluid hypothetical notion that happens to explain otherwise unexplainable behavioural effects rather well. But language, for Lacan at this stage, is the labyrinth into which psychoanalysis and all its characteristic concepts were born and from which they can never expect to escape. Analysts who teach otherwise are deluded in ways that their discipline should have allowed them to recognise and circumvent.

When Lacan speaks in these terms, he seems to be appointing himself as the official remembrancer of the psychoanalytic movement, a self-denying spokesman for its original insights in their original form. And he often suggests that loyalty to Freud demands adherence to a language-based creed unambiguously announced by Freud himself. Freud saw clearly that the functions of speech were the central field of his discipline, but more recently that terrain has been left fallow, analytic discourse has deteriorated, and the procedures for initiation into the profession, unquickened by the flame of linguistic knowledge and self-awareness, have become empty ceremonial (244; 36–7). Of these Lacanian claims it may be said that while they return us to a major aspect of Freud's teaching and pay due tribute to the richness of his literary expression, they flatly misrepresent the detail of his arguments.

Freud was willing of course to grant that psychology of

the kind that he and his colleagues pursued was a model-building enterprise and that its models were short-lived creatures of language. 'In psychology', he wrote in *The Question of Lay Analysis* (1926), 'we can only describe things by the help of analogies. There is nothing peculiar in this; it is the case elsewhere as well. But we have constantly to keep changing these analogies, for none of them lasts us long enough' (XX, 195). But to say this is not at all to say that linguistic forms saturate the psychoanalytic domain, and that the analyst who conducts his explorations in words can expect to find nothing other than words at the end of his quest. For Freud language had as its crowning capacity that of ushering the theorist and the therapist to the threshold of another world, and that world – for which 'the unconscious' was an appropriate shorthand designation – mattered because it was the mute, unstoppable and unappeasable inwardness of human desire. The unconscious was the fountainhead of psychoanalytic thinking, and it was verbal as soon as it made any form of public appearance. But the fact that its outward effects were discursive ones did not mean that it was itself a discourse or imaginable only by pretending that it was. Putting Freud's claims for the unconscious in their minimal but not their most modest form, we could say that it was an explanatory device or manoeuvre whereby human speech and conduct could be made continuously intelligible, but that there was no need for the unconscious to be speech, or closely to resemble speech, in order to perform this role successfully.

The history of the term 'unconscious' in Freud's writings is long and complicated. But if the metapsychological paper 'The Unconscious' (1915) is thought of as occupying a special place in that history, it cannot be doubted that the question 'where do words stop?' was of central importance to Freud in his attempts to model the psychical apparatus. This paper summarizes and re-inflects the theoretical account that Freud had been developing from *The Interpretation of Dreams* (1900) onwards, and it reaches an unmistakable climactic point during his discussion of the difference between 'word-presentations' (*Wortvorstellungen*) and 'thing-presentations' (*Sachvorstellungen*). Throughout the paper he insists on the discontinuity between the unconscious and the preconscious-conscious and guards the border between the two systems with fierce vigilance. Many separate characteristics are ascribed to the unconscious: it is, among other things, the timeless realm of the instinctual impulses; it knows 'no negation, no doubt, no degrees of certainty', and allows individual impulses to 'exist side by side without being influenced by one another, and ... exempt from mutual contradiction' (XIV, 186). But the characteristic which overrides all these is that the unconscious is never straightforwardly translatable or commutable into the terms governing the preconscious-conscious. As the paper proceeds, this implacable separation of mental powers takes on and discards many different metaphorical guises, and it is only towards the end of an elaborate argument that metaphor is superseded by a suddenly revealed fact:

> We now seem to know all at once what the difference is between a conscious and an unconscious presentation. The two are not, as we supposed, different registrations of the same content in different psychical localities, nor yet different functional states of cathexis in the same locality; but the conscious presentation comprises the presentation of the thing plus the presentation of the word belonging to it, while the unconscious presentation is the presentation of the thing alone. The system *Ucs.* contains the thing-cathexes of the objects, the first and true object-cathexes; the system *Pcs.* comes about by this thing-presentation

being hypercathected through being linked with the word-presentations corresponding to it ... Now, too, we are in a position to state precisely what it is that repression denies to the rejected presentation in the transference neuroses: what it denies to the presentation is translation into words which shall remain attached to the object. A presentation which is not put into words, or a psychical act which is not hyper-cathected, remains thereafter in the *Ucs.* in a state of repression. (XIV, 201–2)

Freud's distinction between word-presentations and thing-presentations serves a quite specific theoretical purpose, and should not be thought of as involving simply two different kinds of memory – the predominantly visual trace of whole objects on the one hand, and the predominantly auditory trace of the words that designate them on the other. 'Presentations' (*Vorstellungen*) are memory in so far as it is divisible into charged particles, into words or things or 'word-things' intensified and mobilized by desire. Freud makes no claim here or elsewhere to be handling objects in their phenomenal fullness, or in the multiplicity of their actual or possible forms, and has a linguistic interest that is far removed from that of the grammarian, the philologist or the lexicographer. However remote the Greek terms *cathexis* and *hypercathexis* may seem from the ordinary life of the human passions, it is to those passions in their daily exercise and in their moment-by-moment dialectic that the *Besetzung* and *Überbesetzung* of Freud's original text refer us.

Freud's emphasis in this passage is, however, not ordinary, and not the one that his earlier works seemed often to promise. While adhering to his topographical separation of the unconscious from the preconscious-conscious, and while continuing to grant the unconscious special explanatory privileges, he could have allowed words and things a

51

heterogeneous, interactive and mutually complicating existence in the field of desire. Nothing would have been lost, one might easily conclude, by imagining these presentations of word and thing as intricate and unstable at whatever level they occurred within the stratified psychical apparatus. Are not both the 'bottom up' or unconscious-led view of the mind, and the 'top down' or conscious-led view with which Freud periodically contrasts it, more likely to be enriched than impoverished by a proper appreciation of the lability of word-thing relationships? But Freud conspicuously refuses to see things in this way. A separation is necessary, and must be preserved even at the risk of seeming to purge from the operations of the unconscious the astonishing variety of verbal tricks that *The Interpretation of Dreams* had attributed to it. A central contention of 'The Unconscious', and one that reaches its culmination in the passage I have discussed, is not only that the mind continually passes from a muteness that is its own into a readiness for speech that is equally its own, but that this preliminary silence, belonging to the unconscious, is a bulwark of the entire psychoanalytic approach.

Whether the unconscious is thought of as the domain of the fundamental drives, or as a dynamically maintained repository for memories that are inadmissible to consciousness, Freud clearly does not, at this moment of theoretical summation, want speech, or even a ghostly premonition of speech, to penetrate 'down' into it. Much is at stake here. Indeed one might say that a main claim to seriousness made by Freud on behalf of his new discipline depends on distinctions of this kind. For Freud, psychoanalysis proudly keeps watch over the border territories between nature and culture. The drives are an essential part of its subject-matter, and they belong to nature long before they make their oblique and obstructed appearances in the cultural realm.

The bodily processes whereby instinctual force is accumulated and discharged need to be protected from the encroachments of culture if they are to maintain their scientific dignity; the drives need to be silent, inscrutable, unavailable to mere talk, if psychoanalysis is eventually to rejoin biology in a unified science of man. The individual's accession to language, and the continual modulation of his or her desire in interpersonal speech, made psychoanalysis possible as a therapeutic method, but it was the anterior wordlessness of desire that enabled its links with the science of organisms to be preserved.

When Lacan announces and tirelessly re-announces that 'the unconscious is structured like a language' (XI, 23; 20), he is, from the point of view of these Freudian ambitions, simply selling psychoanalysis short. Far from being an inoffensive analogical aid to the perception and articulation of mental structure, his slogan and the project that it summarizes give language a pre-eminent role. And where Freud erected barriers against language inside his mental models, Lacan at first seems to be allowing it to cross all thresholds and run amok. Yet the language-based programme of study for analysts that Lacan sketches in 'The function and field of speech' and 'The agency of the letter' is in no way deficient in intellectual ambition. Psychoanalysis is to be given a new set of organizing goals, and these are daunting ones. Moreover, by a bold rereading of the earliest psychoanalytic texts – notably *The Interpretation of Dreams*, *The Psychopathology of Everyday Life* (1901) and *Jokes and their Relation to the Unconscious* (1905) – Lacan secures backing from Freud for a theoretical project that the metapsychologist of 1915 would scarcely have recognised as speaking the language of psychoanalysis, let alone as soliciting his patronage.

Although Lacan's new programme is presented as an urgent matter of 'getting Freud right', his opening references to the three canonical Freud books are desultory and unfocused:

> Take up the work of Freud again at the *Traumdeutung* to remind yourself that the dream has the structure of a sentence or, rather, to stick to the letter of the work, of a rebus; that is to say, it has the structure of a form of writing, of which the child's dream represents the primordial ideography, and which, in the adult, reproduces the simultaneously phonetic and symbolic use of signifying elements, which can also be found both in the hieroglyphs of ancient Egypt and in the characters still used in China. (267; 57)

This paragraph recapitulates a number of Freud's speculative analogies between dreams and language, but it moves from one term of comparison to the next at great speed. For Freud, new features of the dream-work came into view each time the analogical lens was adjusted or replaced, and to say that dreams had the structure of a sentence was *not* equivalent to saying that they had that of a rebus, or of writing, or of hieroglyphic or phonetic script. With still greater rapidity, Lacan encapsulates the lessons of the *Psychopathology* in the formula 'every unsuccessful act is a successful discourse' (268; 58), and those of *Jokes* in a tribute to the ambiguity that language confers on all mental process. On each occasion Freud's works are forcibly reclothed in linguistic imagery of a kind that they themselves had often had occasion to employ. Lacan summarizes adroitly. But what he excludes from his sketch is any active sense that Freud's account of language had its stubbornly discontinuous registers, or that Freud found many of his own images unsatisfactorily provisional, or that other, non-linguistic, modelling devices also fascinated him and prevented him from thinking of psychoanalysis as a speech-science pure and simple. Lacan's translation of Freud's technical language into linguistic terms may proceed by mere word-magic.

The notion of 'symptom', for example, which for Freud provided a fortunate bridge between psychoanalysis and traditional diagnostic medicine, is blithely refurbished:

> . . . it is already quite clear that the symptom resolves itself entirely in an analysis of language, because the symptom is itself structured like a language, and because it is language from which speech must be delivered. (269; 59)

> The symptom is here the signifier [*signifiant*] of a signified [*signifié*] repressed from the consciousness of the subject. A symbol written in the sand of the flesh and on the veil of Maia, it participates in language by the semantic ambiguity that I have already emphasized in its constitution. (280; 69)

The problem with expressions like these is that they make a single feature of analytic experience resemble very closely a variety of other features: the symptom 'structured like a language' sounds like the unconscious itself, and both sound like a supra-individual and self-propelling process that may or may not have anything to do with the precise times and places where human suffering occurs. The verbal sign, even when divided with apparent technical precision into 'signifier' and 'signified', still casts its net extremely wide. It catches the strictly verbal symptoms that are to be observed in the individual patient's speech, but also the behavioural and somatic events that psychoanalysis is also obliged to confront. Lacan's indifference to distinctions of this sort may in itself be thought of as salutary, in so far as it reminds the practitioner of the specifically verbal exigencies beneath which his task is pursued. Symptoms, whether they are spoken into the air or inscribed on human flesh, are legible and interpretable, and the analyst may well need to have the full range of his interpretative responsibilities memorably resketched for him. But the 'writing' that the symptom comprises begins to speak of another kind of indifference as soon as it takes place 'on the sand' or on Lacan's curious Graeco-Hindu 'veil of Maia'. The vanity of human wishes, and the ultimate helplessness that patient and analyst share, are introduced into the discussion in such a way as to make the search for a coherent theoretical language seem pettifogging and naive.

At moments like this in 'The function and field of speech', Lacan's professional colleagues are brought before a strait gate through which only a rigorously applied linguistic expertise can allow them to pass, and then encouraged to settle for an impressionistic and relaxing metaphysics of the Word. The modern science of linguistics is often invoked, but before it has a chance to offer psychoanalysis a series of testable models it is overtaken by a superior force. This is a merely incipient super-science of 'the Symbolic'. Just as, in the last passage I quoted, the symptom turns into a symbol without being detained at the level of the signifier, so the entire conceptual edifice of psychoanalysis is to be propelled by way of linguistics towards a higher destination that Freud had foretold:

> Freud's discovery is that of the field of the effects, in the nature of man, produced by his relations to the symbolic order and the tracing of their meaning right back to the most radical agencies of symbolization in being. To ignore this symbolic order is to condemn the discovery to oblivion, and the experience to ruin. (275; 64)

Naming Freud as the herald of the Symbolic order brings problems with it, and not least at the level of technical diction. For when Freud speaks of 'symbolism' and 'the symbolic', he nearly always has in mind a stable, two-term relationship. His symbols were frozen meanings that had grown from fundamental human experiences, and they were to a large extent transportable from one individual, or one culture, to the next. Freud sometimes went so far as to claim that when the analyst encountered such symbols in the dream-work, he had no need to consult the patient's private associations in order to understand much of what was going on: the body and sexuality, together with family relationships and fears of pain and death, were matters of universal concern, and symbolizing them was a 'natural' activity of mind by which ready-made 'natural' relationships were continually remotivated. The analyst had of course to become much more subtle-minded as soon as he approached the verbal and experiential grain of individual lives. There, he could no longer expect symbolic relationships to be simple and firm, and he had to employ a set of differentiated concepts if he was to characterize adequately the signifying processes involved.

Freud's fundamental modes of unconscious mental functioning – condensation and displacement[3] – were complementary axes for the production and transformation of meaning, and allowed him to perceive structural regularities in a domain that could otherwise easily appear as an ineffable mental flux. These twin modes comprised a system that was neither too rigid nor too fluid in the kinds of process that it brought into view, and one that allowed the signifying fabric of the individual's desires to be specified. But Freud had no reason to refer to that system as 'the Symbolic', or to use any one label for a series of what were to him logically distinct relationships.

Lacan's difference from Freud is nowhere more evident than in his talk of 'the Symbolic'. This category was important to Lacan precisely because it was versatile and inclusive and referred in a single gesture to an entire range of separate signifying practices. It linked, in what promised to be a coherent and durable fashion, the world of unconscious mental process to that of speech, and both of them to the larger worlds of social and kinship structure. 'The Symbolic', for Lacan in the mid-fifties, is a supra-personal structural order that becomes interesting, from a clinical viewpoint, only when it appears as the medium of individual speech; it produces a perpetual two-way traffic-flow between the inwardness of passion and the social dispensations that weigh upon that passion in its search for satisfaction. But what is strange is that although human language is the *sine qua non* of Lacan's new symbolic science – in that it is the template from which all other varieties of structure are created – Lacan turns not to a linguist but to an anthropologist when he begins to urge a new sense of symbolism *as system* upon his analytic audience:

Since we are practitioners of the symbolic function, it is astonishing that we should turn away from probing deeper into it, to the extent of failing to recognize that it is this function that situates us at the heart of the movement that is now establishing a new order of the sciences, with a new putting in question of anthropology . . .

Isn't it striking that Lévi-Strauss, in suggesting the implication of the structures of language with that part of the social laws that regulates marriage ties and kinship, is already conquering the very terrain in which Freud situates the unconscious?

From now on, it is impossible not to make a general theory of the symbol the axis of a new classification of the sciences where the sciences of man will once more take up their central position as sciences of subjectivity. (284–85; 72–73)

Repeated tribute is paid to Claude Lévi-Strauss as one who perceived the full magnitude of the Freudian discovery, but the linguists to whom Lévi-Strauss himself was indebted in formulating his early anthropological views are not named. Roman Jakobson's definition of the phoneme and Ferdinand de Saussure's of the sign are re-used, but anonymously, as if these notions were already matters of common knowledge. One has the clear impression that at this stage Lacan finds linguistic concepts insufficiently momentous, and linguistics itself too pedantic in its devotion to the minutiae of speech. Under the aegis of Lévi-Strauss, he is able to position himself at the crossroads where all systems meet, and to survey from there the frenzied movements of structure-seeking humankind. Logics, theories of number, mathematical and combinatorial procedures of all kinds – all that is rarefied, abstract and abstruse in the arts of the mind – are reconnected to the primordial symbolic language that speech embodies. This attempt to reimmerse the builders and manipulators of higher systems in the organized chatter from which their systems grow has for Lacan an improving purpose. For a journey back to the 'original symbolism' to be found in language affords a new knowledge of what it is to be human: 'Man speaks . . . but it is because the symbol has made him man' (276; 65).

Freudian 'symbolism' redefined in such ways brings into view a boundless domain of interrelated transformational processes, belonging to the human mind yet always transcending it. In describing the Symbolic order, Lacan insists that it is governed not simply by conventional rules but by inexorable legalities, by impossibilities, absences and exclusions. But he acknowledges only perfunctorily that new structural principles, new rules of exclusion, come into play as one moves from a given system to another, and he does not for a moment suggest that the transition or the translation between systems may present difficulties. Instead, he resorts to a style of semi-theoretical incantation in which differences of logical kind are simply talked away.

For example, at the very moment of postulating a 'primary language of symbols' upon which all other languages depend, he refuses to say what these prepotent symbols are. He refers the reader in search of a definition to the surrounding paragraphs, from which definitions are irrecoverable:

> Hieroglyphics of hysteria, blazons of phobia, labyrinths of *Zwangsneurose* [obsessional neurosis] – charms of impotence, enigmas of inhibition, oracles of anxiety – armorial bearings of character, seals of self-punishment, disguises of perversion – these are the hermetic elements that our exegesis resolves, the equivocations that our invocation dissolves, the artifices that our dialectic absolves, in a deliverance of imprisoned meaning, which extends from the revelation of the palimpsest to the mystery's solution and to the grace of speech. (281; 69–70)

All this is wonderfully witty and malicious. While enumerating certain of the brute facts with which the psychological sciences are obliged to contend, Lacan draws attention to the element of fact-evading word-magic in his own writing. The processes of resolution, dissolution and absolution that he names are at once a set of creditably altruistic goals for the therapist and a set of self-pleasuring devices for the writer. What kind of lesson is this rapturous catalogue seeking to teach? The main emphasis throughout is on codes that are decipherable, problems that have solutions, and strenuous acts of reading that are in due course crowned with success. The analyst is depicted mainly as one who works with stable sign-systems, and as one whose skills in decoding and encoding bring him into an improbable cross-disciplinary peer-group comprising palaeographers, cryptanalysts, alchemists, heralds and hermetic philosophers. In marked contrast to this, the skills of those who exploit the ambiguities of natural language are only lightly sketched, although Lacan's 'labyrinths', 'oracles' and 'equivocations' clearly bring a much more volatile mode of meaning into play. When it comes to depicting the mobility and many-layeredness of the language in which the analytic dialogue takes place, however, the main expressive burden is borne not by any one analogy but by the pace and rhythm of the entire list. In a sense, Lacan overshoots the analytic dialogue here, for stable sign-systems juxtaposed as rapidly and as numerously as this begin to suggest a wild upheaval of the deciphering intelligence and an uncontrollable surplus of meaning.

In such passages, Lacan is remembering and rephrasing a prominent Freudian theme, and re-experiencing the optimism that Freud had derived from it.[4] For Freud, the analyst was the discoverer and restorer of lost orders of meaning, and as he worked he was sustained by the hope that new knowledge and positive therapeutic results would flow from his discoveries; his interpretations restored sense to the patient's world, and in so doing reopened for him a precarious path towards fulfilment. And Lacan's writing retraces the general contour of a successful Freudian interpretation of this kind. But his act of remembrance is a calculatedly imperfect one, and he attends to two dangers of which Freud in his archaeological or palaeographical moods had made little: on the one hand a superabundance of sense that overspills the analyst's chosen exegetical framework and, on the other, not a paucity but an active denial of sense that seemed to be inherent in the analytic method. In 'The function and field of speech' these dangers are announced in epigrams and to some extent enacted in Lacan's writing –

which is by turns strangulated and fluently associative. But they are not yet convincingly located within a theory.

Simplifying the story a good deal, one could say that Lacan, in this paper, moves too freely between the small world of the decipherer and the incipient but already very imposing world of the symbolic scientist. But the ultimate harmony that he foresees between the apparently discrepant structural levels that comprise 'the Symbolic' makes that most ambitious of psychoanalytic categories seem rather lazy, and insufficiently marked by the sharp discontinuities in which clinical psychoanalysis abounds. Lacan's new symbolic science, in so far as it combines ready-made systemic elements into new wholes, is an oddly undialectical affair. Indeed in the stability of the signs that it employs, and in its freedom from internal dissension, it is rather like a metaphysically ambitious version of heraldry or palmistry or phrenology. The theory that would eventually allow Lacan to accommodate the persistent problems of sense-making and system-building in his account of the Symbolic was already available to him, although he chose not to enlist it at this stage: it was the theory of the linguistic sign propounded by Saussure in his *Course in General Linguistics*.[5] And the path towards an appropriately hard-working version of the Symbolic order took Lacan back to the linguistic details that he had impatiently bypassed in 'The function and field of speech'.

In the first section of 'The agency of the letter' (1957), which is Lacan's most ingenious attempt to cross-fertilize Freud's theory and Saussure's, psychoanalytic concepts appear only reticently, and the unconscious, the *primus inter pares* of Lacan's 'four fundamental concepts', is scarcely present at all.[6] He spends a long time creating from Saussurean raw materials a linguistics fit for psychoanalysis to espouse, and this involves casting Saussure in a role that many literal-minded readers of the *Course* will find objectionable. Lacan's Saussure is a student of the sign, but only in so far as the sign articulates meanings of a fugitive and threatened kind. He is the co-discoverer with Freud of a universal mental propensity which, within an inflexible framework of constraints, dooms all human thinking to be provisional and incomplete.

A literal-minded reading of Saussure has much to recommend it, however. His binomial definition of the sign brings together two kinds of mental process and two logically commensurate notions: the *signifier*, which is an acoustic image, and the *signified*, which is a concept. In the sign, a signifier and a signified collide and are bonded. Their relationship is an arbitrary one, but once this bonding has taken place the sign becomes a fixity and occupies a far from arbitrary position in the overall system of a given language. Saussure speaks both of the sound-realm and of the thought-realm as fluid and undifferentiated when considered in isolation, and he expresses wonderment at the idea that a stable meaning-bearing particle should be produced in such an unpropitious place – at the mobile boundary between two otherwise boundless zones. The components of the sign are thought of as symmetrical and interdependent. Even before Saussure has been named in Lacan's paper, however, this symmetry has been disturbed:

> To pinpoint the emergence of linguistic science we may say that, as in the case of all sciences in the modern sense, it is contained in the constitutive moment of an algorithm that is its foundation. This algorithm is the following:
>
> $$\frac{S}{s}$$
>
> which is to be read as: signifier over signified, 'over' corresponding to the bar separating the two stages. (497; 149)

The algorithm $\frac{S}{s}$, which Lacan offers as a fertile résumé of Saussure's contribution to modern linguistics, is at once shown to have a variety of expressive powers that tend in fact to remove it from the Saussurean orbit. Lacan's placing of the signifier in the upper position has little to do with mathematical convention: this position, together with the use of a capital letter and Roman type, is a way of paying homage to the preponderance that the signifier everywhere, allegedly, enjoys. And his placing of the signified *beneath* the signifier, and beneath the algebraic bar, suggests that a moral rather than a simple topographical inferiority is at issue: the signified retreats to the lower position, shrinks into the lower case and withers into italic type. In this first reformulation of Saussure, the keynote of Lacan's entire approach to linguistics is sounded: the potency of the signifier, here symbolized in a single capital letter, is later to be the subject of countless admiring remarks and eulogistic narratives.

Lacan's account of the disproportion that reigns inside the sign has two main themes, and these are not straightforwardly reconcilable. The first is that relations between signifiers are very much more important and informative than linguistic relations of other kinds: meaning comes from a combinatory play taking place within a closed order of differentiated elements, and then only as an impalpable emanation rather than as a series of separable and recombinable notions. The domain of the signifier is independent and self-governing. Anyone who goes in search of meaning at its source, or in its essential forms, has no choice but to travel by way of language, and at every moment on this journey variously connected signifiers extend to the horizon in all directions. When the signified seems finally to be within reach, it dissolves at the explorer's touch into yet more signifiers. The signifying chain of speech comprises the 'rings of a necklace that is a ring in another necklace made of rings' (502; 153).

Lacan's second theme, however, is that 'the signifier', far from being simply a self-bounded system, has an active, colonizing power over the signified. It 'anticipates' the signified, 'encroaches upon it' and 'enters into it'. His examples are disarmingly small-scale and ordinary: empty sentence openings like 'Never do I . . .' or 'It remains the case that . . .' are already creating meaning before the arrival of the key terms that the sentence is to deploy, just as the characterless 'but' in phrases like 'black but comely' or 'poor but honest' causes an entire value-system to come into view (502; 153). But Lacan's general claim is much larger than his examples would suggest. In this second revised version of the Saussurean sign, meaning no longer emerges wraith-like from the impersonal operations of the signifier but acquires from them its force, its local character and the quality that Lacan describes as its *insistence*. Responsibility for the production of meaning no longer falls to both interactive components of the sign but to one component, hugely re-energized.

The discrepancy between these views could have been damaging to Lacan if he had left matters here. At a time when he was attempting to give a new rigour to the psychoanalytic account of language, and using Saussure as his principal theoretical support, it would have been unfortunate to be seen getting Saussure's theory wrong – and in two incompatible ways. But what Lacan is in fact doing is mapping out for himself, by an inventive re-use of Saussurean diction, a distinctive conceptual landscape in which these divergent accounts of language can be dialectically counterposed. He needed a way of describing conjointly two features of language that mattered equally to psychoanalysis but that had not until then been brought into alignment. The first was its obdurate and impersonal systemic force, and the second its fecundity, the pluralizing semantic power that it enjoyed in the speech of individual persons. For these purposes the metaphor of the 'signifying chain' proves to be particularly versatile. It has a suitably penal and correctional air: the chain is what limits the speaker's freedom, and the concatenation of its links speaks of a rigid causal order in which he is powerless to intervene. Yet the chain is also mobile, sinuous and able to loop back upon itself; any one of its links can provide a point of attachment to other chains. Polyphony and poetry are both used by Lacan as additional models for the double life that language leads:

> ... we learn that analysis consists in playing on all the many staves of the score that speech constitutes in the registers of language, and on which overdetermination depends, which has no meaning except in that order. (291; 79)

> ... one has only to listen to poetry ... for a polyphony to be heard, for it to become clear that all discourse is aligned along the several staves of a score.

> There is indeed no signifying chain that does not have, as if attached to the punctuation of each of its units, a whole articulation of relevant contexts suspended 'vertically', as it were, from that point. (503; 154)

The virtue of these models is that they dramatize a difficulty. They do not offer a view of language in which speech is either a vertical or a horizontal affair, or forward-moving at one moment and stationary the next, or rule-bound at one moment and freely creative the next. Their lesson is that the imperious system of 'the signifier',[7] and the embeddings and intrications that are to be observed within it, are the speaker's unchosen and unavoidable home terrain. The analysand's quest for the 'full' or 'true' speech that psychoanalysis fosters strictly resembles the poet's or the musician's search for originality and expressive plenitude within the structural constraints that his chosen medium relentlessly exerts.

Later in 'The agency of the letter', the complexity of Lacan's attitudes to literature begins to be revealed. At first glance, the pattern is simple enough: literature is the teacher and psychoanalysis the pupil. It is only after a protracted detour through the theory and criticism of literature that discussion of Freud is resumed in this paper, and the priority that Lacan gives to such matters in the unfolding of his argument has suggested to many literary scholars that a flatteringly high valuation is being placed upon their professional endeavours. Lacan quotes, and analyses at length, a celebrated line from Victor Hugo's 'Booz endormi' (Booz asleep), takes issue with the Surrealists on their conceptions of metaphor and automatic writing, and brings a virtuoso improvisation upon the word *arbre* ('tree') to its close with a clinching double quotation from Valéry's 'Au platane' (To the Plane Tree) (503–9; 154–9). In all these cases, the message seems to be that poets, by daily frequentation, already know about the Symbolic order. That they already are, to varying degrees, 'masters of the signifier' and that critics who analyse the polysemantic fabric of verse already understand, in advance of the textual lessons they may in due course receive from psychoanalysis, that all signification is the result of a fortunate fall into a prison of signs. Meaning can never be cut loose from its chains, but is endlessly self-replenishing none the less. To amplify this message, Lacan steps forward as a writer and demonstrates his prowess in a self-conscious parade of puns, pleasantries, conceits, learned allusions and whimsical etymologies.

67

But even in these enthusiastic pages on the poet's craft another voice is to be heard, and this speaks much less encouragingly to the literary practitioner. From Lacan's alternative viewpoint, being able to write – badly or well, abundantly or parsimoniously, in the grand manner or in the manner of a sober theoretician – is not a matter of consequence. 'The signifier' is the writer's domain, but it is everybody else's too. And if the signifier is subdivided according to its local modes of action, and thought of as a competitive interplay between the two 'slopes' (511; 160) or rhetorical dispositions that Lacan, following Jakobson, names *metaphor* and *metonymy*,[8] it becomes still more plainly a piece of public property over which the writer has no special rights. Lacan's monosyllabic redefinitions of these terms place them firmly in the copper-coinage of speech: metaphor is 'one word for another' and metonymy a matter of 'word to word' connections within the signifying chain (506–7; 156–7). Literature has the virtue of allowing us to inspect these and other rhetorical devices under laboratory conditions, and in unusually concentrated forms, but rhetoric itself has the corresponding virtue of allowing us to look beyond literature once more – into the lingua franca of human passion as it might be heard in the consulting room or the street.

This preliminary play with linguistics and literature ends upon an abrupt re-introduction of the unconscious, and the remainder of 'The agency of the letter' immerses that central analytic concept in the purifying ocean of language. If *Ecrits* can be said to have anywhere a core – a place where Lacan's main teachings are to be found in their most emphatic and exacting form – then that core is perhaps in these pages, where Lacan's refashioned linguistic notions lock on to Freud's 'psychical apparatus' with extraordinary vigour and tenacity. At first, this process involves an extreme self-effacement on Lacan's part as he contemplates an overriding characteristic of Freud's writings:

> In the complete works of Freud, one out of every three pages is devoted to philological references, one out of every two pages to logical inferences, and everywhere there is a dialectical apprehension of experience, the proportion of analysis of language increasing as the unconscious is more directly involved.
>
> Thus in *The Interpretation of Dreams* every page deals with what I call the letter of discourse, in its texture, its usage, its immanence in the matter in question. For it is with this work that the work of Freud begins to open its royal road to the unconscious. And Freud gave us notice of this; what he confided, in surprise, at the time of launching this book in the early days of this century only confirms what he continued to proclaim to the end: that he had staked the whole of his discovery on this essential expression of his message (509; 159).[9]

The whole of Freud is in *The Interpretation of Dreams*, and the whole of that work is in Freud's devoted manipulation of linguistic materials. To those who would protest at this account, pointing out that Freud the philologist and textual expositor is also, and simultaneously, a student of wordless drives and desires, and that his interpretations of the dream-text invariably depend upon a postulated order of equally wordless 'latent dream thoughts', Lacan at this stage would reply simply: trust the structure of the dreams Freud discusses, rather than the pseudo-biology with which he seeks to underwrite them. Those who are prepared to do this will see at once that 'the dream-work follows the laws of the signifier' and that the signifier has a 'constitutive role' in the unconscious realm to which dreams give access (512; 161–2).

When Lacan speaks in this way about the sense-producing and sense-transforming processes that are to be observed in dreams, he is indeed taking his cue from Freud. For Freud readily used such notions as translation, transcription, inscription and paraphrase in describing movements between one mental 'zone' or 'level' and another, and the more general terms that he chose for the two fundamental mechanisms of the dream-work – *Verdichtung* ('condensation') and *Verschiebung* ('displacement') – harmonized well with the linguistic tendency of his technical vocabulary.[10] Lacan not only reinforces this tendency but attempts to instil a new principle of harmony into the language of psychoanalysis at large. It is a matter of taking Freud literally at moments when he himself had spoken in an uncertain and semi-figurative fashion about the structure of the mind. The dream-work was a signifying domain and, when it came to modelling its action, there existed no terms more suitable than linguistic and rhetorical ones:

> *Verdichtung*, or 'condensation', is the structure of superimposition of signifiers, which metaphor takes as its field, and whose name, condensing in itself the word *Dichtung*, shows how the mechanism is connatural with poetry to the point that it envelops the traditional function proper to poetry.
>
> *Verschiebung*, 'displacement' – the German term is closer to the idea of that veering off of signification that we see in metonymy, and which from its first appearance in Freud is represented as the most appropriate means used by the unconscious to foil censorship (511; 160).[11]

The advantages of this lexical transposition become plain if we re-imagine part of an ordinary analytic encounter: the analysand narrates a dream, reports on the associations that the dream had when first recalled, and produces further associations during the session; the analyst asks questions, re-narrates, re-associates, places constructions upon the analysand's material and, by way of the tensions, delays, detours and skirmishes of the dialogue itself, moves towards an interpretation. All the crucial events here take place in language, and such circumstantial matters as décor, mood and bodily gesture are of significance only in so far as they offer further material for dialogue. What could be more appropriate, in this world where everything is indefinitely, and as a matter of entrenched therapeutic principle, subject to linguistic mediation, than for a technical language to be sought that would be applicable at all discursive levels, and at all interfaces between levels?

Lacan's metaphor and metonymy, together with the lesser figures and tropes that he often enumerates with glee, at once allow connections to be made between the overall structure of the analytic dialogue and the structure of the dream-material on which that dialogue may dwell. And this manner of speaking about analytic speech also serves to demystify the unconscious itself: the unconscious is not an occult quality or a black box but the conjectural sub-text that is required in order to make the text of dreams and conversations intelligible. The unconscious is no longer, in this view, structured 'like a language', for it has no existence outside language and no structure other than the one that language affords. When it comes to the pressure exerted by the unconscious on conscious thought, speech and action, Lacan, like Freud, thinks of this as operating without intermission. But for Lacan there is no hydraulics of the mind: its pressures can be coherently described only in terms of the interference-patterns that occur between one signifying order and another. There is, for analytic purposes, no bio-energetic power-house 'behind' or 'beneath' human speech, and there is no veiled signified-in-waiting that will eventually call the crazy procession of signifiers to order: 'The unconscious is neither the primordial nor the instinctual; what it knows about the elementary is no more than the elements of the signifier' (522; 170). The 'vertical dependencies' (515; 164) of the signifying chain extend as far downwards into the hidden worlds of mental process as it is possible for the speculative imagination to descend. Beyond the last outpost of signification there is nothing at all – or rather there is that boundless and inexpressible vacuity from which many psychoanalytic writers, including Freud himself, had tried to escape with their anxious talk of instincts and biological necessity.

Often, Lacan's pronouncements about the structure of the unconscious are at once categorical in their phrasing and merely approximate in the structural ideas they deploy. The latter quality may be thought of as the price he had to pay for his wayward exploitation of Saussure and Jakobson. For the system-building elements that both linguists bring together in their work may readily be dissociated and recombined, and the Saussurean system in particular may be mapped on to Freudian theory in a variety of ways. The opportunities for bravura invention upon the keyboard of linguistics being as extensive as they are, it is all the more remarkable to find that Lacan should refuse certain of them almost completely. The troublesome category of the signified, for example, could be thought of as available for an obvious and unproblematic use. Psychoanalysis, as is well known, grants singular privileges to repressed memories. Whether thought of as a series of self-contained blockages in the everyday operations of the remembering mind or as a continuous mental zone underlying all the activities of consciousness, such memories cause symptoms. By lifting the mental ban under which they have been placed, the analyst is able to remove or relieve symptoms. What could be easier, once Saussure's bipartite sign has been brought into play, than to regard the repressed contents of the mind as the order of the signified *par excellence*, as the bedrock of meaning that lies beneath the moving surface of the analysand's speech?

But although Lacan sometimes uses phrasing of this kind,[12] he is reluctant to take the equation signified = repressed very far. If the repressed were granted this kind of authority, then it would be entitled to occupy the upper position in his $\frac{S}{s}$ algorithm: it would have the power to encroach upon the signifier and affect its structure. An occult quality would have re-entered the psychoanalytic field, and an immaterial internal puppeteer would have been handed at least partial control of speech. The whole drift of Lacan's thinking in this area has to do with protecting the right of systems to remain systematic. Whereas certain linguistic categories – metaphor and metonymy, for instance – maintain and enhance those rights in respect of the signifier, others infringe them grievously. The signified is the most dangerous member of the second group. Metaphor and metonymy are modes of connection in the signifying chain, principles of structure and cohesion, but the signified is an undercover agent for vagueness and pathos.

This does not of course mean that Lacan removes the signified from the scene, for even the most elastic versions of Saussure require it. But it enters the theoretical picture under severe restrictions. In the main, it appears as that which the signifier almost successfully dispels, and its characteristic motions are those of slipping, sliding, hesitating, fleeing, expiring, dispersing and disappearing. And when Lacan comes to acknowledge the strange power of endurance that certain meanings nevertheless have, and the ability of such meanings to hold human lives together or to wreck them, he speaks not of signifieds that have somehow broken free from their tutelage to the signifier but of 'the point to which signified and signifier come to be knotted together' (III, 303). At moments like this, Lacan is returning his reader to the essential tragic theme of psychoanalysis: patterns of thinking laid down in childhood return to haunt and thwart the adult individual. But although, in his seminar on *The Psychoses*, he draws his main examples from a literary work that is indeed a tragedy, Racine's *Athalie*, the term that he invents for these intrications of signifier and signified belongs to the everyday world of the workshop and the domestic interior. These fixated meanings are *points de capiton* – upholstery buttons, or places where the mattress-maker's needle has worked hard to prevent a shapeless mass of stuffing from moving too freely about.[13] If these points are too firmly implanted they can drive the individual to despair and self-sacrifice, but if they are too few or too loose they threaten him with madness:

> I don't know the figures, but it's not impossible that people will succeed in working out the minimum number of fundamental attachment-points between the signifier and the signified which are necessary for a human being to be called normal, and which, when they are not established, or when they break, produce the psychotic. (III, 304)

Between the extremes of suicide and psychosis lies the fabric of ordinary lives – the upholstery of speech, the impersonal structures of language that weigh upon our freely chosen words and button them down. But wherever upon this spectrum Lacan's eye falls, the signified is still a poor thing. Even when his phrasing seems to restore a certain parity to the two components of the sign, his major emphasis is always upon the power of a speech-system to hold in thrall the speaking creatures in whom it is actualized.

A philosophical polemic runs through Lacan's account of language in psychoanalysis, and the structural notions that he borrows from linguistics are all pressed into the service of this wider campaign. We have already seen the beginnings of his case in Chapter Two. The psychoanalytic movement, Lacan claims, had from the start been too hospitable towards conceptions of selfhood that were in no way compatible with its founding insights. In particular it had treated with undue respect the idea that the self or the ego was the seat of personal identity. It saw a perpetuity of fragmentation and strife within the human individual, and then looked away. As if it had noticed nothing disquieting, it ascribed to the ego a set of self-regulatory and self-reparative powers and prescribed for itself the task of helping the ego to exercise these fruitfully during periods of crisis or malaise. 'Ego' was a principle of constancy in the natural world, and a stabilizing lens through which the behaviour, the emotional dispositions and the intellectual aptitudes of the individual could be observed. Disruptive forces seemingly internal to the mind were of course a fact of life – like thunderstorms, tidal waves, disease and mortality – and provided strenuous daily exercise for the ego's integrative faculties. But the philosophizing analyst, lost in acquiescent admiration for the ego, could easily find himself with little to say about those forces when he began to construct his doctrine of subjectivity. Psychoanalysis was in danger of becoming 'a right-thinking movement whose crowning expression is the sociological poem of the *autonomous ego*' (523; 171). Against all this benign, ego-enhancing talk, Lacan presents himself as standing firm. For him, the distinguishing marks of subjectivity are to be found not in the forces, faculties, aptitudes and dispositions that individuals in varying combinations possess, but in the signifying processes of which they are part. His philosophy of the human subject is self-consciously thin, empty and weightless. He invents a subject without subject-matter.

'The signifier' – in the special enlarged sense that Lacan has given it – is a new broom with which to sweep aside centuries of obsolete psychological speculation:

> If what Freud discovered and rediscovers with a perpetually increasing sense of shock has a meaning, it is that the displacement of the signifier determines the subjects in their acts, in their destiny, in their refusals, in their blindnesses, in their end and in their fate, their innate gifts and social acquisitions notwithstanding, without regard for character or sex, and that, willingly or not, everything that might be considered the stuff of psychology, kit and caboodle, will follow the path of the signifier. (30; *French Freud*, 60)

This paragraph from the celebrated seminar on Poe's 'The Purloined Letter' that Lacan delivered in 1955 performs the delicate task of disengaging the essential Freudian message from the words Freud actually wrote. It is one of numerous formulations in which the signifier becomes a versatile topological space, a device for plotting and replotting the itineraries of Lacan's empty subject. 'The subject' is no longer a substance endowed with qualities, or a fixed shape possessing dimensions, or a container awaiting the multifarious contents that experience provides: it is a series of events within language, a procession of turns, tropes and inflections. 'A signifier is that which represents the subject for another signifier' (819), Lacan was to say a few years later. Just as the hen is an egg's way of producing another egg, so the characteristic sensations of 'being a person' or 'having a personality' come from the self-perpetuating imperative that propels the signifying chain.

Lacan's jargon of signification has as its most conspicuous advantage that of removing minds, and mental processes or apparatuses, from the scene. 'The signifier' and its cognates not only cover the entire field that had previously been designated 'mental' but redramatize the crucial conscious-unconscious distinction and provide a sketch at least of the relations between the speaking subject and the social order. Lacan's new view of the subject is a correction both of Freud himself and of the European philosophical tradition – often personified for Lacan by Descartes – to which Freud had at moments offered his docile adherence.[14]

Lacan sets out to inhabit the linguistic dimension that the Cartesian *cogito* failed to acknowledge. The subject is irremediably split in and by language, but 'modern man' still has not learned this lesson. He thinks himself wonderfully astute for parading his doubts and uncertainties – where Descartes had striven merely to rescue himself from his – but does not understand that the trust he places in language, even as he prates about his doubts, is in direct line of descent from the *cogito*. After Freud, there is no one 'thought' on which to base the existential proposition 'I think therefore I am' or such modern derivatives as 'I am in the very act of saying "I am what I am"' or 'being lost, I nevertheless am'. And after Lacan, there is no simple, single signifying level that would allow an appropriate psychoanalytic counter-proposal to be made. Hence the *cogito* is not flatly repudiated; its terms and its propositional structure are refashioned in a sequence of parodic alternatives:

I think where I am not, therefore I am where I do not think.

I am not wherever I am the plaything of my thought.

I think of what I am where I do not think I'm thinking. (517; 166)

This is the general import of psychoanalysis mockingly translated into Cartesian language, but it is also a peculiarly Lacanian tribute to the power of the signifier: Descartes's formula is a short signifying segment that can be extended and embellished indefinitely. The unconscious is a language that can be made and remade from any language at all, or from any fragment of discourse containing at least two discrete elements. Philosophical statements made by Descartes, Hegel or Heidegger, or poetic statements made by Shakespeare, Góngora or Hugo, have no special status in the eyes of the unconscious. He who would interpret its productions must be 'an encyclopaedia of the arts and muses, as well as an assiduous reader of the *Fliegende Blätter*' (521; 169), and he who would produce models of the unconscious must heed the call of structure that is to be heard wherever the human voice sounds – in the modulated cries of a child as much as in polysyllabic adult conversation. A child's alternating exclamations *fort* and *da*, as reported by Freud in *Beyond the Pleasure Principle* (XVIII, 14–17), offer psychoanalysis, among other things, a lesson in theoretical parsimony. In these counterposed vocal gestures is to be found an intimation of the unconscious in the full range of its structuring capacities. So much from so little.

There is, then, a central paradox in Lacan's handling of the *Course in General Linguistics*. The technical language of linguistics, as purged and codified by Saussure, has an appealing economy about it, and even when Lacan carelessly misuses Saussure's terms, or deliberately alters their meanings, his 'sign', 'signifier' and 'signification' bring a new harmony to the cacophonous psychoanalytic lexicon. But once 'signifier' has risen to its preponderant rank, and in the process usurped so many other notions, it can afford to scatter itself across the firmament. For the Lacanian signifier is no ordinary technical term: it migrates into all other terms, potentiates them and silently propels them as they perform their tasks. Lacan speaks of the 'law of the signifier' and in so doing exploits the ambiguity of the genitive: this is at once the law from which the signifier comes and the law that the signifier in its turn exerts upon the desiring subject. Subjects who happen to be theorists are bound by it quite as much as their fellow human beings, and benefit quite as much from the peculiar grace that it dispenses: this is a law that cannot not be obeyed, and that applies with sovereign indifference to all speech. It both binds and liberates; it both cramps desire and sends it on an endless journey. Saussurean jargon, as manipulated by Lacan, stands at the threshold of all other language and invites the theorist in. Once its harmonizing office has been performed, it makes a new richness of implication – a new chromatic plenitude, one might say – possible within and beyond the language of psychoanalysis. The analyst becomes a knight errant in the world of words, and everywhere he goes he finds new models of the unconscious to tilt at.

Lacan's self-appointed task in 'The function and field of speech' and 'The agency of the letter' is, as I have said, to redescribe the entire Freudian enterprise, and to bring into focus its inveterately linguistic character. In performing this task, however, he finds that Saussurean notions, for all the versatility they display in giving voice to the unconscious, are subject to a severe limitation elsewhere. For psychoanalysis is a science not of isolated minds, but of minds that are co-present and interactive; the speech it studies takes place between individuals and bears the marks of their conflict. While 'the signifier' is in one sense perfectly public – it is an encompassing social order that individuals inhabit and are inhabited by – it has very little to say about the intersubjective dramas that occupy ordinary life and that analytic therapy seeks to restage in schematic and condensed form. In order to find appropriate dramaturgical tools

79

for this part of his linguistic project, Lacan had to go outside linguistic theory altogether.

He went to Hegel and to the 'Other'. But not to the thinly diffused Hegel who had already made it possible for analysts to speak knowingly of the 'existence of the other' and a 'feeling of otherness', and to describe their role as that of being 'the other' for each of their patients in turn. Lacan's Hegel is the author principally of the *Phenomenology of Spirit* (1807), who had been made available to Lacan and others of his generation by the combined scholarly efforts of Alexandre Kojève and Jean Hyppolite. He is, that is to say, the supremely resourceful poet of an otherness that haunts consciousness and finds endless echoes and analogues in the public sphere. This Hegel is introduced into the arguments of *Ecrits* in two distinct ways. On the one hand, he inspires many arresting statements on the desiring transactions that take place between individuals and on the constitutive role that other people have *ab initio* in the formation of the subject:

> For in this labour which he undertakes to reconstruct [his imaginary being] *for another*, he rediscovers the fundamental alienation that made him construct it *like another*, and which has always destined it to be taken from him *by another*. (249; 42)
> ... man's desire finds its meaning in the desire of the other, not so much because the other holds the key to the object desired, as because the first object of desire is to be recognized by the other. (268; 58)

In sentences of this kind the Subject–Other encounter takes place not in language but in the glare and counter-glare of desire; Lacan's writing reminds us of language, and of its multifarious modes of action, simply by being so conceited and self-aware. On the other hand, the Hegelian dialectic of

Subject and Other may be recast much more directly in terms of its spoken and unspoken verbal content:

> What I seek in speech is the response of the other. What constitutes me as subject is my question. In order to be recognized by the other, I utter what was only in view of what will be. In order to find him, I call him by a name that he must assume or refuse in order to reply to me. (299; 86)
>
> The Other is, therefore, the locus in which is constituted the I who speaks with him who hears, that which is said by the one being already the reply, the other deciding to hear it whether the one has or has not spoken. (431; 141)
>
> . . .this other is the Other that even my lie invokes as a guarantor of the truth in which it subsists. (524; 172)

Speech – true or false statements, questions, answers, names – has now become the necessary and inescapable medium of desire, the place where Subject and Other come into being conjointly, and under pressure each from each.

To some extent Lacan's Hegelian manner serves simply to glamorize ideas that are already present in Freud's work. Freud would never have spoken of 'the radical ex-centricity of one to himself with which man is confronted' or of 'a radical heteronomy gaping within man' (524; 171–2), but he did describe, patiently and with restraint, the emergence of selfhood from the individual's earliest identifications with others, the influence that the 'others' of childhood continued to exert upon the individual's later life and the elaborate defensive negotiations that were necessary in order to sustain a sense of self in the face of a coercive social group. 'Ex-centricity' and 'heteronomy' were Freud's themes, we might say, without being his words.

Lacan is not, however, simply restating certain aspects of Freud's teaching with portentous and memorable brevity:

he is reconnecting analytic topics that had previously drifted apart. When he says that 'the unconscious is the discourse of the Other' (379), for example, he is knotting into an enigma a group of individually forcible postulations: the human subject is divided; the unconscious has a linguistic structure; the subject is inhabited by the Other; psychoanalysis is a variety of speech. And he is hinting at a kinship, developed at length elsewhere, between the structure of language and the structure of the subject: both are articulations of difference; neither has a centre; both involve endless displacement; neither has a point of plenitude or stasis. In sententious statements of this kind Lacan is using Hegel as a particularly expressive form of shorthand. Despite their pared-down syntax, they allow the ruminative murmur of an entire, complex theory to be heard.

But they offer an escape from complexity too. 'This, then, was the complete game', Freud writes of the child's *fort* and *da*, '– disappearance and return' (XVIII, 15). And Lacan's complete game has, beneath the riddles and ornaments of his style, a comparably simple rhythm: the other-infested subject can have no other destiny than that of successive disappearance and return, entity and non-entity, sense and nonsense, concentration and dispersal, being there and being gone. The subject's language is not a late-coming and accidental vehicle for this rhythm: for language was there from the beginning, as the condition of the individual's subjecthood, and supplies the underlying vacillatory pattern for all his adventures in being. Language may of course be construed as an abstract system, and for that purpose may be drained of its personal content. But as soon as language takes again the form of speech it reassumes its intersubjective character: it becomes a 'third locus' (525; 173), the endlessly mobile space in which the Subject and its Other are made, dissolved and remade.

Lacan's 'Other' is a pliable and sometimes confusing

notion. For it designates now one member of the dialectical couple 'Subject–Other' and now the limitless field and overriding condition in which both members find themselves – 'alterity', 'otherness'. When Lacan writes, for example, 'it is the signifier itself that must be articulated in the Other' (551; 195), the term is clearly being used in this second sense, while in most of the formulations I quoted a moment ago it is equally clearly being used in the first. The oracular power of such sentences as 'the unconscious is the discourse of the Other' comes, in large part, from the hesitation they encourage in the reader between these long-range and short-range definitions. What does the sentence mean? That the unconscious is where the Other performs his darkest deeds, as an occupying force or a fifth column, or that the unconscious is otherness pure and simple, the 'other scene' by which our conscious thought and action are constantly shadowed?[15]

In either sense, and in both senses at once, 'the Other' has a crucial place in Lacan's theory. Like all dynamicists of the mind, he needs something to make things move. But he adamantly denies himself the support of nature as a source of propellent energy: the instincts are accorded no explanatory power in the discussion of human desire, and 'natural' analogies between the human and non-human worlds are continually devalued. 'The Other' propels, where nature, instinct and nervous excitation do not. It is that which always insinuates itself between the individual and the objects of 'his' desire; which traverses those objects and makes them unstable; and which makes desire insatiable by continuously moving its target. And as language is the site of desire – the supreme mechanism for its production and transformation, the complete tease – the Other takes language as its field of action. Where 'natural' analogies, and symbolism based upon them, offer the promise of completion, fullness, symmetry and repose at the end of the signifying process, the Other keeps the signifier perpetually on the move.

Lacan's account of language in psychoanalysis seems remarkably efficient and economical when we consider the sheer variety of disconnected topics that he chooses to discuss. And he forcibly recalls his colleagues to a sense of professional responsibility: if language is to be your main source of clinical data and your main therapeutic instrument, you must rid yourselves of your superstitions about it and seek to understand its efficacy. Yet the manner of his own assent to the linguistic imperative that he spells out for others is, in at least one important respect, disconcerting. He speaks in his Poe seminar of 'the supremacy of the signifier in the subject' and 'the pre-eminence of the signifier over the subject' (20, 39; *French Freud*, 50, 70), and draws upon a rich stock of near-synonyms to make the same point elsewhere. In the life of individuals, and in the world beyond, the signifier has priority, precedence, primacy, predominance, insistence, amplitude, autonomous power . . . Although Lacan often derides the psychoanalytic quest for the primordial in human affairs – for early formative events to which clinical explanations may be anchored, for the first mental causes from which an indefinite sequence of effects smoothly flows – and recommends the notion of 'signifying chain' precisely for the superior subtlety of the causal schemes that it makes available, it is primordiality, yet again, and in a particularly blatant form, that is to be heard reasserting itself in this recurrent tribute to the signifier.[16] Wherever you go, whatever you do, the signifier is already there. It is the power behind the power that individuals and groups exert. It is inexorable. Even as it allows its subject populations the sensation of 'free' play, it is in fact tightening its grip upon them, and its authority is no less complete for being exercised with discretion and

guile. Lacan's gloating, self-righteous 'not-I-but-the-signi-
fier' refrain brings him dangerously close to the language of
fundamentalism and to an acquiescence before supra-
human authority that sounds out of place both in Freudian
scholarship and in the practice of psychoanalysis.

'The signifier' is of course a convenient catch-phrase.
Lacan uses it, in his papers of the nineteen-fifties, as a way
of suggesting the existence, within the noise of human
language, of a fundamental level of structuration, by
recourse to which the manifold flowering of social and
cultural forms may be understood. 'The Symbolic' is an
equally convenient way of sketching the entire range of
those levels, from lowest to highest, and the common
structural principles that allow them to intercommunicate.
Yet an undifferentiated pseudo-technical noise is always
threatening his discussion. 'The signifier' and 'the Symbolic', together with the notion of 'structure' that each of
them seeks to enforce, shade at moments into a perfectly
metaphysical 'language', 'discourse' or 'speech'. Lacan's
rhetoric catches up all these terms in a single enthusiasm,
and the overwhelming potency he ascribes to the signifier
flows bountifully into its dependent concepts.

The final paragraphs of 'The function and field of speech'
contain Lacan's most expansive homage to the new Logos
that psychoanalysis has revealed, and his grandest gesture
of self-identification with a transcendent power:

> When the Devas, the men and the Asuras were ending
> their novitiate with Prajapâti, so we read in the second
> Brâhmana of the fifth lesson of the Bhrad-âranyaka
> Upanishad, they addressed to him this prayer: 'Speak to
> us.'
>
> '*Da*', said Prajapâti, god of thunder. 'Did you hear
> me?' And the Devas answered and said: 'Thou hast said
> to us: *Damyata*, master yourselves' – the sacred text

85

meaning that the powers above submit to the law of speech.

'*Da*', said Prajapâti, god of thunder. 'Did you hear me?' And the men answered and said: 'Thou hast said to us: *Datta*, give' – the sacred text meaning that men recognize each other by the gift of speech.

'*Da*', said Prajapâti, god of thunder. 'Did you hear me?' And the Asuras answered and said: 'Thou has said to us: *Dayadhvam*, be merciful' – the sacred text meaning that the powers below resound to the invocation of speech.

That, continues the text, is what the divine voice caused to be heard in the thunder: Submission, gift, grace. *Da da da*.

For Prajapâti replies to all: 'You have heard me.' (322; 106–7)

Could there ever be a more fortunate outcome for the analytic enterprise, concerned as it routinely is with the abjection of human desire and the threadbare language in which that desire speaks, than to find itself the agent of an authority so exalted that even the Gods are subject to its law?

Looked at in one way, Lacan's valediction is an encouraging retort to the final pages of T.S. Eliot's *The Waste Land* (1922), which make use of the same Sanskrit text. And it seems to have a charitable purpose – that of softening the impact of signifying law upon practitioners of the word. Lacan thunders at his professional peers, but offers them reassuring practical advice. 'Submission, gift, grace' states three analytic guidelines that could be amplified in any number of constructive-sounding ways. For example: 'you must recognise the unyielding framework of constraints that language places upon the analytic dialogue'; 'you must help your patient to acquire speech that will as far as

possible be full, flowing and commensurate with his wishes';
'you must treat him with compassion'. Yet Lacan-Prajapâti's
message descends upon everyone indifferently. Whether or
not human beings listen, whether or not they listen well,
they cannot but hear. This *'da da da'* is not simply a
mnemonic device with which to summon up three cardinal
virtues: it is the sound language makes when it has become
blah-blah, jaw-jaw, a passing susurration within the cosmic
process. It is language that has become a hobbyhorse (*un
dada*), or an enemy of hierarchy in all its forms (Dada). And
above all, in the immediate context of Lacan's 'Rome discourse', it is an answer to the *fort/da* of *Beyond the Pleasure
Principle*. Lacan has just been discussing the structuring
capacity of Freud's elemental 'symbolic couple', and the
model of signification that it provides. But against the strong
rhythmicity of the contrasted sounds *fort* and *da*, he now sets
the enfeebled rhythm, the near-noise, of *da da da*. This is the
language of prophecy moving towards a final emptiness.

The gesture is characteristic, and the conclusion that it
provides for Lacan's seminal paper is appropriately ambigu-
ous. On the one hand, the Symbolic relentlessly pre-ordains
and organizes human experience, but on the other hand it
cancels experience. It creates meaning, yet also withdraws it.
It vivifies, yet also mortifies. The unconscious 'structured
like a language' exists, for Lacan, in conditions of extreme
peril, and the broader lessons that he attaches to his slogan
are often extremely uncomfortable ones. The real scandal of
psychoanalysis, he says in 'The agency of the letter', and the
factor that has provoked public resistance to it from the start,
'is the abyss opened up at the thought that a thought should
make itself heard in the abyss' (522; 170). But the abysmal
realm that psychoanalysis obliges us to contemplate is not,
as we shall see, merely the ultimate vacuity over which all
language runs: it is a deathliness written into the Symbolic
order and present at all its functions.

4 Symbolic, Imaginary, Real . . . and True

When, in 1923, Freud proposed a new, triadic structure for the mind he began to experience what was for him a new kind of theoretical difficulty. At the outset the differentiation of the mind into an id, an ego and a super-ego marked a clear advance in the theory of mental dynamics: where the division between the unconscious and preconscious-conscious systems had come to have a straitening effect upon Freud's discussion of the mind's internal action, the new triad re-energized the whole picture. Where earlier all mental forces or agencies had had to belong to one or other of the postulated 'systems',[1] it was now possible to be much more flexible and, by a prudent sub-division and recombination of the three main power-zones, to produce a complex set of intercommunicating transmission lines. But connections between id, ego and super-ego could easily become unmanageably elaborate, especially as those that belonged to the here-and-how of the mind in action often recapitulated moments or stages from that mind's developmental history. Although the thinking in threes upon which Freud embarked in *The Ego and the Id* had certain obvious advantages over the thinking in twos that had dominated his psychological writings until then, it could bring an enveloping air of complication to the most straightforward-seeming descriptive tasks.

One of Freud's responses to this complication was poetic and dramatic in character. It was a matter of re-employing certain of the simple images that had been present in psychoanalysis from the start. The entire edifice of analytic theory rested upon a singular initial choice of subject-matter: within the indefinitely extending world of natural process, Freud focused his attention on the human organism, and within that organism on those structures and functions familiarly called 'mental'. If the mysteries of the universe had anywhere a point of special intensity, one where the explanatory zeal of the scientist seemed particularly worth applying, that point was to be found in the individual mind, isolated for experimental purposes from the rest of the natural world. The *person* gave Freud's new science its subject-matter, and the person's 'psychical apparatus' became the essential point of re-entry to the larger worlds of nature and society. Freud's attempts to control the fertility of his later mental model were often made in strict accordance with this original focus: memorable images of mental process could be produced by envisaging the mind as a group of persons in restless co-existence or open strife. An impersonal language of force – one that spoke, for instance, of quantifiable excitation and its modes of discharge – was still attractive, especially as it held out the promise that psychoanalysis might eventually become a 'hard' science, but when it came to the phenomenology of mental process there was no contest: dividing the mind into *dramatis personae* made sense in theoretical terms because being divided in that way was what it felt like to have a mind.

The extraordinary last chapter of *The Ego and the Id* (1923), which is devoted to 'The Dependent Relationships of the Ego', teems with such stage characters. Discussing melancholia, for example, Freud writes:

. . . the excessively strong super-ego which has obtained a hold upon consciousness rages against the ego with merciless violence, as if it had taken possession of the

89

> whole of the sadism available in the person concerned. Following our view of sadism, we should say that the destructive component had entrenched itself in the super-ego and turned against the ego. What is now holding sway in the super-ego is, as it were, a pure culture of the death instinct, and in fact it often enough succeeds in driving the ego into death, if the latter does not fend off its tyrant in time by the change round into mania. (XIX, 53)

Where the super-ego here acts upon the ego as an Attila or a Tamburlaine, the ego itself is generally confined to more modest roles. It resembles a constitutional monarch 'without whose sanction no law can be passed but who hesitates long before imposing his veto on any measure put forward by Parliament'; a 'sycophantic, opportunist and lying' politician; a physician during analytic treatment; a submissive slave (XIX, 55–7). And although the ego does on occasion play much more glorious and much less glorious parts – at one extreme it can take over from the id as the 'representative of Eros' and at the other resemble protista 'destroyed by the products of decomposition that they themselves have created' – it is in these unremarkable human characters that its ordinary powers, weaknesses and dilemmas are figured. Freud's intricate mental dynamics are simplified, then, by the idea of a *person in whom there are persons*, and the implication of the individual in worlds larger than himself is correspondingly understated. The turbulent and threatening id is the ego's 'second external world' and Freud's attention is much more readily drawn to this outside that is inside than to the external world proper or to the desiring, speaking subjects who populate it.

During the nineteen-fifties Lacan developed his own triadic style of thinking, and this may be seen in large part as a complement to Freud's: it is an attempt to extend psychoanalytic discussion into a fully intersubjective dimension. The Symbolic, the Imaginary and the Real are not mental forces, personifiable on the model-builder's inner stage, but *orders* each of which serves to position the individual within a force-field that traverses him.[2] The term *order* itself has for Lacan a number of important connotations. It suggests that a hierarchical arrangement of classes is taking place, as in a botanical or zoological taxonomy; that internal principles of similarity and congruence govern membership of each class; that higher classificatory levels have superior cognitive status; and that from some undetected source a series of orders or commands is being issued to the theorist. But, although Lacan's three orders often seem to be seeking the approval of natural science, they are as firmly centred upon mind-stuff as Freud's three agencies had been: it is only in the interaction of minds that the variously related orders begin to acquire explanatory depth.

Again like the id, the ego and the super-ego, Lacan's Symbolic, Imaginary and Real have an air of undisguised ambition about them. Indeed within the human sphere no limitations are placed upon their warrant. They can be used to pinpoint the sources of conflict in all kinds and conditions of men and women, and are available for the study of ordinary mental functioning no less readily than for the treatment of neurosis and psychosis. And just as a physicist would not be content with a theory of superstrings that worked well in San Francisco but badly in Los Angeles, or well on Earth but badly on Neptune, so Lacan expects the permutations of his triad to be enlightening across the entire range of human classes, societies and cultures. At moments, moreover, the three orders slip their human moorings altogether, and become warring principles in a grandiose cosmological allegory.

Each of the three, considered alone, may be defined in fairly straightforward terms. What is more, each keeps a firm core of meaning over the later decades of Lacan's career, despite the invitation to semantic slippage that his account of the signifier offers. Both the Imaginary and the Symbolic were arrived at after long periods of varied theoretical speculation, and each came to stand as a one-word summary of the gestatory processes involved. I have surveyed those processes in Chapters Two and Three respectively. The Imaginary is the order of mirror-images, identifications and reciprocities. It is the dimension of experience in which the individual seeks not simply to placate the Other but to dissolve his otherness by becoming his counterpart. By way of the Imaginary, the original identificatory procedures which brought the ego into being are repeated and reinforced by the individual in his relationship with the external world of people and things. The Imaginary is the scene of a desperate delusional attempt to be and to remain 'what one is' by gathering to oneself ever more instances of sameness, resemblance and self-replication; it is the birthplace of the narcissistic 'ideal ego' (*Idealich, moi idéal*). Lacan's 'Imaginary' thus creates a bridge between inner-directed and outer-directed mental acts, and belongs as much to the objects of perception as to those internal objects for which the word is usually reserved in ordinary speech. The term has a strong pejorative force, and suggests that the subject is seeking, in a wilful and blameworthy fashion, to remove himself from the flux of becoming.

The Symbolic order, on the other hand, is often spoken of admiringly. It is the realm of movement rather than fixity, and of heterogeneity rather than similarity. It is the realm of language, the unconscious and an otherness that remains other. This is the order in which the subject as distinct from the ego comes into being, and into a manner of being that is always disjoined and intermittent. In the Symbolic order 'nothing exists except on an assumed foundation of absence.

Nothing exists except in so far as it does not exist' (392). Gaps have as much signifying power as plenitudes, and neither has such power without the other. Whereas the inhabitant of the Imaginary ventures into the world of others only to freeze, foreshorten and incorporate it, the Symbolic is inveterately intersubjective and social. It is a *res publica* that does not allow any one of its members to be himself, keep himself to himself or recreate in his own image the things that lie beyond him.[3]

To some extent, the Symbolic and the Imaginary are a contrasting and interdependent pair: on numerous occasions in *Ecrits* and the *Seminar* each is implicated in the redefinition of the other. Moreover the moral qualities associated with the two orders are themselves polarized, and often seem to rest on a categorical separation of virtue from vice that is of doubtful worth to psychoanalysis either as a mental science or as a therapeutic method. Yet in so far as the two orders become symmetrical in such ways, they come under suspicion from their author, who is not only temperamentally hostile to dyadic patterns of thought but seems to have forged his notion of the Imaginary precisely in order to discredit them. 'All two-sided relationships are always stamped with the style of the imaginary,' Lacan and Wladimir Granoff announce in their co-written paper on fetishism (1956).[4] The 'style of the imaginary', when it is described in terms as broad as these, is of course difficult to expunge from intellectual pursuits, and we need not be surprised to find Lacan lapsing into it from time to time. Even in the heartlands of the Symbolic order, the Imaginary may retain a foothold. When Lacan writes, for example, 'The unconscious is that discourse of the Other where the subject receives, in the inverted form which is appropriate to the promise, his own forgotten message' (439), a thinly disguised imagery of mirroring and noise-free telecommunication may be seen reclaiming for the Imaginary at least

93

part of the terrain that the aphorism as a whole is staking out for the disjunctive Symbolic order. But it would be unwise to become agitated about phrasing of this kind. For Lacan himself introduces all manner of snags and discrepancies into his would-be dualism, and moves boldly from the dyadic to the triadic style. A third order, a 'third locus' that cannot be assimilated to either of the others, is postulated as a permanent agent of disharmony between them. The gravitational pull exerted by the Real upon the Symbolic and the Imaginary is such that their relationship can never be other than skewed and unstable.

Lacan's account of the Real is marked by a solemnity of utterance not often to be found elsewhere in his writings. Dance as one may in the chequered shade of the signifier, parade as one may the plumage of one's own literary style, there yet exists a world that falls entirely and irretrievably outside the signifying dimension. And this world must be spoken of in terms appropriate to it if the verbal performances of the speaking subject are not to have preposterous claims made on their behalf: 'For the real, whatever upheaval we subject it to, is always in its place; it carries it glued to its heel, ignorant of what might exile it from there' (25; *French Freud*, 55). 'The real is that which always comes back to the same place' (XI, 49; 49) is a convenient formula, but it understates the degree to which Lacan's concept is separate from 'reality' as it is usually understood in psychoanalysis. For Freud 'reality' is the world external to the human mind, and the 'reality principle' lies in the individual's recognition that this world places limitations upon him as he pursues his pleasures. For Lacan, on the other hand, the Real is that which lies outside the symbolic process, and it is to be found in the mental as well as in the material world: a trauma, for example, is as intractable and unsymbolizable as objects in their materiality. Language has powers over the Real:

It is the world of words that creates the world of things
– the things originally confused in the *hic et nunc* of
the all in the process of coming-into-being – by giving
its concrete being to their essence, and its ubiquity to
what has always been: κτῆμα ἐς ἀεί.(276; 65)

But allowing the structure of the Real to emerge against the
background of a primitive, undifferentiated All is not the
same thing as being able to name it, process it symbolically
and put it to work for one's own ends:

For the real does not wait, and specifically not for the
subject, since it expects nothing from the word. But it
is there, identical to its existence, a noise in which
everything can be heard, and ready to submerge in its
outbursts what the 'reality principle' constructs within
it under the name of external world. (388)

This noise in which one can hear 'everything' is the All re-
emerging in triumph as that surface upon which human
beings can never achieve purchase. The Real, that is to say,
is the endlessly daunting power which supersedes the
already very considerable power that Lacan ascribes to the
Symbolic. For Lacan, the Real thus comes close to meaning
'the ineffable' or 'the impossible', but this does not lead him
to adopt daunted or resigned attitudes towards it. On the
contrary it is a practical analytic tool. The importance of
the concept lies not only in the additional work that it
compels the Symbolic and the Imaginary to perform inside
a self-enclosed system, but in the contribution that it makes
to the discussion of vexed psychoanalytic issues.

Before we look more closely at these uses of the concept,
and at the range of interactions that Lacan brings about
within his triangular arrangement of orders, I must make it
clear what kind of triadic thinking we are concerned with.
On first noticing the Hegelian undercurrent that runs

through so much of Lacan's work, the reader could suspect him of wishing to mitigate the harsher teachings of psycho-analysis. For Freud, all hopes of perfect self-possession were idle, and the dealings between id, ego and super-ego could never be expected to reach a final point of settlement. His tripartite mind, like its bipartite predecessor, had conflict as its inescapable native condition. The mind had integrative capacities, of course, and the skilled therapist could co-operate with these during treatment, but no peaceable kingdom, where all mental ghosts and demons would finally be laid to rest, awaited the human subject and his travelling companions at the end of their journey. Analysis was the enemy of such illusions, and offered the mind no release from its unceasing internal dialectic other than the one that death had already promised it.

Psychoanalysis was not, and could never be, an idealism, Lacan insisted (XI, 53; 53). How could Hegel, of all improbable antecedents, help him to remain steadfast in this refusal? For Hegel's *Phenomenology* is the story of a sublimely successful integrative exploit, carried out upon itself and on its own behalf by a representative individual consciousness. The progress of that consciousness is figured as a circular upward movement towards absolute knowledge. The destination towards which the mobile and variously self-divided consciousness relentlessly tends is not simply that of a final inclusiveness, a condition in which all its previous and all its potential states survive in harmony, but that of a union, at last consummated, with Spirit at large. And the workaday instrument of this progress, and the key to Hegel's entire philosophy of growth and development in the *Phenomenology*, is, of course, the dialectical triad. What is more, the process whereby two previously contrasted states or postulations reach their moment of synthesis has its own three-in-oneness. The essential dialectical operation is one by which oppositions are *aufgehoben* – simultaneously annulled, preserved and raised to a higher level. All moments of resolution reached in this way, with the sole exception of the very last, re-begin the dialectic one level up and add a further twist to the ascending spiral. A metaphysical project of this kind seems bound to bring the contagion of idealism to psychoanalysis, and to show its disputatious agencies or orders a delusional upward path towards reconciliation.[5]

In 'Position of the unconscious' (1960), Lacan is to be seen simultaneously accepting and rejecting Hegel, in a passage whose mood of high-minded ambivalence will be familiar from many of his declarations of allegiance to Freud himself:

> . . . the use we made of Hegel's phenomenology involved no allegiance to the system, but preached by example in order to counter the obvious facts of identification . . .
>
> Beyond that, the Hegelian utterances, even if one confines oneself to the text of them, are propitious for saying always an Other-thing. An Other-thing that corrects their linkage by phantasmatic synthesis, while at the same time preserving the effect they have of exposing identifications in their illusoriness.
>
> This is our personal *Aufhebung*, which transforms that of Hegel, which was his personal illusion, into an opportunity to pick out, instead and in place of the leaps of an ideal progress, the avatars of a lack. (837)

Hegel in this account is both a critic and a victim of the identificatory mechanisms that underlie the Imaginary order. On the one hand, the narratives of unhappy and alienated consciousness that fill the early sections of the *Phenomenology* are trenchant indictments of human folly, and have a cautionary lesson to teach: the 'beautiful soul'

97

(*schöne Seele*, *belle âme*), for example, identifies the law of his own heart with the law of Nature and thereby comes to adopt absurd postures of conceit or self-absorption.[6] And even though the overall dramatic structure of Hegel's book requires that consciousness pass through such stages as these – they are its necessary ordeals, stations on its way – his tone as he describes them is far from sagacious and all-forgiving. Hegel is a merciless satirist of what cannot strictly be other than it is, and attacks from the vantage-point afforded by later and superior modes of awareness the earlier and inferior modes without which the entire dialectic of Spirit, and the eventual beatification to which it conduces, would not have been possible. Yet, on the other hand, this abrasive Hegel, who 'exposes identifications in their illusoriness', is himself subject to the temptation he denounces: the threefold *Aufhebung* that propels his dialectic mildly contests the authority of the mutually reflecting and mutually confirming couple, but overall, in the 'linkage by phantasmatic synthesis' that the dialectic enacts, the principle of identification reasserts itself in a crazily over-weening form. Hegel could have been the pure poet of otherness and its ubiquity, but his nerve failed. He gave every appearance of having understood the lacunary and lack-ridden character of the Symbolic, but lapsed from his own insight and strove for the fraudulent intactness of the Imaginary.

Lacan's triadic style resembles Freud's but not Hegel's, then, in that it seeks to cover the entire human field without promising the individual mind any final consolidation of its powers or removal of its deficiencies. The Symbolic, the Imaginary and the Real pressurize each other continuously and have their short-term truces, but they do not allow any embracing programme for synthesis to emerge inside or outside the analytic encounter. The three orders together comprise a complex topological space in which the characteristic disorderly motions of the human mind can be plotted. Plenitude is to be approached not by ever more ambitious movements of dialectical synthesis in the Hegelian manner, but additively – by reading off one by one the interferences between Symbolic, Imaginary and Real by which 'being human' is defined.

Despite their clear differences of temperament and literary style, Freud and Lacan in general manipulate their tripartite models in similar ways. Both offer us world-systems that have mind-systems at their core, and each is defiantly unsystematic in pursuing certain topics. Both are moralists – not moralists of the barrack-room kind but professional students of human conduct who expect their studies of mental structure to reveal a set of principles to live by. And each chooses an appropriately malleable technical language. Freud's terms *Es*, *Ich* and *Über-Ich*, unlike the id, ego and super-ego which replace them in most English translations but like Lacan's terms, exploit the expressive resources of ordinary usage and are able at any moment, and with an ease that is sometimes alarming, to become the tools of informal reflection or exhortation.

Before discussing the things that Lacan's model can do when working at full stretch, I shall pause for a moment to review some of the more localized contributions that it makes to psychoanalytic discussion. Here are three brief examples. (i) The Imaginary is not the same thing as the illusory in that the phantasmatic constructions comprising the Imaginary order are highly durable and can have effects in the Real. If they are 'illusions' at all, they are firmly structured and fully operant ones that the analyst must learn to recognise; he must also help each analysand to submit them to symbolization. (ii) Although the Symbolic has 'priority' over the Imaginary, the latter gives it content, and work to do. The analytic dialogue is a way of coercing the false fixities of the Imaginary order into movement, and those who monitor the techniques that practitioners employ must remain aware of the extent to which those techniques may themselves be re-infiltrated by Imaginary constructions. (iii) One cardinal virtue of the Symbolic is that death is intrinsic to it: 'the symbol manifests itself first of all as the murder of the thing, and this death constitutes in the subject the eternalization of his desire' (319; 104). Death is the eventual triumph of the Real, but is already homeopathically present in speech. If analytic practice places its main stress on the Imaginary, and on the bolstering of the ego, it will find itself purging death-fears and death-desires from its activities. At worst, it will collude with the analysand in creating an empty and demeaning sense of immortality. A stress on the Symbolic, on the other hand, allows the individual's mortality to speak and be spoken; it allows him to be unillusioned in his desire, and, for a time, to fly in the face of the Real.

These and numerous other permutations of the triad are interventions in an existing professional controversy. At moments the strands of Lacan's argument come together in writing that seeks simultaneously to restructure the theory of psychoanalysis, to redraft its clinical agenda and to re-imagine its moral responsibilities:

> The specular relation to the other . . . can successfully subordinate all the phantasmatic activity revealed by analytic experience only by interposing itself between the near side that is the Subject and the far side that is the Other, in the place indeed where speech inserts it, in so far as the existences that are based in the latter are completely at the mercy of its faith.

It is by having confused these two couples that the legatees of a praxis and a teaching that has settled, in the decisive fashion that one can read about in Freud, for the fundamentally narcissistic nature of all being-in-love (*Verliebtheit*) have been able to deify the phantom of so-called genital love to the point of granting it the oblational virtue which has given rise to so many aberrations in therapy.

But by simply suppressing all reference to the symbolic poles of intersubjectivity in order to reduce treatment to a utopian rectification of the imaginary couple, we have now reached a practice in which, beneath the 'object-relations' banner, something is being consummated that in men of good faith cannot do other than stir up a feeling of abjection. (53–4)

This passage from the continuation of the seminar on 'The Purloined Letter' stages a noisy tournament between the lion of the Symbolic and the unicorn of the Imaginary.[7] The errors of one major lineage within the psychoanalytic movement have all involved a depletion of the symbolic dimension, in theory and in practice, and a monstrous over-promotion of the 'imaginary couple' in all its multifarious but mutually confirming forms. At an earlier stage the language of intersubjectivity was simply not mentioned, but now the 'object relations' theorists are intent on abolishing it altogether and making 'imaginary identifications' into the cult objects of their doctrine.[8] Sexuality itself has been reduced to imaginary couples and to the act of genital coupling that sanctifies them. Lacan's answer to all this not only spells out the neglected claims of the Symbolic but gives textual form to the sensations of intersubjective strife. This is writing that wants to become what it describes – a proudly resurgent Symbolic order, decked out in neologism and archaism, seasoning technical discussion with sarcasm, and catching its wretched but resourceful Imaginary prey in the wild convolutions of its syntax. Each sentence is also a paragraph; each paragraph a self-contained assertive gesture and a rehearsal in miniature of Lacan's entire argument.

'Magnificent, yes . . . but is it war?', the reader may find himself asking during these elaborately orchestrated battles between the two orders. The polarization is too neat, and the pervading tone too much that of the pamphleteer. Energies that could have been expended on the difficulties and paradoxes inherent in the analytic project are being lavished by Lacan on a narcissistic exaltation of his own superior insight. He removes himself from this duel with dualism, as I have already said, by introducing a suitably recalcitrant third term. And this term, the Real, is handled with an acute sense of paradox – with a sense indeed of the unthinkable being thought.

Nowhere in his work does Lacan 'discuss' the Real more exactingly or more inventively than in the fifth chapter of *The Four Fundamental Concepts of Psycho-Analysis* (1964). I hesitate over the verb 'discuss' because the singular force that this chapter possesses comes in large part from Lacan's ability to reinvent the concept from moment to moment, and to embody the weight and the recurrence that he ascribes to the Real in the ponderous repetitions of his text. He draws his chapter-title, 'Tuché and Automaton', from Aristotle, and under the aegis of these contrasted notions sets out to restate the most severe difficulty that psychoanalysis faces.

Although the terms τύχη and αὐτόματον as used in the second book of the *Physics* have been translated in a variety of ways – as 'fortune' and 'chance', or as 'chance' and 'spontaneity', for example – Aristotle's essential distinction is clear: *tuché* and what results from it 'are appropriate to agents that are capable of good fortune and of moral action generally'[9] whereas *automaton*, the wider term, refers to chance events that take place in the natural world at large. At first sight, Lacan may seem to have these terms the wrong way round, for he glosses *tuché* as 'the encounter with the real' and *automaton* as 'the network of signifiers'

(XI, 51; 52): 'the real' sounds rather like 'nature' and 'signifiers' suggests the presence of a human subject. Lacan's recourse to the *Physics* and his metaphorizing of Aristotle's terms may seem still more hazardous and inopportune when we remember that Aristotle himself had found the terms something of a nuisance. His enumeration of the causes and modes of causation that were to be seen at work in nature was already, in his judgement, complete before he began asking whether 'fortune' and 'chance' should be included among them. But on this occasion Lacan is a wise metaphorist, for it suits his purposes well to describe the generality of the signifying machinery in terms appropriate to the generality of nature and 'the encounter with the real' as a happy or unhappy accident befalling the subject but irreducible to the signifiers that define him: 'The real is beyond the *automaton*, beyond the return, the coming-back, the insistence of the signs by which we see ourselves governed by the pleasure principle. The real is that which always lies behind the *automaton*' (XI, 53–4; 53–4). Lacan's *tuché* is in one sense very simple: it is a tile falling on to the head of a passer-by, a person from Porlock bringing a creative trance prematurely to its end, or, to take one of Lacan's own examples, a knock on the door that interrupts a dream. The network of signifiers in which we have our being is not all that there is, and the rest of what is may chance to break in upon us at any moment.

Falling tiles are not without interest to psychoanalysis, and the analyst is required to come from the Porlock direction into the analysand's phantasies. But another kind of painful intrusion is at the centre of its concerns. This, as I have said, is the traumatic event proper, which is as extrinsic to signification, as unassimilable to the pursuit of pleasure, as any foreign body encroaching upon the human organism:

Our experience then presents us with a problem, which derives from the fact that, at the very heart of the primary processes, we see preserved the insistence of the trauma in making us aware of its existence. The trauma reappears there, indeed, frequently unveiled. How can the dream, the bearer of the subject's desire, produce that which makes the trauma emerge repeatedly – if not its very face, at least the screen that shows us that it is still there behind?

Let us conclude that the reality system, however far it is developed, leaves an essential part of what belongs to the real a prisoner in the meshes of the pleasure principle. (XI, 55; 55)

This account of trauma differs markedly from Freud's in *Beyond the Pleasure Principle*, which is Lacan's 'key' text in this first section of *The Four Fundamental Concepts*. For Freud the external trauma initiated a huge defensive and reparative operation by the organism, and caused the pleasure principle to be 'for the moment put out of action' (XVIII, 29). And in a certain class of dream also, he found himself obliged to admit, this same principle, the founding statute of the unconscious, could find itself suspended. These dreams, in which the psychical traumas of childhood were repeated, could be provoked by analytic treatment, but could occur outside analysis as well. They were a main source of supporting evidence for the view that the pleasure principle had its 'beyond', irremoveable exceptions to its rule. It would be too simple to say that Lacan is traumatizing the unconscious, turning Freud's exceptions into a new rule, but there can be no doubt that he is sketching an extremely wide area of application for a term that for Freud had had precise clinical uses only. The hard, durable traumatic residues that are caught up in the 'meshes' of the pleasure principle, or in the 'network' of signifiers, are an accidental catch – no one was fishing for them; and they cannot be put to use – no one can knit them into a net. Yet these encounters with the Real, in their obtuseness and their acuity, are essential to an understanding of the mind. They are stray events, stragglers, in which the march of an overwhelming necessity may be glimpsed. In them the mind makes contact with the limits of its power, with that which its structure cannot structure.

Lacan chooses as his central instance of events belonging to this class the 'burning child' dream discussed by Freud in *The Interpretation of Dreams*. A father falls asleep in a room adjoining the room where his dead son lies. An old man has been left to watch over the son's body, but he too falls asleep, and does not notice when a candle falls over and begins to burn the bedding and the child's arm. The father dreams that his child is standing by his bed, and hears him whisper reproachfully '*Father, don't you see I'm burning?*' (V, 509). The words 'I'm burning', Freud suggests, may have been spoken 'during the fever of the child's last illness', and Lacan agrees that the phrase could be overdetermined in this way. But the special eloquence of this dream for Lacan is that the entire scenario described by Freud is placed between two 'reals': the sound of the falling candle on the one hand and the phantasmal sound of the son's voice on the other. If we grant provisionally, Lacan says, that there may be something of note in the otherwise rather facile Freudian notion that the sleeper's main wish is to stay asleep, then a reasonable way of differentiating between stronger and weaker forms of the real would be to ask 'which of them has the power to wake the dreamer up?' Of the three characters involved in this miniature drama, the one who emerges, according to this test, as pre-eminently real is the dead child himself:

> When everybody is asleep, including the person who wished to take a little rest, the person who was unable

to maintain his vigil and the person of whom some well intentioned individual, standing at his bedside, must have said, *He looks just as if he is asleep*, when we know only one thing about him, and that is that, in this entirely sleeping world, only the voice is heard, *Father, don't you see I'm burning?* . . . (XI, 58; 59)

But this dream-voice is remarkable not simply for the physical effect that it produces on the father, who wakes up, but for the fact that it repeats, in its clarity, incisiveness and cruel efficacy the moment of bereavement itself: it is an accident that repeats an accident, an irreducible fragment of the real that speaks of irrecoverable loss, an encounter that is peremptory and brutal and yet one that can now never, outside dreams, take place. Is the real outside or inside? Is it a vacuum or a plenum? Does one chance to meet it, or chance not to meet it? In Lacan's rereading of Freud's celebrated dream-narrative, the undecidability of the concept 'Real' is scrupulously preserved. The Real is an uncrossable threshold for the subject, and not one that can be sidestepped in the analytic encounter: 'This is the real that governs our activities more than any other and it is psychoanalysis that designates it for us' (XI, 59; 60).

The varied clinical uses to which Lacan's 'Real' could be put were already in evidence in the nineteen-fifties, in the seminar on *The Psychoses* (1955–6) and in the long and densely argued manifesto 'On a question preliminary to any possible treatment of psychosis' (1958). To a certain extent, these works continue and amplify the attack that Lacan had launched in his doctoral dissertation on paranoia (1932).[10] The most regrettable error made by clinical psychiatry in its discussion of psychosis, Lacan had argued in the early thirties, was that of excluding the personality of the individual from its field of enquiry: the patient was all too often simply the site where a ready-made 'psychical process', or a given nexus of psychological characteristics, had taken up residence. The paranoiac was not a person, endowed with family relationships, an emotional history, ambitions, intentions and intellectual capacities, but an embodiment of this or that typological or 'characterological' category. Lacan's goal in his dissertation had been to restore a complex missing dimension to the discussion of psychosis, and his argument had drawn extensively on his patient's writings as revealers of this dimension. What he did not have at this stage was a theory that could continuously connect the structure of personality with linguistic structure or explain fully how mere writing came to enjoy its high evidential standing. By the mid-fifties, he was in a position to do both things, and to present madness as a mode of meaning, an articulation of signs, in which the individual sufferer was held captive.

The Symbolic, the Imaginary and the Real provide this new phase of discussion with its indispensable conceptual framework. Lacan's main innovation in his 'On a question preliminary to any possible treatment of psychosis' and its associated documents is the idea of *forclusion* ('foreclosure').[11] This is in part Lacan's translation of Freud's *Verwerfung* ('repudiation'), although the French term soon came to occupy a stable position in Lacan's thinking on psychosis that no single German term had had in Freud's. The distinction between *Verwerfung* and *Verdrängung* ('repression') is plain for both writers. Where foreclosure seeks to expel a given notion, thought, image, memory or signifier from the unconscious, repression seeks to confine it there. Where repression belongs to the ordinary functioning of the mind and in certain conditions may produce disabling neurotic effects, foreclosure is a violent refusal of symbolization and its effects are catastrophic. It is an operation that gives psychosis a structure distinct from that of neurosis.

In 'Psycho-Analytic Notes on an Autobiographical Account of a Case of Paranoia' (1911), Freud, not using the verb *verwerfen* on this occasion, had said of Schreber's hallucinations: 'It was incorrect to say that the perception which was suppressed internally is projected outwards; the truth is rather, as we now see, that what was abolished internally returns from without' (XII, 71). Lacan's response to this is twofold. First of all he condenses it, and translates it into his own terms: 'that which has not emerged into the light of the symbolic appears in the real' (388). And then, in a move that proved decisive for all his subsequent thinking on the matter, he said what it was that, having escaped or been expelled from symbolization, had the power to unleash, early or late, psychotic effects. For it was not just any repudiated signifier that produced the catastrophe: it was the Name-of-the-Father, as Lacan called it, in what was at first a semi-facetious allusion to the Christian liturgy and its celebrated triad but soon became a crucial reference-point in his theory.

The Name-of-the-Father was the symbol of an authority at once legislative and punitive. It represented, within the Symbolic, that which made the Symbolic possible – all those agencies that placed enduring restrictions on the infant's desire and threatened to punish, by castration, infringements of their law. It was the inaugurating agent of Law, but also gave birth to the mobility and the supple interconnectedness of the signifying chain. Once this fundamental signifier was expelled the entire process of signification was thrown into disarray:

> For the psychosis to be triggered off, the Name-of-the-Father, *verworfen*, foreclosed, that is to say, never having attained the place of the Other, must be called into symbolic opposition to the subject.

It is the lack of the Name-of-the-Father in that place

which, by the hole that it opens up in the signified, sets off the cascade of reshapings of the signifier from which the increasing disaster of the imaginary proceeds, until the level is reached at which signifier and signified are stabilized in the delusional metaphor. (577; 217)

The Name-of-the-Father is the 'paternal metaphor' that inheres in symbolization and thereby potentiates the metaphorical process as a whole; and it is an essential point of anchorage for the subject. Without it, metaphor, in the form of 'voices' and visual hallucinations, comes at the subject from without, from a 'Real' that is perfectly delusional yet cruelly concrete in its impact. The missing Name-of-the-Father leaves a hole in the symbolic universe – Lacan's account is haunted by this image – and the effort to fill the hole provokes, during periods of psychotic crisis, an escalating series of misfortunes.

In the case of the Schreber material that Lacan re-examines at length here and in *The Psychoses* the always uneasy relationships between Symbolic, Imaginary and Real reach a point of grotesque incoherence. The signifier is 'unleashed' and gives birth not to an abundance of sense but to a vociferous tribe of imaginary beings. The imaginary becomes real, we might say, by passing through the symbolic dimension without being submitted to its exactions and obliquities. Schreber's untrammelled journey towards the real is an exemplary one: he is not a cosmologist but a creator of worlds, not a student of kinship structure but an indomitable populatory force. And the causes of his delirium may be traced back to an initial mispositioning of Subject and Other: the Other should be intrinsic to the signifying chain but has been moved to a position outside it. The Other should be exercising its legislative authority silently and invisibly in human speech – twixt cup and lip, between one syllable and the next – but instead has relocated itself beyond speech, over and against the Subject, 'in the Real'. There, it becomes not a law-maker but a tyrant, not one who maintains the threat of judicial punishment but one who exercises and withholds punishment in accordance with its own unfathomable whim.

The essential ambiguity of Lacan's *tuché* is thus already present in this account of psychosis. The peculiar anguish to which the ejection of the paternal emblem exposes the psychotic subject is one in which the Real is endlessly encountered yet endlessly foreign to him. It lies beyond the network of signifiers, yet causes an uncontrollable upheaval within it. It is firm and obdurate, yet its intrusions upon the subject cannot be anticipated or forestalled. For the subject, the Real is more forcible than anything else in the world, yet it is phantasmal, shallow and fortuitous. All this is to some extent a resourceful attempt on Lacan's part to strengthen the campaign that he had launched on the psychotic patient's behalf in the early thirties. He is now making his point about the 'reality' of mental illness not simply by reinstating the concept *person* as an instrument of clinical description but by putting the terminology that is familiarly reserved for the real, measurable contents of physical space to work on the private spaces of hallucination and delusion. The Real is inward and outward at once, and belongs indifferently to sanity and to madness. In all its modes, it successfully resists the intercessions of language.

This is much more than a philanthropic attempt to speak up for the mad. For the 'preliminary question' that Lacan addresses to students of psychosis is shown to be of interest to a much wider audience too. In his concluding remarks, he restates a familiar but often neglected question: in the world of symbolization *à deux* that analytic therapy comprises, what can be done for the psychotic patient? If psychosis is a disastrous disturbance in the Symbolic order, by what means can the transferential dialogue between clinician and sufferer achieve positive results? In such conditions of extremity, can mere dialogue alleviate pain? Yet the interplay between Lacan's three orders, even while it is being used to redraw with a new precision chosen sections of the clinical map, is presented as the foundation for a new science of man. Where Freud, in discussing the causes of paranoia, had placed a strong emphasis on repressed homosexual wishes, Lacan presents homosexuality as an effect rather than a cause: the decisive, properly causative moment is to be found in the act of foreclosure itself. He moves the attention of his colleagues, that is to say, from the declared content of the patient's delusions, and the latent content that psychoanalysis has trained them to detect, towards the exact configurations of Symbolic, Imaginary and Real which trigger such delusions and determine their structure. And a further movement of the same kind is implicit in much of his phrasing elsewhere: the three orders *are* the human world, and if they are aligned, interconnected and disjoined with appropriate subtlety they will tell the whole story of mind in action. Once the 'preliminary question' has been faced squarely, answers – some of them encouraging, others not – will begin to accrue for 'conjectural scientists' of all persuasions.

This grafting of an ambitious philosophy of 'the human' on to an argument purporting to be a technical contribution to the study of specific mental disorders is characteristic of Lacan's impatient intellectual style. And in his willingness to switch between registers in this way he resembles Freud. In the works of both writers the varieties and sub-varieties of 'the human', the mind-types that a new anthropology might study, are often described with the seeming disinterestedness of a natural scientist. 'Truth', if it is an issue at all, resides in the aptness, economy and inclusiveness of the classifications proposed. The important thing is to say what

111

the human world comprises, and everything that it comprises is, in a weak but handy sense, 'true'. Lacan's three orders, especially when their joint action is modelled upon the conventions of classificatory science, remain neutral on the question of truth: it would make no more sense to say that the Symbolic was truer than the Imaginary or the Real than to say that the Pleistocene was truer than the Eocene or the *Reptilia* truer than the *Mammalia*. Besides, each of the three orders is singularly ill-equipped to be a guarantor or even a responsible custodian of Truth. The would-be truth-seeker will find that the Imaginary, the Symbolic and the Real are an unholy trinity whose members could as easily be called Fraud, Absence and Impossibility. But despite these impediments, and despite the fact that mental structures can be exhaustively described and classified without being submitted to an independent truth-test, Truth is of crucial importance to Lacan: recognising, respecting and speaking it are for him unequalled acts of virtue. Moreover the Lacanian True does not accidentally adhere to other notions; nor does it serve to complete them or to accredit them from afar. For it offers its own separate route to completeness. It pertains not to the world as it is for the scientist, but to the world as it was, is and shall be for the speaking subject.

Lacan's fullest account of Truth, in the special sense that he gives the term, is to be found in 'The Freudian thing' (1955). This paper is a literary performance of extraordinary brilliance, and one in which theoretical positions that are in their ordinary forms already extreme find themselves re-expressed in a vein of supercharged and exacerbated hyperbole. The paper, which was originally an address commemorating Freud's achievement, delivered in the Viennese neuro-psychiatric clinic, has a grandiose programme: to restate Freud's discovery, to recapitulate Lacan's extensions of it, to arraign and excoriate those in the profession of psychoanalysis who have betrayed it, and to sound a key-note for all those who would maintain their loyalty to a doctrine that can never be less than profoundly disquieting. Doing all this in a short space involves Lacan in a series of rapid metamorphoses. He changes from historian into theorist, and from theorist into jester, medicine-man, fabulist and hanging judge. And in the middle of it all the polymorphous narrator becomes, in an extended imitation of Erasmus's *Praise of Folly*, Truth – not its spokesman or its defendant but its incarnation. Where Erasmus had begun his celebrated encomium with the words 'Folly speaks', Lacan begins 'Men, listen, I am giving you the secret. I, truth, will speak' (409; 121).

An extended quotation will give the flavour of this writing as it levitates towards the threshold of madness:

Whether you flee me in fraud or think to entrap me in error, I will reach you in the misapprehension against which you have no refuge. In that place where the most caustic speech reveals a slight hesitation, it is lacking in perfidy, I am now publicly announcing the fact, and it would from then on be rather trickier to pretend that nothing had happened, in good, or for that matter, bad company. But there is no need to tire yourselves keeping a closer watch on yourselves. Even if the conjoint jurisdictions of politeness and politics were to declare unacceptable whatever is associated with me by presenting itself in so illicit a way, you will not get off so lightly, for the most innocent intention is disconcerted at being unable to conceal the fact that one's unsuccessful acts are the most successful and that one's failure fulfils one's most secret wish. In any case, is it not enough, to judge of your defeat, to see me escape first from the keep of the fortress in which you are so sure you have me secured by situating me not in you yourselves, but in being itself? I wander about in what you regard as being the least true in essence: in the dream, in the way the most Gongoresque conceit, the nonsense of the most grotesque pun defies sense, in chance, and not in its law but in its contingency, and I never do more to change the face of the world than when I give it the profile of Cleopatra's nose. (410; 122)

The madness here is that of a speaker who wishes to lodge in the unconscious in the full knowledge that the unconscious is not a residence or a habitat. If truth belongs anywhere and to anything it belongs in and to the unconscious – of this the entire grain of psychoanalytic thinking seeks to convince us – but for that very reason it can be had only in part, in disguise and intermittently. In this passage, Lacan reconstructs in brief format the impact of Freud's books on dreams, slips and jokes. Truth is to be found in errors and misapprehensions of all sorts, in nonsense and word-play, in the wanderings of sense through the labyrinth of the dream-work. It cannot inhere in individual states of mind or states of affairs, and can only be syncopated and spasmodic. It is composite, heterogeneous, the common province of Subject and Other, and can as easily be fabricated from lies and evasions as from a plain man's report on things as they are.

Even such statements as 'I am lying' or 'I am deceiving you' reveal the truth-directedness of the subject's speech. It is quite wrong, Lacan proposes in *The Four Fundamental Concepts*, to respond to 'I am lying' by saying 'If you say *I am lying*, you are telling the truth, and therefore you are not lying' (XI, 127; 139), for this would presuppose a unified speaking subject where no trace of one is to be found: 'I am lying' irreparably divides the subject who enunciates from the subject who is enunciated, as did Descartes's 'I think'. But to the analysand's 'I am deceiving you', the analyst, recognising his own role in the production of the statement, is nevertheless able to reply 'You are telling the truth': 'On the path of deception where the subject is venturing, the analyst is in a position to formulate this *you are telling the truth*, and my interpretation has meaning only in this dimension' (XI, 128; 140). Translating this into Lacan's linguistic idiom of the time, we could say that truth is an effect of the signifying process as a whole, that it is intersubjective and interlocutory wherever it appears – in the fertile outpourings of a literary soliloquist quite as much as in the analytic dialogue itself – and that it is the action of the unconscious upon language that makes a given procession of signifiers or of symptoms 'true'. Truth in this sense is contrasted with the exactitude of the exact sciences: it has a 'fictive arrangement' (17; *French Freud*, 46), a 'structure of fiction' (451, 808; 306); it demands of the truth-seeker an 'unbending discipline' in following its mobile contours (365).

In works like 'The Freudian thing', however, doctrine and performance are not necessarily at one. On the surface at least, Lacan's emphasis is upon the lack and discontinuity that constitute the Symbolic order, and his enigmatic conjuring with truth-notions and time-notions often seems designed to create in the reader a lively sense of meaning under threat of cancellation. He seems to be adhering to a principle that he had laid down in 'The function and field of speech':

> The ambiguity of the hysterical revelation of the past is due not so much to the vacillation of its content between the imaginary and the real, for it is situated in both. Nor is it because it is made up of lies. The reason is that it presents us with the birth of truth in speech, and thereby brings us up against the reality of what is neither true nor false. At any rate, that is the most disquieting aspect of the problem. (255–6; 47)

115

The truth is made from the not-true; the present from the not-present. The ability to tell the truth when truth no longer has 'falsehood' or 'lies' as its antonyms comes from a willingness to accept that everything falling into the domain of speech is hybridized in the process, and to make a pact with the schism and incompletion that all speech entails. But if this doctrine is a useful and fitting one for analysts to re-espouse – in that it may make them look to their own lacking language and so discourage them from assailing their patients with ready-made wisdom – it is not necessarily respected in Lacan's truth-intoxicated writing.

His imitative tribute to the *Praise of Folly* is revealing in this respect, and not quite in the way that his own remarks on Erasmus in 'The agency of the letter' would lead one to expect. Erasmus as evoked in this paper knew that in changing 'the relation between man and the signifier' you could change the course of history, and the historical importance of his own satire lay in the common ground that it marked out between two signifying zones that had previously been considered incommensurable – the language of folly and the language of reason (527; 174). In doing this he anticipated the later revolutionary moment that saw the publication of *The Interpretation of Dreams*. But in 'The Freudian thing' the Erasmian characteristic that Lacan most admires is *copiousness*, and his manner of truth-telling is often one that seeks to 'say it all' rather than observe literal-mindedly a doctrine claiming that every *all* is a worthless and untrappable prey. Telling the truth, if we pay due attention to the overflowingness of this writing and to its tireless enumerative pulse, is a matter of actualizing the possible forms of the world. An ecstatic sense of plenitude is being sought. Gaps and spaces of all kinds are to be filled. Besides Erasmus, Lacan's kinsmen at these moments are Rabelais, the Apuleius of *The Golden Ass* and the Joyce of *Finnegans Wake* – those writers who endeavour to capture the transformations of human identity in an end-lessly playful and self-transforming literary text, and who propel themselves with abandon towards the supreme moment of abundance that their verbal skill seems to promise.

This cult is celebrated by Lacan in improbable places. An important element in his account of the psychoses is, as we have seen, the linguistic impairment that these conditions bring. Despite the fact that the sane and the mad inhabit the same embracing Logos, the mad face penalties that their fellow humans can only guess at. Their language is intoler-ably broken and dispersed. But Lacan, speaking on their behalf, submits this damaged language of theirs to a magical process of repair:

> Further still, the father's relation to this law must be considered in itself, for one will find in it the reason for that paradox, by which the ravaging effects of the paternal figure are to be observed with particular fre-quency in cases where the father really has the function of a legislator or boasts of it, whether in fact he is one of those who make the laws or whether he poses as a pillar of the faith, as a paragon of integrity and devotion, as virtuous or as a virtuoso, as a servitor of a work of salvation, of whatever object or lack of object, of nation or of natality, of safeguard or salubrity, of legacy or legality, of the pure, the impure or of empire, all ideals that provide him with all too many opportunities of being in a posture of shortcoming, inadequacy, even of fraud, and, in short, of excluding the Name-of-the-Father from its position in the signifier. (579; 218–19)

The naming of penalties becomes its own reward, and a new cornucopia comes into view in the very act of listing the privations that afflict the psychotic. During Lacan's perora-tion this list is extended and ornamented in a last surge of

117

word-play: 'we will be able to regard as past the limits at which the native and the natal extend to nature, to the natural, to naturism, even to naturalization, at which virtue becomes vertigo, legacy the league, salvation saltation . . .' (581; 220). In part this writing is of course a benign attempt to show the psychotic patient the return road to a 'full' and anchored language, but it also offers the spectacle of a writer in search of his own truth-as-fullness and willing to leap to the stirrups at the least provocation.

Truth conceived of in this way requires the constant tribute of irony and mirth from its devotees. Speaking the truth becomes a lost cause if the possible is merely itemized. Truth must be catalysed by a comic intelligence that can measure and savour the distance between one actualized form of the possible and the next. Lacan responds wholeheartedly to this invitation. He becomes Proteus, and Procrustes. Truth demands that he be both an exalted visionary and a buffoon. He identifies with Freud as the mouthpiece for 'an immense truth' (527; 174), and as the author of a true book, and does not shrink from the grandest identification that recent European civilization can provide. 'You would not be looking for me if you had not already found me,' he says in one of his truth-personifying moods, quoting words that Pascal in his *Pensées* had given to Jesus (298; 85). 'I can get away with the grandeur of this', Lacan seems to suggest, 'because – just look at me – I'm not the Saviour alone but a chattering ragamuffin and a fluent salesman too. Truth obliges me to be everyone and to speak in all tongues.'

In 'Science and truth' (1965), looking back upon the initial impact of 'The Freudian thing', Lacan reports that one response to his paper had been 'why doesn't he tell us the truth about truth?' He answers that he had already told everything about it that could be told, for 'there is no metalanguage . . . no language could ever speak the truth about truth, since truth is founded on the fact that it speaks and that it has no other way of achieving this' (867–8). Later in this paper, Lacan toys relentlessly with a single pun, on the word *cause*: the unconscious is the cause of truth (causes it, makes it happen) and analysis has sole responsibility for defending truth's cause (its interests, its standing). This piece of word-play is confidently executed, and has the support of etymology: the Latin *causa* had both senses and also, for that matter, gave birth to the thing (*chose*) so elaborately played upon in 'The Freudian thing'. But does the pun display or disguise its own incoherence? The two senses of *cause* can scarcely have equivalent and co-active roles in the *causerie* of psychoanalysis. For truth, defined in the full rigour of the Lacanian perspective, under the aegis of the unconscious, has no need of defenders, and, unlike fresh air, brown bread or the universal franchise, offers no basis for a political programme. Indeed it is an inescapable destiny for the speaking subject: it is ubiquitous in speech, as a promise when speech is empty and as an audible triumph when speech is full.

I said earlier that Lacan's 'truth' did not adhere to or inhere in any one of his three orders, and suggested that it represented for him an alternative path towards the goals of completion and inclusiveness. What the orders achieve by repeated triangular mapping, truth seeks to achieve by instantaneous assumption. But there is a much closer connection than this between the two styles of thought. For the Symbolic is the order of the unconscious and without it truth is impossible. The dominant tendency of Lacan's triadic thinking is to present the Symbolic, wedged between the immediacy of the Imaginary on the one hand and the weightily recurrent Real on the other, as a realm of unavoidable lack and indirection – the full recognition of which is bound to produce salutary effects upon the symbol-born(e) subject. 'Truth' in the lesser of the two registers that I have sketched is by way of being an uncomfortable home-truth about the Symbolic: it tells us where our losses come from and suggests measures for limiting them. But 'truth' in its maximising and plenary register is an answer to the Symbolic; in its copiousness and its comedy it strives to repair the damage that the Symbolic has caused; it is speech exultant. When the theorist has completed his long apprenticeship, and travelled far along the *via negativa* that psychoanalysis recommends to all those who would presume to construct theories, he is eligible for his reward. In Lacan's case the reward is to become a writer, and in his writing to discover not the foothills of Truth but its delirious summits.

Lacan in his truth-as-fullness comes very close to Hegel, who wrote in the preface to the *Phenomenology*: 'The True is thus the Bacchanalian revel in which no member is not drunk; yet because each member collapses as soon as he drops out, the revel is just as much transparent and simple repose.'[12] The dramatic structure of the *Phenomenology*, as we have seen, is that of a long and arduous quest for knowledge, one that passes through numerous dialectical stages and can be crowned with success only if the rigours of each consecutive moment are courageously faced. No cheating is allowed. But the questing consciousness that is the book's hero cannot resist looking ahead, and knows in advance what its final consummation will be like. The preface recapitulates the whole story before the story has begun. Lacan's bacchanal is similarly a song of rejoicing that an eagerly awaited and long-deferred outcome has been reached and at the same time a pre-emptive seizure of that outcome. It is the dance of possibility being realized in time, and in the literary text, yet also a frieze of isolated figures immobilized and in repose. Looked at in either way, it is a complete answer to the *danse macabre*, the *Totentanz*, of the Symbolic. Lacan denies himself the cognitive satisfactions that Hegel had promised in the *Phenomenology*, and will not allow his triad of Symbolic, Imaginary and Real to be dialecticized in the Hegelian manner. Yet 'Truth' of a kind that Hegel had foretold breaks in upon him, momentarily relieves him of the need to say 'always an Other-thing', and breathes upon his writing an unmistakable air of bliss.

5 The Meaning of the Phallus

Lacan's papers of the nineteen-fifties are often cast in an abstract and unfleshly vein. They are 'about' sexuality, of course, as Freud's works were, but Lacan is much less concerned than Freud had been to explain and classify sexual inclinations. Rather than furnish a detailed account of what sexual beings do, he propounds an eroticized science of meaning, modelling devices for which are derived from logic, rhetoric and topology. Lacan's Eros finds its primary expression neither in physical sensations nor in desirous mental states, nor yet in the organs and erotogenic zones that, for other theorists of sexuality, allow the pursuit of pleasure to be mapped and logged on the surface of the human body. Indeed the attributes of Eros are often negative ones: it is not an instinct, not a quasi-biological 'libido', not a variable flow of neural energy or excitation, not an appetite, not the concealed source from which appetites derive and not, as it had been for the later Freud, the life-principle itself. The sole positive attribute that Lacan sets against all these negative ones seems at first fragile and empty: desire, as he came to call it in preference to all other terms, is what keeps the chain of signifiers moving. It is the dynamo, everywhere in motion and nowhere at rest, that propels all acts of speech, all refusals to speak and all conscious and unconscious mental representations.

For a large number of theoretical tasks, it was sufficient to describe desire in this way. It was the postulated insatiable force that fuelled the mind's transformational machinery – sustaining the endless play of condensation and displacement among ideas, or of metaphor and metonymy among signifiers – and nothing was to be gained by giving it further characteristics. From the analytic point of view, the transformations themselves were in any case more interesting and of much sharper clinical relevance than the propellent energy that all minds shared. Yet the body and its organs existed; organs were not all equal and not all sexual; and physical needs and appetites seemed worth distinguishing from the elaborate erotic gambits that analytic treatment revealed. For Lacan these facts of life posed two theoretical questions: how could organs acquire the power to signify? and how could the desire of *homo significans* be differentiated from those needs, urges, impulses and cravings that he shared with his fellow animals? These questions are addressed, and related to each other, in a number of papers, but nowhere more ingeniously than in 'The meaning of the phallus' (1958), the original German text of which was delivered at the Max Planck Institute in Munich.

The first question is exceptionally vexatious and, however it is answered, is likely to bring further theoretical difficulties in its wake. For a start, the Symbolic dimension can contain only symbols. Organs, like all other physical objects, notable or not, can gain entry to it only by being symbolized. Once symbolized, however, they are subject to the systemic law which holds that no signifier can exist alone, and that, under pressure from its neighbours, any signifier's existence will be unstable and multiform. What is required, if the stability of the organ is to be preserved and respected in the Symbolic, is a signifier that will to some extent resist this law and enjoy a position of privilege among its fellows. The phallus is Lacan's only serious candidate for this role. And he is at once adamant that he has in mind the ancient emblem and its countless modern successors rather than the penis:

> For the phallus is a signifier, a signifier whose func-
> tion, in the intra-subjective economy of the analysis,
> lifts the veil perhaps from the function it performed in
> the mysteries. For it is the signifier destined to desig-
> nate as a whole the effects of the signified, in that the
> signifier conditions them by its presence as a signifier.
> (690; 285)

Freud too had spoken of the *phallus* and, as Lacan points
out, had taken pleasure in the antiquity of this symbolic
device. Moreover in the successive phases of libidinal organization that Freud had outlined, the penis was the only
bodily part to receive this accolade: mouth, breast, anus and
vagina were named in accordance with ordinary polite usage
and no nimbus of cultural or historical value surrounded
them. Yet there is a major difference between the two
writers. For Freud the 'primacy of the phallus' was not
placed at a point of culmination in sexual development: the
'phallic phase' superseded the anal and oral phases of infantile eroticism and was itself, in adulthood, to be superseded
by the phase of 'genital maturity', which was almost
entirely that of no-nonsense heterosexual coupling.[1] Against
this background, Lacan's portrayal of the phallus as the
signifier that holds all signifieds in thrall seems simply
regressive, or the sign of an infantile infatuation that has
not yet been outgrown.

Besides, even if one grants for a moment that the male
organ may possess some quite special capacity to create
meaning, the claims of the 'real' penis as distinct from the
'symbolic' phallus seem to be understated:

> It can be said that this signifier is chosen because it
> is what sticks out the most in the real of sexual
> copulation, and also the most symbolic in the literal
> (typographical) sense of the term, since it is equivalent
> there to the (logical) copula. It might also be said that,

by virtue of is turgidity, it is the image of the vital flow
as it is transmitted in generation. (692; 287)

The penis here provides a stepping-stone between sex and
logic, but otherwise its characteristics – even such a
straightforwardly organic one as the capacity to ejaculate
semen – are made over to the phallus. What of the everyday
uncertainties that beset the male member? If we remind
ourselves of these a promising 'Lacanian' scenario may
begin to emerge. The penis may be rigid or flaccid, and
either condition may arise opportunely or not. Its discharge
may be premature or indefinitely delayed. It may be short
and wished longer, or long and wished shorter. It may be
proudly displayed, or apologetically concealed. It may be
the instrument of will or seem to possess will of its own; an
object of fear, disgust, admiration, envy ... This capacity
for variation within pre-ordained limits seems to make it
into a dialectician *par excellence*, a nexus of signifying
opportunities, a fine example, in all its modes, of the
Freudian *fort/da*. And the fact that these are features of a
mere organ does not disqualify that organ from entering the
Symbolic. For the word *penis* is no less a signifier than the
word *phallus*, and its relative lack of cultural dignity cannot
be of consequence in the rigorously non-elitist world of the
signifying chain.

Yet Lacan refuses to adopt these promising perspectives
and insists on using the term *phallus*. In doing so he has
two principal motives: to maintain the coherence of a
structure and, more paradoxically, to maintain the neutrality of that structure on questions of gender. In pursuing
this programme, he borrows elements from Freud's Oedipus
and castration complexes and seeks to make these two
cornerstones of the psychoanalytic approach fully compatible. For Freud, as is well known, the triangular relationship
between child and parents had a profound determining

power over the individual as he or she grew towards adult-hood: the warring passions and anguished self-division that the child experienced between the ages of three and five created a problem that, incompletely solved or not solved at all, could leave its tragic mark on the remainder of his or her life. But this early stage was not to be understood simply in terms of the loving and aggressive wishes that the child entertained towards each of its parents: at the centre of the drama was the organ of pleasure itself, and the phantasy of punishment by castration played a crucial role in the child's efforts to understand not only the anatomical difference between the sexes but the severe legal constraints that were placed on its pursuit of sexual gratification. Where other analysts sometimes sought to attenuate the fear and threat of castration by making them less literal – by presenting them, for example, as merely one episode in the history of loss and separation that begins for each human being at the moment of birth – Freud himself attributed to castration a singular and irreducible explanatory power.[2] Where the castration complex in boys hinged on an imagined future event, in girls the event was imagined as already having taken place. Boys and girls were in agreement that originally both sexes had possessed the penis. Mothers either had lost what was rightly theirs, or possessed it still, or re-embodied it in a monumental form, in their entire person.

While keeping a certain distance from the troubled con-cept of 'penis envy', Lacan takes up a phallocentrist position akin to Freud's: 'Freud revealed this imaginary function of the phallus, then, to be the pivot of the symbolic process that completes *in both sexes* the calling into question of sex by the castration complex' (555; 198). What he is doing, however, in statements of this kind, which pass for simple summaries of Freud, is giving to the phallus a pivotal role that is quite new. For Freud the Oedipus and castration complexes mattered so much because, as I have said, they had crucial consequences for the later life of the individual; mapping the developmental routes by which they could be satisfactorily resolved was a delicate theoretical task. In Lacan's paper, on the other hand, the two complexes are conflated and redramatized as a primordial intimation of structure. Against a clear normative pattern of staging-posts through which the individual must pass, he sets a complex, wayward and indefinitely extendable dialectic. From an original structure, all other structures grow. The phallic 'moment' launches a series of signifying practices and combinatorial procedures that the individual can never expect to outgrow.

'But where is the *structure* here?', one might reasonably ask. Lacan seems to be outlining, in a loosely associative way, a number of distinct infantile experiences – discovering one's own genitalia, inspecting those of others, speculating about sexual difference, feeling secure or insecure in one's erotic pursuits. Yet is it not the case that these features of childhood will acquire collective explanatory force only if they are considered in relation to the other than sexual desires of the child? For the child wishes to avoid pain, remain physically safe and gain the nourishment required to sustain life. These too are passions of the body and when disregarded or thwarted can produce perplexity, anxiety and rage. Lacan answers such objections by stressing two essential differences between instinctual wishes of this kind and the 'desire' that is already fully in place in the infant's sexual world.

First, whereas wishes can be met, there is something in the sexual situation itself that even in the midst of seeming satisfaction speaks of insatiability. The child does not desire any one thing exclusively; it is faced with a multitude of potentially gratifying objects; and it can never know enough about its own sexual goals to perform an efficient cost-benefit analysis on the various pleasurable options that are available to it. Secondly, in the case of male children, the most intense sexual pleasure is to be had from a protruding and detachable bodily part. The phallus is the only signifier that has an origin of this kind, in an organ belonging, in phantasy at least, entirely to the surface of the body and bereft of all inwardness. But its detachability, the combined presence and absence that it enshrines, means that it is not simply a signifier which must await the advent of another signifier before structure can be achieved: in so far as it weaves together the antithetical states of possession and non-possession, it is already, in itself, an articulation of structure. The phallus is the promise of meaning organized by an organ and, equally, it is the loss or cancellation of meaning perpetually being foretold. For children of both sexes, it is the emblem, only trivially 'masculine', in and through which human desire finds form. In due course, the clitoris is discovered by the little girl and given its own signifying function, but it cannot be a primary signifier and is recognised and esteemed as a secondary one only because the phallic obsession has prepared the way. In the beginning, only one organ could mean.

Lacan's use of the term *phallus* depends upon a conceit. In embryology, the phallus is the primitive structure from which penis and clitoris are in due course fashioned. And in Lacan's doctrine it is the undifferentiated afterlife, in the Symbolic, that the male and female organs together enjoy (690; 285): the phallus is again a primitive structure, but by now it has been elevated from anatomy to a universal semantics. Sexless it once was, and now, after passing for a time through the human body and creating sexual difference on the way, sexless it has again become. But this tale of a voyage beyond male and female is disingenuously told, and often contradicted. For Freud and Lacan both seek the patronage of Priapus and write with unashamed enthusiasm of his magical powers. 'The remarkable phenomenon of erection', Freud says in *The Interpretation of Dreams*, 'around which the human imagination has constantly played, cannot fail to be impressive, involving as it does an apparent suspension of the laws of gravity. (Cf. in this connection the winged phalli of the ancients)' (V, 394). Yet this object of wonder, comparable to rainbows, tornadoes or solar eclipses in its apparent flouting of natural law, is not presented to all human spectators on the same terms. Certain of them have it among their possessions and others have not; in certain of them the wonder is incarnate, in others not.

Lacan's *phallus* wings its way upwards to the intellectual sphere and at the same time, rather in the manner of Descartes's pineal gland, is the essential point of junction between thinking and the human body. But where Descartes's point, though concealed in the third ventricle of the brain, had been present in everyone, Lacan's, though perfectly available for empirical inspection, is seriously deficient in generality. In overcoming this drawback, Lacan repeats the classic Freudian manoeuvre: what is absent in fact is present in phantasy. The phallus is what women want, and beyond their wishful imaginings they have concrete ways of acquiring it – either directly, by incorporation of the male organ during intercourse, or indirectly, by producing a baby, a substitute phallus that travels in the opposite direction along the vaginal canal and is obedient to gravity as it moves. The world-picture is not incomplete, therefore, simply because the female body as a primary source of symbolism – and as a primary object of fear, disgust, admiration and envy – is excluded from it. Thanks to the prefigurative capacity that the phallic *ur*-structure possesses, vulva, womb, breasts, milk and menstrual flow have, and need to have, no independent symbolic tone. They say again, in their richly circumstantial dialect, what the phallus has already said. Lacan's re-endorsement of Freud's

129

phallocentrism is forthright. And there is perhaps nowhere in the corpus of psychoanalytic doctrine where the 'scientific' modelling of mental structure bends more compliantly to a prevailing current of sexual opinion than in these paragraphs of Lacan's 'The meaning of the phallus'.

This is a qualified and guileful Priapic cult, of course. Neither Freud nor Lacan is interested in constructing theories that would simply boost conventional notions of male potency and fecundity: it is only under the shadow of the knife that the male member can, for either of them, be a useful theoretical tool. Yet once it has been placed under threat, and become the token of an absent presence and a present absence, an unlimited explanatory range can be claimed for it. Indeed from late infancy onwards the whole of human experience can be thought of as plainly or covertly phallomorphic. Lacan takes sides in a debate that is already several decades old.[3] He aligns himself with Freud, and against Otto Rank, Ernest Jones, Melanie Klein and Karen Horney, and translates into his own terms a Freudian principle that all these heterodox theorists of female sexuality had, in their individual ways, had occasion to dispute: that the phallus 'is the signifier destined to designate as a whole the effects of the signified' (690; 285).

I said at the start of this chapter that Lacan's positive account of desire was somewhat 'thin'. The notion that desire could be usefully imagined as a simple natural force, as a restless animal energy that happened to mobilize human beings in their thoughts, words and deeds, is attacked by him with great vehemence, and it often suits his critique well to leave his own contrasting notion as an insubstantial *je ne sais quoi*. When he came to set forth at some length his own definitions, it was important for desire to remain mobile and multiform. Over and against the leaden instinctualism that much analytic thinking seemed to encourage his *désir* was to be the purest quicksilver. And,

presented in its full volatility, in a shimmer of inconse-
quential semi-definitions, it allowed him to theorize a
quality of Eros on which his analytic predecessors had been
all but silent.

Desire is delineated, and given a secure place in Lacan's
now rapidly developing theory, in the three closely related
papers that he was working on in the early months of 1958:
'The meaning of the phallus', 'The direction of the treatment and the principles of its power', and 'A remark on
Daniel Lagache's report "Psychoanalysis and the structure
of personality"'. In this group, Lacan performs a feat that
coming from another, less paradoxical, writer, would be
strange and incongruous: in the thick of his masculinising
theoretical exposition he works out a view of desire that
not only discards all distinctions of gender but makes them
unthinkable. As we shall see, this is not a casual hesitation
between equally elegant and compelling conceptions. Still
less is it a prudent attempt on Lacan's part to disguise a
contentious political standpoint. This embedding of alternative views inside each other is a sign that Lacan's psychoanalysis, always so proud of its certainties, has struck again
upon an issue that it cannot resolve.

How can the theorist make sure that gatecrashing terms
and suppositions from biology will be excluded from his
definitions of desire? A simple precaution, and one that
Lacan often takes, is to characterize desire as no more than
a secondary postulate, or a learned addendum, for those who
have already been convinced that 'signifying chain' is an
essential and well-founded analytic notion. Thus desire is
the moving mover of all signifying processes, the insinuat-
ing genie that runs through the endless concatenations of
language:

> And the enigmas that desire seems to pose for a
> 'natural philosophy' – its frenzy miming the abyss of

the infinite, the secret collusion with which it envelops the pleasure of knowing and of dominating in *jouissance*, these amount to no other derangement of instinct than that of being caught in the rails – eternally stretching forth towards the *desire for something else* – of metonymy. Hence its 'perverse' fixation at the very suspension-point of the signifying chain where the memory-screen is immobilized and the fascinating image of the fetish is petrified. (518; 166–7)

Where the 'natural philosopher' might talk of instinct, the analyst has to talk of that which is unnatural, fabricated, rigid. A railway system for example. Metonymy keeps desire on the rails, and always pressing ahead to the next destination, but metaphor supplies a limitless profusion of junctions, loops and branch-lines. This is a network that goes everywhere, and those who travel have no choice but to use it, however little it can be relied upon to take them where they want to go. The scientist might talk of the indefinite plurality of worlds, or life-forms, or epochs, but the student of desire has his own vision of unsubduable otherness, his own 'frenzy miming the abyss of the infinite'. A partial arrest of the metonymic function produces a screen-memory (behind which there is a missing childhood memory) or a fetish (behind which there is a missing organ), but these motionless statuesque forms are no more than a perverse attempt to refuse what cannot be refused – the omnipresent desiring motion of speech.

Lacan's writing in passages like this belongs to the genre of the self-authenticating theoretical statement. If what I am saying about language is right, he clearly suggests, my own language must bear it out; in sentences that have desire as their theme the metonymic displacement of desire must be seen and heard. In certain places, this double exposure of theoretical writing to the desiring imperative of language is performed with gleeful verbal dexterity. For example, Lacan asks in 'The direction of the treatment' a question that may be paraphrased roughly as 'Where did Freud find the structure of language when he had no Saussure to help him look?' and then answers himself in these terms:

> He discovered it in a signifying flow [*flux*], the mystery of which lies in the fact that the subject does not even know where to pretend to be its organizer.
>
> Being made to discover oneself there as desirer is the opposite of getting oneself recognized as the subject of it, for it is as a derivation of the signifying chain that the channel of desire flows [*court le ru*], and the subject must have the advantage of a crossover [*voie de bretelle*] to catch his own feed-back. (623; 259)

The 'signifying flow' that Freud discovered was the common medium of the dream itself, the waking associations that the dream prompted and the dialogue between patient and analyst in which all this material might be elaborated further. Far from being able to control and organize this flux, the subject is at its mercy and 'his' desire is not his. Desire is not the neural or emotional raw-material that the subject supplies but something secondary – abstract, deduced, inferred, derived – to which he is subjected. *Ru* is an antiquated and seemingly inappropriate term: how can the unceasing flood be reduced to a mere streamlet? But the phrase *court le ru* brings as its guest *courir les rues*: desire roams the town and is ordinary enough to be found on every street corner. And connected to this now rather impressive and populous channel is another section not of road or waterway but of the rail network. The *voie de bretelle* joins together two adjacent sets of tracks, and what is it in the analytic encounter that enables one to remove oneself momentarily from the rails of one's desire if not the *voix* ('voice') of the therapist? A *flux* that is a *ru(e)* that is a *rail*;

133

a railway crossover that melts into a feedback loop. By water, by road, by rail, by cybernetic circuitry, desire is perpetually in transit and writing is one of its most eventful routes.

But if writing about desire contains too much transport it will begin to lose contact with the tragic and intractable content of Freud's teaching. And if the anatomy of desire is too closely dependent on the inventions of an individual verbal practitioner, it will begin to seem a matter of concern merely for the talented few, for those charismatic personalities who rush in where dull, timorous folk fear to tread. Lacan draws attention to himself as a writer, as an exemplary verbalising vessel through which your desire and mine may be seen to flow, but he also, and in the same papers, diverts attention from himself by constructing a sequence of impersonal models and describing them in what is, for him, a thoroughly dry and self-effacing manner. These models continue the attack on biology, but employ a much more direct method. They do not put on a display of cultivated artifice, designed to make instinct-based accounts of Eros seem crude, but trace and retrace the limits of biological explanation.

The underlying task was not an easy one. For, as I have already suggested, it involved Lacan in the enterprise of describing a universal mental fact that none of his predecessors – dedicated though they were to the study of such facts – had thought worth bothering with. It was not that they had failed to notice the thing: they had chosen not to discuss it. The troublesome feature of desire was not its 'metonymic displacement', for this had been well caught by Freud on a number of occasions. He had called it, in his biologizing way, the 'plasticity of libido' (XVI, 345),[4] and had sketched specimen paths for it in his dream analyses and case-studies. What Lacan had in mind was the 'paradoxical, deviant, erratic, eccentric, even scandalous character' of desire 'by which it is distinguished from need' (690; 286). The error of his colleagues lay not in a simple refusal to talk about these observable characteristics but in their tendency, both as theorists and as clinicians, to reduce desire to need. Their uncriticized model was that of a bodily appetite, the perfectly achievable goal of which was satisfaction, the pleasurable relief of an unpleasurable physical tension, and they spoke as if wishes that did not conform to this model did not, for practical purposes, exist. Yet one had only to look again at the classic case-material of psychoanalysis, now securely enthroned in its text-books, to see that human beings did not always or even mainly wish in this way. Indeed it was only because passions were 'deviant, erratic and eccentric' that analysis had clinical work to do: patients, and not patients alone, could be found desiring to be ill or dissatisfied; in success they could desire their own failure; in pursuit of one goal they could stumble upon another not reconcilable with it, and strive confusedly towards both at once.

To make matters worse, Lacan announces, a fundamental Freudian insight is suppressed by the theoretical over-promoters of need. There is no point in talking as if other people merely held the key to the individual's satisfaction and could decide whether to turn the key or not. Other people do of course have powers of this kind. The breast, for example, can be given to the hungry child or withheld; once given, it can be withdrawn on time, or too early, or too late. We can be offered shelter before the storm starts, or during it; or we can be abandoned to the rain. But something else is always going on in dealings between the need-driven subject and the other who may or may not provide satisfaction. A demand for love is being made. The divided subject, haunted by absence and lack, looks to the other not simply to supply his needs but to pay him the compliment of an unconditional *yes*. If mere need were at stake in these interpersonal encounters a suckling machine or a public umbrella service would satisfy the individual quite as well as an interceding person. But the paradox and the perversity to be found in any recourse to persons is that the other to whom the appeal is addressed is never in a position to answer it unconditionally. He too is divided and haunted, and his *yes*, however loudly it is proclaimed, can only ever be a *maybe*, or a *to some extent*, in disguise.

Desire has its origin in this non-adequation between need and the demand for love, and in the equally grave discrepancy between the demand itself and the addressee's ability to deliver. In setting forth this paradigm, Lacan makes extensive use of a single geometrical figure. This is articulated neatly by the French adverbs *en deçà* and *au delà*, which can also serve as prepositions (*en deçà de, au delà de*) and nouns (*l'en-deçà* can be produced by analogy with *l'au-delà*, 'the beyond', 'the hereafter'). Things are not as neat in English, but 'on the near side'/'on the far side', 'short of'/'in excess of' and even, when one is speaking of measurable intensities, 'below'/'above' are rough equivalents and give some idea of the expressive power that the polarized French phrases possess.

Here are three passages from 'The direction of the treatment' in which the human passions are spatialized in this way:

> Desire is that which is manifested in the interval that demand hollows on the near side of [*en deçà de*] itself, in as much as the subject, in articulating the signifying chain, brings to light the want-to-be, together with the appeal to receive the complement from the Other, if the Other, the locus of speech, is also the locus of this lack.
>
> That which is thus given to the Other to fill, and which is strictly that which it does not have, since it,

too, lacks being, is what is called love, but it is also hate and ignorance.

It is also . . . what is evoked by any demand beyond [*au-delà de*] the need that is articulated in it, and it is certainly that of which the subject remains all the more deprived to the extent that the need articulated in the demand is satisfied. (627; 263)

Desire is produced in the beyond [*l'au-delà*] of demand, in that, in articulating the life of the subject according to its conditions, demand cuts off the need from that life. But desire is also hollowed on its near side [*son en-deçà*] in that, as an unconditional demand of presence and absence, demand evokes the want-to-be under the three figures of the nothing that constitutes the basis of the demand for love, of the hate that even denies the other's being, and of the unspeakable element in that which is unknown in its request. (629; 265)

Desire, although it always shows through demand . . . is nonetheless beyond it [*au delà*]. It also falls short of [*est en deçà de*] another demand in which the subject, reverberating in the locus of the other, not so much effaces his dependence by a return agreement as fixes the very being that he has come there to propose. (634; 269)

On each occasion desire, announced at the outset as a term in search of a definition, is conscientiously removed from view during the defining process: it is not a state or a motion but a space, and not a unified space but a split and contorted one. Need and demand are its co-ordinates, but they cannot be co-ordinated. It is a dimension in which the subject is always destined to travel too far or not far enough, in which any 'above' is always a new 'below', and in which

137

each anticipated moment of plenitude brings with it a new vacancy. Desire-space is not just mobile and unmappable by the subject: it is a place of permanent catastrophe. Psychoanalysis, alone among the intellectual disciplines of the modern age, has the concepts with which to theorize that catastrophe, but has for the most part, in defiance of its own discoveries, chosen to cultivate a stable Euclidean garden instead.

When this geometry of *en deçà* and *au delà* reappears in 'The meaning of the phallus' it acquires a ghostly historical axis. Early on, in the primordial relationship between child and mother, demand is 'on the near side' of need – in that the child constructs an Other whose first obligation is to be present, and who is called upon only secondarily to exercise the 'privilege' of satisfying its needs. At an unspecified later moment, something re-appears 'on the far side' of demand. This is the residue of non-satisfaction that is left when the meeting of a need has been turned into a proof of love: 'the power of pure loss emerges from the residue of an obliteration' (691; 287). Another name for this 'power of pure loss', which survives the deceased need, is of course *desire*. But by now the spatial models are accumulating so fast and the definition of desire is sprouting so many volutes and traceries that the plain fact of the thing, its relentless daily urging, is in danger of being lost. At a culminating moment in this paper, Lacan attempts to escape from his own ingenuities by turning back to kindergarten arithmetic:

> . . . desire is neither the appetite for satisfaction, nor the demand for love, but the difference that results from the subtraction of the first from the second, the very phenomenon of their splitting (*Spaltung*). (691; 287)

From the upper air in which we were led from one fantasticated geometry to the next, we now descend to earth and to the abacus: take need from demand and desire is your remainder. In its context, this formulation is not as plain as it might seem if read in isolation, for the simple subtraction to which Lacan refers has, strictly speaking, already been ruled out. Need and demand are conceivable only in so far as each espouses the other's outline or uses the other as its alias. But the reassurance that the sentence affords is nevertheless very powerful: desire is what everyone already knows. It belongs to children and to adults, to men and to women, to Don Juan and to Bob Cratchit. And although it may appear in human experience only in oblique and evanescent ways – in a gap, at a tangent, as a residue – it is always there and cannot be got round, or shelved, or evicted. Above all, desire, though infinitely malleable, is not divisible or destructible. For Lacan there can be only one desire, just as for Freud there was only one libido.

The term *Spaltung* on which Lacan's 'definitive' definition ends is itself revealing, and allows us to pinpoint a major difficulty in his account of the passions. For it is one of his favourite pseudo-technicalities and moves between arguments with astonishing ease. The term has among many virtues that of allowing Lacan to declare allegiance to Freud at moments when he is in fact pursuing a line of thought quite different from his. Freud used the term *Spaltung* ('splitting') from time to time in his early career to denote the self-dividedness of the human mind, but it was only later, and then in quite specialized discussions, that it came to resemble a technical term. *Ichspaltung* or 'splitting of the ego' was the mechanism, of particular note in the theory of fetishism and the psychoses, whereby the ego could maintain in uneasy co-existence two distinct attitudes towards the external world – those of acceptance and disavowal.[5]

Lacan's *Spaltung*, while picking up the resonances of Freud's usage, is altogether more ambitious and carries a pronounced metaphysical charge. It is the primal condition of the human subject. Lacan speaks of 'the split (*Spaltung*) which the subject undergoes by virtue of being a subject only in so far as he speaks' (634; 269) and 'a subject divided by the signifying *Spaltung*' (693; 288). In the beginning, so Lacan's perpetual refrain runs, there was a split. And there are two ways of describing it: as a separation visited upon the speaking subject by the very language he uses, or as a separation inherent in the human passions and datable, for each individual, to an epoch before his language had been acquired. The *Spaltung* between need and demand in the nursling somehow predestines him, we are to suppose, for his later divided subjecthood.

As a metaphysical principle, Lacan's *Spaltung* or *refente* resembles the Strife (νεῖκος) that Freud had borrowed from Empedocles in 'Analysis Terminable and Interminable' (XXIII, 246). But where Empedocles had set Strife against Love (φιλία), and Freud Thanatos against Eros, as combatants in a ceaseless cosmic struggle, Lacan gives *Spaltung* a solitary inaugural force.[6] Desire is not its opponent but its derivative. All that we can know of Eros, and of ourselves as subjects, comes to us from our ability to travel back, studiously and with passion, from our current self-division to its earliest antecedent state. Yet for Lacan there is something profoundly unsatisfactory as well as profoundly tempting about this retrospective movement. And the problem lies in the fact of possessing two seemingly independent routes back to the primal moment of Strife. At first this seems to bring a clear benefit. If the dialectic of the 'naked' passions and the dialectic of subjectivity as articulated in language could be shown to enact twice over the same sort of future-directed motion from an original split, through an indefinite series of upheavals, towards an always unrealisable cessation of desire, did one not, in a sense, know the structure of the human subject twice as well? But Lacan becomes distrustful as soon as the idiom of 'need', 'demand'

and 'desire' begins to have too little linguistic content. It must not begin to sound like the language of an introspective psychologizer who imagines himself to have immediate access to the wordless states, activities and dispositions of his mind. It must not seem like an attempt to unshackle oneself from the signifying chain, or to jump from the train of speech while it is still in motion. The two routes to the *Urspaltung* cannot, then, be allowed to be merely parallel, or their two underlying structures merely homologous. The dialectic of desire must become in its own way a dialectic of signification, and for this to happen there must be a crossover and a set of points.

The phallus performs this role. It is of course available as a rough non-verbal emblem of need, demand and desire – and allows us to imagine a world of mute desiring transactions between human individuals – but, as we have seen, it is also for Lacan, and much more impressively, a signifier and an elastic structural idea. But giving the phallus this crossover role, and giving an equivalent role to no other signifier, is exceptionally problematic. I said earlier that two views of desire were present in 'The meaning of the phallus', but the general drift of Lacan's thinking in the late fifties is yet stranger and more undecided than this. For the phallus, and the entire 'masculinist' discourse that it unleashes in these papers, are at odds not with one but with two models of perpetual mobility and incompletion, neither of which has any particular bias on matters of gender. 'The subject', divided in and by language, is genuinely neutral in Lacan's analysis, despite the masculine gender that the term happens to bear in French. ('The person' and 'the personality', much favoured at an earlier stage, were equally fortuitously feminine.) Desire, born of the impossible confluence of need and demand, is genderless in the same way. But the agent that is called upon to tie the two views together, to give the subject 'his' desire by signifying it for him, is the male genital, transcendentalized. No other volunteer has stepped forward.

Lacan's peroration in 'The meaning of the phallus' endorses and amplifies a view of the masculine principle that Freud had expressed in his *Three Essays on the Theory of Sexuality* (1905). Freud had written in his chapter on 'The Differentiation between Men and Women': 'if we were able to give a more definite connotation to the concepts of "masculine" and "feminine", it would even be possible to maintain that libido is invariably and necessarily of a masculine nature, whether it occurs in men or in women and irrespectively of whether its object is a man or a woman' (VII, 219). But Lacan goes much further, disregarding the hesitations both of Freud's main text at this point and of the long footnote that he added in 1915:

> Correlatively, one can glimpse the reason for a characteristic that had never before been elucidated, and which shows once again the depth of Freud's intuition: namely, why he advances the view that there is only one *libido*, his text showing that he conceives it as masculine in nature. The function of the phallic signifier touches here on its most profound relation: that in which the Ancients embodied the Νους and the Λογοσ. (695; 291)

There is something desperate about this apotheosis of the phallus. It is of course agreeable to see the relations between Mind and Word turning for a visionary moment upon a single hinge, but the reader will need more than a tribute to 'the depth of Freud's intuition' if he or she is to be persuaded that any one notion (or organ, or symbol) is entitled to such glory.

Lacan repeats without comment Freud's *non sequitur*: if desire is one it must also be masculine. But a still more obliging discipleship is also at work in these final pages of the paper. Much of Freud's argument in the *Three Essays* leads directly to the view that sexual types or constitutions have to be thought of as an extensive connected series rather than in terms of simple polarities such as male–female, heterosexual–homosexual, sadistic–masochistic or normal–perverse. Yet in spite of this his book abounds in stereotyped images of Woman and Man and the 'natural' inclinations of each. Lacan, for all the dialectical nicety that he earlier brought to the discussion of sexuality, in the end speaks in similar ways. Women are less subject than men to the '*Verdrängung* [repression] inherent in desire'; infidelity is 'masculine'; women turn themselves, by way of their self-adornment, into signifiers of desire: they try to become the phallus that they lack; a fondness for masks and masquerades is 'feminine', and for that reason manly self-display is itself perceived as a feminized form of behaviour (694–5; 289–90). And so it goes on. These are scattered sociological observations being passed off as a theory of sexual difference. And it is the phallus, now conceived as the primal *Spaltung* from which all others descend, that promises structure, coherence, economy and elegance to what could otherwise be mistaken for a dictionary of received ideas about sex. Sexual types and dispositions are constructed within the Symbolic order, Lacan vigorously announces, not vouchsafed to humankind by physiology or by nature at large, and an appropriately complex view of the phallus will allow us to see the construction taking place. This being granted, it is all the more surprising to find that Lacan's typology of socially fabricated sexualities is rather ordinary, and that it coincides in so many of its categories with the views of those who think that an essential 'femininity' and 'masculinity' are indelibly inscribed in the book of nature.

In all Lacan's writings on feminine sexuality phallocentric arguments are advanced and, at least implicitly, criticized. The signifying phallus is now the key to any understanding of human sexuality, now merely a prominent structural model that can be variously employed in the conjectural science of psychoanalysis. A particularly fertile version of this divided theoretical approach is to be found in the 'Guiding remarks for a congress on feminine sexuality' that Lacan wrote in the same year as the other papers that I have considered in this chapter. The congress itself was held in Amsterdam in 1960, and Lacan's paper appeared for the first time in 1962. These remarks take the form of a draft curriculum for future psychoanalytic research and cover a wide variety of theoretical and clinical topics: the universal 'psychical bisexuality' postulated by Freud; the clitoris and the vagina as alternative sites of sexual pleasure; masochism; fetishism, and its absence; frigidity; female homosexuality; the social context of sexuality.

In a sense, the entire paper is a plea for cool, non-prescriptive thinking about the construction of human subjectivity. Such thinking, so expertly performed by Freud himself, has had two main enemies in the analytic tradition: stage-by-stage models of human development and essential-ising views of the individual subject. For Lacan these are the plainest of intellectual vices, and the damage they have done to the discussion of female sexuality is grave. There has been much talk, for example, of the masochism and passivity of women, but talk too of 'the castrating and devouring, dislocating and stupefying effects of feminine activity' (731; MR, 92).[7] The discrepancy between the two views, where it has been noticed at all, has not been thought worthy of discussion. What is needed is a model that will make the two modes of action jointly intelligible. There-after it will be possible to ask serious questions about the role that masculine phantasy has had in creating and main-taining the notion of feminine masochism, or of any other 'inherent' feminine characteristic.

A similar operation is performed on aspects of Melanie

144

Klein's theory. Lacan finds this theory especially uncongenial, but recognises in Klein an adversary who cannot simply be ignored or pilloried. Her main errors are plain: she re-attributes the powers of the phallus to the maternal body, and in so doing backdates the Oedipal drama to earliest infancy; and she refuses to elucidate the underlying structural principles that govern the interplay of her 'good' and 'bad' part-objects. Yet the displacements and substitutions that her developmental narratives contain make her a dialectician without knowing it, and important advances may perhaps be made by switching her copious description of internal objects from the Imaginary to the Symbolic register. If discussion of feminine sexuality is to be taken beyond the point where Klein, and Ernest Jones in her wake, had left it 'a theory is needed of how the phallus is assigned the function of equivalence in the emergence of all objects of desire' (729; MR, 91).

It is clear from this account that the phallus is entitled to its extraordinary structuring and dialecticising role only if it is thought of as un-male, as a terrain that both sexes inhabit and a pivotal point for their countless mutual determinations. In Lacan's longest discussion of a clinical topic – frigidity – this supposed neutrality of the 'phallic signifier' provides the basis for an optimistic view of analytic therapy:

> Analysis alone mobilizes [frigidity], at times incidentally, but always in a transference which cannot be contained by the infantilising dialectic of frustration, that is, of privation, but one which always brings symbolic castration into play. In which context it is worth recalling a basic principle.
>
> A principle which can be simply stated: that castration cannot be deduced from development alone, since it presupposes the subjectivity of the Other as the place

145

of its law. The otherness of sex is denatured by this alienation. Man here acts as the relay whereby the woman becomes this Other for herself as she is this Other for him.

It is in this sense that an unveiling of the Other involved in the transference can modify a defence which has been taken up symbolically.

By which I mean that, in this case, defence should first be conceived of in the dimension of masquerade which the presence of the Other releases in its sexual role. (732; MR, 93–4)

Frigidity is treatable analytically – where other procedures notoriously fail – because the cancellation of pleasure that the condition involves has already been grasped by analysis in its most radical form: as castration, as the threatened abolition of the pleasure-providing organ itself. Where others might speak, when confronted by frigidity, of a sexual need and its frustration, Lacan speaks of an intersubjective process in which a fateful 'thou shalt not enjoy' passes from one partner to the other. In the transference, the legislating and pleasure-denying power of the Other can be unveiled, and an experimental sequence of unveilings and re-veilings can itself become a return route to interpersonal sexual enjoyment. Although Lacan associates this *ballo in maschera* with feminine sexuality in particular, it is clear that his structural model can be applied elsewhere in the sexual sphere as well. The hope that the transference offers the frigid woman is offered on equal terms to the impotent man. Viewed in a perspective of this sort, the phallus does indeed begin to seem neutral, and only adventitiously connected with the male body. It becomes the indispensable theoretical device that allows sexual difference to be measured – not an organ but a structure, not a token of virility but the foundation for a new combinatorial science.

All this would be unexceptionable if Lacan's plea for dialectic did not also involve him in a monomaniacal refusal to grant signifying power to the female body. His model could of course be speculatively re-invented from the female point of view without losing its explanatory force: the drama of possession and privation, of absence and presence, of promise and threat, could be retained and perhaps even enhanced if the principals were breast, clitoris, vagina and uterus. If these organs were allowed to become signifiers too a new and more inflected geometry of *en deçà* and *au delà* could come into view; and the parallel worlds of passion and signification could acquire a more elaborate and more telling pattern of crossovers. But Lacan himself tirelessly suggests that any such transfer of symbolic power to the female would be heresy, and bring the Symbolic order itself to the verge of ruin.

Looking back to the Kleinian views that he had criticized earlier in his paper, he refers to them as a 'monstrous' conceptualization; and this strangely overburdened adjective chimes with certain of the phrases he had used in his original summary. He had spoken of the 'perfect brutality' of Klein's concepts, and of the 'fantastic phallophagia' to which the bad breast was subjected, according to Klein, by the suckling child.[8] There is an unmistakable tremor of fear in this writing. Freud in a celebrated paragraph of his essay on 'Female Sexuality' (1931) had compared the surprising discovery of a pre-Oedipal phase in girls to 'the discovery, in another field, of the Minoan-Mycenean civilization behind the civilization of Greece' (XXI, 226). Klein takes Lacan on a similar but for him intolerable imaginative journey into the ancient past and brings him face to face, in the labyrinth of female sexuality, with a true monster: the breast that is also a phallus. Where hybridization had produced in the Minotaur an emblem of supercharged virility, it had acquired in Klein's phantasy an emasculating force. The breast-phallus was the object of the young child's cannibalistic rage, but the psychoanalyst who had invented it, and had dared to make over to the female body powers that could only ever be male, was driven by a vengeful 'phallophagia' of her own. Lacan's answer to Klein is cast as a list of questions that he proposes to 'modulate upon the lyre' of her theory. By way of a sonnet by Gérard de Nerval,[9] he is here remembering Orpheus, the sweet singer and devoted lover whose fate it was to be torn limb from limb by the women of Thrace . . .

The sexuality of women is to be understood, therefore, from within the phallic dimension, and attempts to think of it differently are likely to be interpreted as the sign of a 'devouring and castrating' womanhood at work. Yet there is an aspect of Lacan's thinking that does not harmonize with this at all. Women reveal to him something about desire itself that would otherwise be unknown to his theory. At the end of his discussion of lesbianism, for example, he writes of those lesbians who adopt a conventionally 'male' role:

> We still have to draw a lesson from the naturalness with which such women appeal to their quality of being men, as opposed to the delirious style of the transexual male.

> Perhaps what this reveals is the path leading from feminine sexuality to desire itself.

> Far from its being the case, indeed, that the passivity of the act corresponds to this desire, feminine sexuality appears as the effort of a *jouissance* wrapped in its own contiguity (of which all circumcision might represent the symbolic rupture) to be *realised in rivalry* with the desire which castration releases in the male by giving him its signifier in the phallus. (735; MR, 97)

On the surface this seems to keep the phallocentric message intact: such women, by imitating men and entering into rivalry with those who 'possess' the phallus, confirm that desire is activity and activity male. But *'jouissance* wrapped in its own contiguity' is not simply a point of departure for the sexual act, a circle that has to be broken if the subject is to begin the ascent towards orgasm: it is the blissful suspension of desire that all sexual agents seek, and therefore the destination towards which they travel. Women in general – and not just the lesbians who serve as their advance guard – set out in quest of something that they, unlike men, already have.

Lacan's reference to circumcision brings male sexuality into the argument as a pathetic counter-theme. He speaks of 'all' varieties of this practice, but clearly has in mind the symbolic mutilation of the penis rather than the real acts of castration that Western commentators have chosen to describe, with unseemly delicacy, as 'female circumcision'. Where men are energized by the threat of castration and know only the phallic route towards sexual pleasure, women, when they experience pleasure, are empowered from within, 'contiguously to themselves'. They are perpetual motion machines programmed to produce their own rapture. We have come a long way from the idea that females perceive themselves, and are perceived by males, as bereft of the penis and doomed to an endless pursuit of substitutive satisfaction. Lacan has in these paragraphs come close to reversing the terms of this description, and to claiming that women, freed from the servitude of the phallus, have already got what men will always crave. Wherever it is that men want to be, women are already there.

There is something knowingly outrageous about this attempt to construct an encompassing view of sexuality from an endless contrastive play with the notions 'male'/

'female' and 'masculine'/'feminine'. And Lacan does suspend the game from time to time. It is clear that much of his writing in these papers is concerned not with gender and not with sexual difference in the usual sense, but with the construction of the subject and with the different rhythms, intensities and styles of delectation to which sexual subjects have access. There is much that is acknowledged as rough and arbitrary in his distribution of genders: the masquerade is feminine, but men practise it too; the *mille e tre* objects of male desire pass in procession before women too. Besides, the universal bisexuality postulated by Freud places a continuous blur upon all such definitions.[10] Provided always that the centrality of the phallus is accepted, a spectrum of sexualities is possible. Yet it would be quite mistaken to say that Lacan is merely a compulsive ironist in these matters, or that he toys with traditional gender notions in order to enforce an extreme form of sexological relativism. Mistaken because a durable sexual polarity is at work in his writing, and because the difference between speaking, acting or enjoying 'as a man' and doing the same things 'as a woman' offers him a unique way of keeping that polarity in focus.

Lacan's most radical attempt to construct a distinctive and irreducible 'feminine sexuality' is to be found in the central chapter of *Encore*, the twentieth volume of his *Seminar*. This chapter, 'God and the *jouissance* of the Woman' (XX, 61–71; MR, 138–48), is the transcript of a densely allusive and self-referring verbal performance and, from its title onwards, poses exceptional problems for the reader and for the translator. For his 'discussion' – if such a word can be used of a text that lurches between catechism, riddle-book and Pindaric ode – is organized around a series of puns, and of these the most overt are far from being the richest, although they certainly make their mark. In speaking, for example, of his over-dutiful followers and their fondness for such phrases as 'the lack of a signifier' and the 'signifier of a lack of a signifier', he uses the terms *cafouillage* and *bafouillage*: their language is an imitative floundering and spluttering, and they do not understand that they must renounce or disrupt Lacanian diction if they are to adhere to Lacan's message. His word-play nudges these docile mimics towards the language they dare not speak. Or again, to refer to the vagina as having different zones of sensitivity is, he suggests, to indulge in *conneries*, or nonsense and 'cuntishness'. Whatever triggers female sexual arousal is to be found somewhere between *secouer* ('to shake') and *secourir* ('to aid'). Lacan's bawdy in cases like these hesitates between anti-feminine derision and an exaltation of women as artists in physical rapture.

But the main provocations of Lacan's chapter are to be found in its undertow of monosyllables. Woman is not an all, or an All. She is not all there. She is not-at-all. She is not a One, but less than one, and more. She is also a moreover, a what-is-more. She is not a universal, and the definite article that in French would make her into one is struck out to make the point. For women and for men, 'woman' is an endless sequence of projections and fabrications. What is feminine sexuality, then, if there is no Woman, no eternal femininity, to enshrine it? At the most primitive level of phantasy, the proliferating puns tell us, it is to be found in not having a penis, in not being 'all there'. But this minus is also a plus, for not having the small all that defines the 'phallic function' means having access to that greater all which is undulating and overspilling diversity, the joy and frenzy of unstoppable change. Philosophies of the one and the many, from the pre-Socratics to the neo-Platonists, are caught up in Lacan's continuous *bafouillage*. For the discussion of his cancelled Woman, Lacan has invented a language that is weighty and flashy, solemn and mischievous, mythopoeic and disabused.

151

Running through the whole tirade, however, there is a much more candid strain. Lacan displays unaffected wonderment in reporting that the female orgasm exists and that he feels obliged to situate it 'beyond the phallus'. How can this be so? After all, the phallus is the one signifier that has no 'beyond' and that places an uncrossable boundary around human sexuality. Rather than develop an argument against this view – his own view of many years standing – Lacan offers a succession of disconnected counter-proposals. These culminate in an invocation to Bernini's Saint Teresa that is remarkable for having nothing of note to say:

> . . . you only have to go and look at Bernini's statue in Rome to understand immediately that she's coming, there is no doubt about it. And what is her *jouissance*, her *coming* from? It is clear that the essential testimony of the mystics is that they are experiencing it but know nothing about it. (XX, 70–71; MR, 147)

Lacan resists the temptations to discourse offered by Bernini's Cornaro chapel. He refuses to be elaborate or abundant in imitation of this masterpiece of the Baroque, and in particular has nothing to say about its complex figuration of the masculine. There are no Cornaro males kneeling by; there is no seraph, no divine radiance flooding the scene. Teresa writes of the seraph in her *Life*: 'In his hands I saw a long golden spear and at the end of the iron tip I seemed to see a point of fire', and Bernini, while commuting spear to dart, gives this weapon a prominent place in his design.[11] Lacan removes it. He focuses attention on the blissful figure of Teresa, and describes her enraptured movements as 'mystical jaculations'. The removal of the phallus could scarcely go further than this: *éjaculations* has been shorn of its detachable prefix, and the distinction between inside and outside that is central both to the heterosexual encounter and to the male orgasm, has been lost. Teresa and her fellow mystics are borne along on an uncaused, unlocalizable and ineffable pleasure-spasm.

Charcot and others of his generation, Lacan goes on to say, had thought that mysticism was all a matter of 'come'. But no, not at all. *Jouissance* of the kind that Lacan chooses to call feminine is to be found in the sinews, in thinking, in writing – wherever *signifiance*, the combined production of meaning and pleasure, occurs. Enjoying oneself and not knowing anything about it is 'feminine' in a way, but this does not mean that men are debarred by their gender from reaching such states. The unanswerable proof that feminine sexuality migrates between the sexes is to be found in the fact that 'The *Ecrits* of Jacques Lacan' is itself a mystical jaculation, a 'Jacques-ulation'. The book may resemble 'chatter' and 'verbiage', but it is in fact made of stronger stuff: the body's joy, and the mind's (XX, 71; MR, 147).

Although Lacan clearly thinks of this description as a *coup de théâtre*, those who are familiar with his earlier writings are unlikely to be surprised by it. An identification with the feminine had been visible from his first publications onwards. Indeed the article that he wrote on the Papin sisters for the Surrealist journal *Minotaure*,[12] and the extended discussion of a female patient ('Aimée') that figures in his doctoral dissertation, already show him not just as an observer of women but as one who, when they are mad, wants to share their madness. Diana in 'The Freudian thing', the Queen in Poe's 'The Purloined Letter' and Marguerite Duras's Lol V. Stein, in Lacan's review of the book, are in the same lineage.[13] They are patron saints of extremity and indecipherability. To some extent this chapter of *Encore* is simply the latest and grandest identification in the series and differs from the others in degree rather than kind: it is more manic than they were but is continuing to mythologize Woman as a foil to the ratiocinative, knowledge-seeking and system-building intelligence that Lacan unself-consciously thinks of as male. For a long time an argument has been taking place within him, it might be said, between two intellectual styles or sensibilities and now, as a *maître-à-penser* at the height of his fame, he feels able to lay that argument bare before an admiring public.

But something much more interesting than this is also going on, and the 'God' of his title gives us a clue to it. 'God' means two things at once in the chapter itself: it is 'the One' that male sexuality ordains, and that psychoanalysis, in temporary partnership with Christian theology, is able to unmask in an indefinite variety of human contexts. Yet is is also the Other, whatever inextirpable impediment it is that comes between the partners in the well-known arrangement that one is not strictly entitled to call a 'sexual relationship': 'why should the materialists, as we call them, be indignant that I place God as third party, and why not, in this affair of human love? After all, doesn't it ever happen, even to materialists, to know something about the *ménage à trois*?' (XX, 66; MR, 141). There is no such thing as a sexual relationship, Lacan repeatedly announces at this time, because, although each partner plays the role of Subject to the other's Other, this dispensation can never produce symmetry or reciprocity: language always creates between them an intractable and unsheddable surplus cargo of otherness, a third party ubiquitous and powerful enough to be called God. It is the special virtue of feminine *jouissance* to outplay both these Gods. It is always supplementary to the One and an enemy of any system that may be erected in its honour, and at the same time swoons away from Otherness and its nefarious works. Orgasm has seldom been asked to bear a philosophical burden as heavy as this.

What is still more extraordinary, however, than the theological penumbra that envelops this argument is the way in which its main thrust and its countless polemical annexes are centred on the person of Lacan himself. The chapter begins with a reply to Jean-Luc Nancy and Philippe Lacoue-Labarthe's *Le Titre de la lettre* (*The Title of the Letter*), which is a critique of 'The agency of the letter' conducted from the viewpoint of Derridean deconstruction. The authors of the book, who are referred to as 'underlings', are not named in Lacan's rebuttal, and neither is Derrida. All three are to be the anonymous recipients of Lacan's benediction:

> Earlier you saw me wavering, drawing back, hesitating to come down on the side of one meaning or the other, on the side of love or of what is called hate, when I urged you to share in a reading whose express objective is to discredit me – which should hardly deter someone who speaks of nothing but dis-consideration, and who aims at nothing less. (XX, 64; MR, 139)

This is an exalted version of the 'evenly suspended attention'[14] with which the analyst is required to listen to the patient's speech. Having received the wound of *Le Titre de la lettre*, having been its guileless victim, Lacan now reaches beyond martyrdom to become the public stage on which love and hate play out their conflict. Let the underlings and their master publish their spiteful squibs, for here is an impersonal vengeance that will seek them out and an unconditional love that will embrace them in their wretchedness. Lacan is already moving into a God-like position and preparing for his final Teresan self-apotheosis. But the whole chapter is cast in this vein: here we have a theorist who dares to say 'I' and who can at any moment reinforce his vatic authority by displaying his wounds.

The wounds that hurt most, however, are not those that come from his critics. These are Lilliputian pinpricks when measured against the damage that such a writer can do to himself. He has created a system, and now wants to disown it. He has invented a cant – of the signifier, the phallus and the rest – and can no longer bear to hear it spoken. Above all, he has created an infinitely menacing world-picture that it would not be improper, he concedes, to call 'ahuman' (827; 324): the subject is divided from the beginning and forever, desire is the unhappy pursuit of an impossible goal, and the reign of the phallus is an empty display founded upon craven anxiety and fear. He must now find a way out. He looks back to pleasure for an alternative view of things. *Jouissance*, which had made many seductive appearances in his earlier work, is now the central redeeming notion:

> Might not this *jouissance* which one experiences and knows nothing of, be that which puts us on the path of ex-sistence? And why not interpret one face of the Other, the God face, as supported by feminine *jouissance*? (XX, 71; MR, 147)

A beneficent power is being called upon to rescue him from the severity of his own theory. We could say, remembering Crashaw's great Hymn to Saint Teresa, that Lacan's wounds 'weep/Balsam to heal themselves with' and that this remedy is nothing better and nothing worse than literature. Women in their 'ex-sistence' guide him back to the pleasures of the text.

Does Lacan's hyperbolical account of Woman show us phallocracy being overthrown from without, or undermined from within, or lingering on under an alias? When Lacan has finished his sport with what he calls 'feminine sexuality', the female body scarcely exists. The hand of Brancusi rather than Bernini has been at work upon it, smoothing away its organs and polishing its surfaces into yet another mirror for the male. Women *are* their ecstasy, and envied for it by men, but when their transport ceases they have little to do and nothing at all to say. Not so Lacan himself. For when he descends from the glorious excesses of *being a writer* and *being a woman*, he finds himself the possessor again of primal structures, or splits, or ruptures, that are either without gender or male. When they have no gender – as in the *Spaltung* that separates need and demand – and have to be given one in order to become fully capable of signification, there is only one direction in which it is worth looking: towards the phallus. Should your gaze move from *lingam* to *yoni*, it will move not from one structure to another but from structure itself to its ineffable and boundless *au-delà*, to that *jouissance* 'the absence of which would make the universe vain' (819; 317).

If Freud's sense of tragedy often makes psychoanalysis seem centuries old, and a worthy inheritor of the Sophoclean vision, his speculations on gender make it seem young, sportive and provisional. He presents himself as travelling, in the *Three Essays on the Theory of Sexuality*, from a dark age of sexual superstition towards a new enlightenment. But how far does he get? He sees clearly that sexualities are cultural products, and that their ideological supports can be analysed, but the sexuality of the patriarchal male is curiously resistant to investigation. It keeps on returning as the unanalysed grid that allows other sexual dispositions to be sorted and evaluated. Lacan, dissident in so many ways, is steadfastly loyal in this area of enquiry. Indeed much of his writing on sexual difference is a sophistical reworking of the *Three Essays* and Freud's later works on 'Femininity' (*New Introductory Lectures*, XXII, 112–35) and 'Female Sexuality' (XXI, 225–43). Yet if there is something derisory about the Lacano-Freudian phallic cult, we should nevertheless remind ourselves of what it has achieved. It has helped to make human sexuality into a thinkable subject for the West, and one for which a coherent and encompassing theory might in due course exist. And it has become an indispensable prolegomenon and cautionary tale for a later generation of theorists – the feminist thinkers who are at last bringing the discussion of sexual difference out from the dark ages.

6 Theory without End

By the early 1960s Lacan's theory was complete in at least two senses. On the one hand, it was a coherent transformation of Freud's entire doctrine. Lacan's 'return to Freud' could be thought of, at this period, either as an attempt to be uncommonly faithful to the letter of the original texts, or as a simple catch-phrase designed to disguise an entirely different purpose – that of building a new psychoanalysis to rival Freud's own. But it was by now plain to upholders of either view that Lacan had revisited all the main points on Freud's itinerary and reconceptualized all the main psychoanalytic issues. Lacan's theory, that is to say, was complete in that it did not leave relevant things out. On the other hand, it was complete in the sense that it had no outer boundary: there was nothing in human experience on which it was obliged to maintain a principled silence. It could travel in all weathers, fish in all streams and sit down at any table. For it was a theory of the desiring speech in which all human beings live and die. And it was not one theory among others, amicably conversing with its neighbours. It was a listening station for the whole conversation of mankind, a working model of the human world, a contrapuntal portrait of things as they are.

A charitable onlooker from the Anglo-American analytic tradition might have said at this point: 'This is all very well, but we have work to do with our patients. If your "desiring speech" and your "dialectic of intersubjectivity" are derived from your own experience as a clinician, please tell me what clinical consequences they can be expected to have for me. What changes in the way I and my patients talk should I seek to bring about as a result of reading Lacan?'[1] Lacan's published works of the period 1960–75 do not contain a clear answer to questions of this kind. Indeed they show him becoming more theoretical not less, and adding numerous subordinate mechanisms to his already 'complete' model. He develops further his account of desire and returns with new vigour to two topics – the object in psychoanalysis, and the structure of human temporality – that had been dormant for a number of years. I shall be devoting most of this chapter to these extraordinary last adventures of Lacan's theoretical imagination, and attempting only in my concluding remarks to answer in any detail the question raised by my imaginary observer.[2]

It will already be plain, however, that Lacan, who so often thinks in terms of discontinuity and division, does not think of theorizing and clinical practice as split off from each other. Theories get complex because the raw materials of psychoanalysis are already so: 'Analysis accustoms us to recognising that insignificant beings are inhabited by a dialectic as subtle as this, which can also be explained by the fact that the least of the *ego*'s failings is its banality' (733; MR, 95). And Lacan's language itself constantly reminds us of the daily return journey that the analyst must be prepared to make from the pure logic of subjectivity to the gaps, redundancies and confusions of ordinary speech. Such speech, in the form of slang, proverbs, slogans, exclamations and jokes, permeates Lacan's theoretical writing and refers us at every turn to the verbal rough-and-tumble that takes place between analyst and analysand. Indeed we could go further than this and say that spoken speech enjoys a special advantage over the extenuated language of 'theory', and continues to enjoy it even when the theorist seasons his writing with the vernacular. Theory, for Lacan, does not make anything happen, or get things done, or make certain things matter more than others. The more complete a theory is, the more powerless it becomes. The theory-maker can easily fall victim to his own success: having been animated at the start by an array of precise local issues, he can end up as the hapless proprietor of a gratuitous verbal universe. He can lose all sense of there being causes to defend, follies to expose, sufferings to alleviate and pleasures to pursue. The noise of theory can be as forlorn as the rustle of dry leaves on a dull day. Against this background, speech itself becomes glorious: the subject is in question, and *jouissance* breaks cover even as death threads its way invisibly from one syllable to the next. In speech, everything is still to play for. It is the complacent theorist's land of lost discontent. The often highly abstract extensions of Lacan's theory to which I now turn all need to be understood by reference to the interpersonal communicative activity that by circuitous paths they seek to rejoin.

The works that I shall be drawing on for the most part are those collected in the final section of *Ecrits*: 'The subversion of the subject and the dialectic of desire in the Freudian unconscious' (1960), 'Position of the unconscious' (1960–64), 'On Freud's *Trieb* and the desire of the psychoanalyst' (1964) and 'Science and truth' (1965). I shall also be referring to Book XXII of the *Seminar* (*RSI*) and returning to Books XI and XX: *The Four Fundamental Concepts of Psycho-Analysis* and *Encore*. 'Desire and its objects' would be an appropriate collective title for these works, although these terms and the axis connecting them are characteristically unstable.

Much of Lacan's work on the further refinement of 'desire' itself is of a philological kind, and less far-reaching than his account of its objects. Lacan was conscious, long before scholarly fashion caught up with him, that certain of Freud's technical terms had changed their meaning during translation and transmission, and he became expert in detecting the hidden ideological shifts that such changes imply. Freud's *Trieb* offers a particularly absorbing case in point. The editors of the Standard Edition chose to translate it as *instinct*, thereby losing the firm distinction that Freud had made between *Trieb*, which belonged to the dynamics of the human mind, and *Instinkt*, which belonged to zoology. In doing this they had, for Lacan, provided the term with a set of false identity papers, and made it sound much more biological than it was. The term *drive*, and its approximate French equivalent *pulsion*, were plainly to be preferred, but in both cases additional precautions had to be taken in order to protect the 'dissident' character of Freud's concept (543). *Dérive* ('drift') would be an accurate French translation, Lacan suggests (803; 301 and VII, 132, XX, 102), punning between the Teutonic and Romance languages (*drive – dérive – derive*), but if that proves unacceptable the usual French term *pulsion* will have to be put under strict surveillance. This term, which was created from *impulsion*, in the early years of the century, for the specific purpose of translating Freud's *Trieb*, has in ordinary professional usage one clear failing: it suggests that human desire is subdivisible into a stable set of fundamental types or elements, each of which may be characterized by reference to a similarly stable set of relationships between its bodily source, its aim and the object or objects by which that aim can be satisfied. Freud had begun to isolate such elements – in the form of *Partialtriebe* or 'component drives' – in the first edition of the *Three Essays* (1905).[3] And Lacan understates by far the part that Freud himself had played in encouraging further classificatory work of the same kind, even while he acknowledged that the psychoanalytic theory of the drives was a 'mythology' (XXII, 95).

Lacan's philological disquisitions on *Trieb* have a very broad underlying aim: to rewrite the history of desire from its farthest shores, from the viewpoint of its 'impossibilities' (852). Where those who allow *Trieb* to be annexed by *Instinkt* are setting up for themselves a safety net, a 'natural' community of interests between wishful human beings and instinct-driven organisms, Lacan returns Freud's readers to the unprotected brink of an original *béance*. There is nothing mysterious about this journey back to the abyss, for it is a matter simply of continuing to take Freud literally at a point where he himself had been literal: 'it is the assumption of castration that creates the lack upon which desire is instituted' (852). Desire comes into being not at the moment when 'source', 'aim' and 'object' enter into alignment, but when an already desiring Other intervenes to say *no*. The 'assumption' of castration is at once an acquiescence in this Other's law and an envious appropriation of his desire – an 'impossibility', therefore, at the very moment of its inception.

Desire is of course subject to fixation, and the cause of psychoanalysis may in some respects be well served by thinking of its relatively fixed forms as separately nameable drives. But the way of looking at things that Lacan by now much prefers is one that places lack and interdiction at the centre of the picture and has the drives circulating round them. Each drive, if and when it is individually considered, bears the mark of impossibility: each is desire seeking and failing to find its point of satiation. Failing to find this point, it pursues or half-pursues its own extinction: 'every drive is virtually a death drive' (848). Here and in numerous other contexts Lacan simplifies Freud's *Todestrieb* ('death drive') by deeming that its action is merely immanent to the signifying chain.[4] The subject comes into being 'barred' by the signifier and thereby injected with a sense of death. And this is poisoning rather than inoculation. The taste for death is not something that the subject acquires through experience, as one might say, or reaches towards as a last

despairing manner of delectation, for it has been there from
the start as a perilous gift from the signifier, and one that
cannot be refused. The drive, as it circles round the exca-
vated centre of being, is pulled outwards towards the objects
that promise gratification, but inwards too towards the
completest form of a loss that it already knows.

It is not immediately clear why Lacan, having ventured
to this extremity, needs to add anything other than a
rudimentary sketch of the objects upon which desire plays.
For desire characterized in this way has become the mental
fact *par excellence*: it calls the tune and all kinds and
conditions of object rush forward to join a variegated but
theoretically uninteresting dance. Besides, Freud and his
early followers had developed a view of the matter that
Lacan was scarcely in a position to dispute. In speaking of
'the object' or 'objects', they had had in mind a range of
differentiated entities that still possessed an essential
common feature. The object could be thought of as that
towards which drives were directed, as that to which the
emotions of love or hate were fastened, or as that which –
in the spheres of perception and cognition – was separate
enough in its existence and stable enough in its qualities to
override the wishes of the individual and remain 'objec-
tively' there. From the psychoanalytic point of view, the
common feature was that of inwardness: even the object of
perception was of interest only in so far as it figured in the
inner theatre of individual passion and affectivity. Analysts
were in general agreement that inner objects – part or whole,
real or phantasized – were indispensable subject-matter for
their discipline, and they were then of course free to disagree
on the ways in which those pockets of inwardness could be
sorted and hierarchized. Lacan, who had by now redefined
so much of the basic Freudian terminology, could surely
afford to leave 'the object' alone.

He chose a different path. If desire was drift and deviation, aberration and eccentricity, the object in its traditional range of mutually confirming senses was likely to provide a discordant counter-suggestion of tranquillity and order. Indeed the 'object of perception', seemingly so innocent, could be thought of as a systematically misleading under-cover notion, and an unsafe bridge between the languages of philosophy and psychoanalysis. What was there, after all, in the Freudian household that in any way resembled the medium-sized dry goods to which philosophers and psychol-ogists of perception so often resorted when they felt obliged to name representative items from the material world? Where were its tables and chairs, its cups and saucers? Where were the mental images and after-images of such things? They existed for psychoanalysis only if they became caught in the meshes of desire, and once they had been caught their prized characteristics of stability, constancy, completeness and separateness began to dissolve.

In his writings of the nineteen-sixties Lacan went to great lengths both to protect discussion of the object from what one might loosely call the 'perceiver-percept' model and to mark the object itself with the sign of its own mutability. His technical diction already contained a suitably versatile general term – the 'Other', yet again – but Other-talk like signifier-talk could easily become blunt and cumbersome, and reintroduce in a thinly Hegelianized form the very qualities of the object that he was seeking to dispel. If the Other was to be kept other, and the object mutable, an entirely new rhetoric was needed – one that would enable Lacan to reinvent, as he moved from one theoretical occasion to the next, what he saw as a universal propensity towards decay among the objects of desire. He set off, therefore, in search of a special kind of *memento mori*. Yorick's skull would not have been suitable, and neither would the tomb that Poussin's shepherds seem just to have come upon in the Louvre version of his *Et in arcadia ego*. It had to be a death's head that belonged to all speech, and one that 'theory' was at last bold enough to allow into its own text. It was an intimation of mortality that resided both in the baleful message inscribed on Poussin's Arcadian tomb and in his shepherds' attempts to decipher it, both in the patient's speech and in the interpretative interventions of his therapist.

The object conceived of in this way was given a name: the *objet a*, the *Autre* with a lower-case *a*, the little-other-object. And this name eventually reached its final state of depletion when Lacan and his followers began speaking, quasi-algebraically, of the *a*. Although limitless expressive power came to be ascribed to this term – it was the alpha of human experience already overprinted with the omega of death – Lacan's choice was in one respect unfortunate and confusing. For he had spoken much earlier of a little-other-object and then had meant something quite different by it. This *a* was 'the other which isn't an other at all, since it is essentially coupled with the ego, in a relation which is always reflexive, interchangeable' (II, 370; 321). It was an effect of the Imaginary not of the Symbolic. The problem in Book II of the *Seminar* – *The Ego in Freud's Theory and in the Technique of Psychoanalysis* (1954–5) – had been that of preventing the couple Ego–Counterpart from seeming too simple and peremptory. For the parties in a specular relationship did not come into being merely in the two-way glare of like upon like: the space between them was full of relay-stations and alternative conductive pathways. This earlier *a* was the world at large in so far as it could be 'specularized', or distributed along the imaginary axis. The dialectical couple Subject–Other also needed to be rescued, by an intervening detail, from a fondness for the broad brush. But whereas the later *a* also came between two counterposed parties, and also stood in for the world at large, its mode of action was quite different: it was caught up in language, and was a relay-station that distorted all messages passing through it.

The *objet a*, then, like the earlier 'little other', can be anything at all, but is none the less governed by rules of exclusion. It is anything and everything that desire touches, and cannot exist where desire is not. In 'A remark on Daniel Lagache's report' (1958–60), Lacan sketches the combined breadth and narrowness of the term:

> *a*, the object of desire, at the departure-point where our model places it, is, as soon as it functions there . . ., the object of desire. This means that if it's a partial object it is not just a part, or a detached component, of the device that's here imagining the body, but an element of structure from the very moment of origin, and, if one can put it this way, present in the way the cards were dealt for the game that's in progress. In so far as it has been chosen from among the appendices of the body as an index of desire, it is already the exponent of a function, which sublimates it even before it has been exercised – that of an index finger raised towards an absence of which the *est-ce* [is it] has nothing to say, unless it says that the absence in question belongs to the place where it speaks. (682)

The model to which Lacan refers is an optical one, and the *a* is that which perpetually undermines its intelligibility. The human body can be mirrored, whole or in part, but certain of its zones always escape the mirror's grasp. The 'appendices of the body' are the phallus together with its substitutes and derivatives, and these are at once indicators of desire and objects of desire. They are caught up in a structure and hover there; in their continual waxing and waning no optical device can achieve purchase upon them. Lacan's paragraph ends on a figure that not only combines these motifs but enacts within itself the refusal of 'specularity' by which the *objet a* is constituted. The raised index finger which appears so often and with such firm iconographic purpose in Renaissance painting now vacillates. Where in Raphael's *School of Athens*, for example, the figure of Plato points upwards to a realm of otherworldly Ideas, in Lacan's text an 'appendix' points at once to its own fragility and to the this-worldly conditions of absence and loss in which its desiring gesture takes place. And in the same sentence he adds a further dimension to a pun that he has often used before.[5] S, pronounced 'ess', which is already the subject, the symbol, the signifier, and *das Es*, the id, now acquires in addition an epistemological resonance. If you raise an enquiring finger you can expect nothing by way of reply other than your own question *est-ce*? ('is it?'): you cannot speak otherwise or elsewhere than from within the penumbra of your *Es* and this confines you by force to the interrogative mode.

Lacan's descriptions of the *objet a* are composed in the spirit of carnival, and have a rule-breaking insolence and *élan* that can often be bewildering. In 'Subversion of the subject', for example, he constructs a spectral anatomical museum in which the *objet a* is displayed as a triumphant last exhibit. Lips and other erotogenic zones, Lacan first announces, occur at the margins of the body – in places where a cut (*coupure*) or a discontinuity is to be observed. A cut also brings into being the part-objects that analytic theory has often isolated. But to the standard list of erotogenic zones and representative part-objects ('nipple, scybalum, phallus (the imaginary object), the urinary stream') Lacan adds his own unkindest cut, a further list that seems to break with all notions of logical propriety: 'the phoneme, the gaze, the voice – the nothing' (817; 315). This is the category mistake considered as one of the fine arts. When Lacan in due course supplies the missing category that will

167

allow his mistakes to be seen as an act of rectification gradually declaring itself, and in so doing opens up a continuous path connecting lips, excreta, nipple, gaze and nothingness, the wildness of his enumerative procedure is still untamed.

What all these objects have in common, Lacan says, is that none of them possesses a specular image. But a prominent discontinuity remains between his 'own' list and those that he adopts ready-made from earlier psychoanalytic discussion. For his own list comprises items that are at one and the same time members of the class 'unspecularisable objects' and symbolic representatives of the class itself. The voice and the gaze are an uncontrollable litter of *objets a*, and nothingness, upon which the list resoundingly closes, is the prevailing condition in which all such 'objects' appear. The Subject, in this formulation, is no longer spun out along a signifying chain that is powerless to refer to, or otherwise make contact with, a world lying outside it. For Lacan now allows the ghost of referentiality to regain admission to his scheme. With the ragged remainders and evanescent margins of the world desired by the subject the subject himself is fashioned and upholstered; *objets a* are 'the "stuff", or rather the lining, though not in any sense the reverse, of the very subject that one takes to be the subject of consciousness' (818; 315).

Lacan's longest and most enticing account of the object as known to psychoanalysis is to be found in *The Four Fundamental Concepts*, and in that volume the act of looking, and of looking at paintings in particular, seems to be given an exemplary status. There are of course numerous ways in which visual experience could have been exploited for didactic purposes, and numerous schools of painting that could have helped to bring Lacan's abstruse concepts back within the pale of ordinary experience. Impressionism could have shown the object in motion in a mobile visual field;

surrealism could have revealed an underlying structure of paradox at work in innocuous-looking everyday scenes. But although Lacan refers briefly to a wide variety of painters – Arcimboldo, Caravaggio, Cézanne, Dürer, Goya, Leonardo, Matisse – he does not accept the invitation to aesthetic tourism that his new theory of the object might be thought to issue. His account of painting is at once austerely self-limiting in the examples chosen for detailed discussion and prodigal in the consequences that it draws out for visual experience at large, and indeed for experience *tout court*.

I can perhaps best illustrate this by taking a straightforward parallel case. These remarks on seeing and not seeing are from the great American painter Frank Stella:

> This ephemeral quality of painting reminds us that what is not there, what we cannot quite find, is what great paintings always promise. It does not surprise us, then, that at every moment when an artist has his eyes open, he worries that there is something present that he cannot quite see, something that is eluding him, something within his always limited field of vision, something in the dark spot that makes up his view of the back of his head. He keeps looking for this elusive something, out of habit as much as out of frustration. He searches even though he is quite certain that what he is looking for shadows him every moment he looks around. He hopes it is what he cannot know, what he will never see, but the conviction remains that the shadow that follows but cannot be seen is simply the dull presence of his own mortality, the impending erasure of memory. Painters instinctively look to the mirror for reassurance, hoping to shake death, hoping to avoid the stare of persistent time, but the results are always disappointing. Still they keep checking.[6]

Stella's *Working Space* (1986), in which this passage occurs, is both an impassioned history of spatiality in Western painting, from Caravaggio to the present, and a series of trenchant notes from the artist's own workshop. The overlap between Stella and Lacan at this point is striking, especially as there seems to have been no direct influence: Stella's death-haunted painter, striving towards an impossible completeness of vision and retreating periodically to the consolations of the mirror, lives out by the sweat of his brow the dialectic of Symbolic and Imaginary. And the huge, brightly coloured and many-planed constructions that Stella was working on at this time are a tribute to the erotic power of the cut and the margin. His surfaces, whether they are coated in a uniform wash of colour, or geometrically patterned, or stippled and randomized, gain their energy from the countless edges and intersections they produce. The three dimensions of the construction as a whole collapse into the two of each surface and then into the one of each separating line. But this process is reversible at any moment: lines explode back across surfaces to reproduce an unfocusable manifold. Each of these works is a litter on the basis of which the 'stuffing' of vision is reinvented. Whatever it is that is present to the artist without his being quite able to see it – the *objet a*, as Lacan would say – has been provided with a multi-dimensional labyrinth in which to run endlessly.

Yet a problem arises when we begin to 'apply' Lacan in this way, even if we choose an artist with whom he seems to have a marked affinity. The relevance of Lacan's theory to Stella's art falters as soon as we remind ourselves that for Lacan the labyrinth of desire already exists everywhere in the human sphere and that no ingenious conjoining of metal, fibre-glass and acrylic paint can expect to improve upon it. The problem is a familiar one. Notions of desire-at-large and algebraic representations of its innumerable evanescent objects are all very well, but they are of doubtful value to the kind of criticism that attends closely to the grain and coloration of individual works. Yet desire, largely conceived, has been the chosen business of psychoanalytic theory from the start. If it comes to a choice, Lacan sides with theory against criticism. He has formidable critical skills, but reins them in as soon as they make individual art-works seem disproportionately interesting: the generality of desire needs to be protected. The question that haunts Lacan's discussion of 'The gaze as *objet a*', in *The Four Fundamental Concepts*, is 'can a theory cast in these terms any longer have applications?'

In this section of the seminar, Lacan pays particular attention to one painting – the double portrait by the younger Holbein usually known as *The Ambassadors* – but in introducing the work he makes it plain that he is turning to it because he expects it to yield a parable:

> The gaze may contain in itself the *objet a* of the Lacanian algebra where the subject falls, and what specifies the scopic field and engenders the satisfaction proper to it is the fact that, for structural reasons, the fall of the subject always remains unperceived, for it is reduced to zero. In so far as the gaze, *qua objet a*, may come to symbolize this central lack expressed in the phenomenon of castration, and in so far as it is an *objet a* reduced, of its nature, to a punctiform, evanescent function, it leaves the subject in ignorance as to what there is beyond the appearance, an ignorance so characteristic of all progress in thought that occurs in the way constituted by philosophical research. (XI, 73; 76–77)

The project outlined here is uncommonly audacious: to write into the text of psychoanalysis the terms and conditions of its own impossibility. Where philosophers have made a poor show of things by ignoring their own ignorance, or by acquiescing in it in the interests of intellectual progress, Lacan seeks to construct a theory within which ignorance, and worse, can circulate freely and be called by an appropriate name. The unperceivable 'fallenness' of the subject – the inescapable lack and destitution that castration ordains for it – is to re-enter the theoretical picture; the goal of psychoanalysis must be to rescue the sciences of mind from their myths of plenitude and redemption. Holbein's panel is introduced as a comparably bold adventure in the visual domain – an attempt to paint the unpaintable and to make the spectator see what prevents him from seeing.

The Ambassadors, which now hangs in the National Gallery in London, was painted in England in 1533 and much is now known about its subject-matter and the circumstances in which it was executed.[7] Jean de Dinteville and Georges de Selve were painted by Holbein while they were on separate missions from France to the English court. Each mission was a delicate one – this was the period of Henry VIII's marriage to Anne Boleyn and of an unparalleled crisis in Christendom – and Holbein has taken pains to represent the professional mobility and vigilance of the diplomatic eye. Two pairs of eyes, neither of which has a stable focal point. And between them, on a two-tier table, an array of objects symbolizing religion, the fine arts and the sciences of measurement. The table joins the two men and its contents disjoin them: the Renaissance encyclopaedia that Holbein has assembled in the centre of the work contains too many viewpoints and too many intersecting planes for any act of vision taking place nearby to be simple, clear and direct. And the entire design teems with allusions to events offstage, and with pregnant details – a lute with a broken string, a half-concealed crucifix, Luther's translation of *Veni Creator Spiritus*, a terrestrial globe. There is a great deal going on in this painting but Lacan concentrates on one detail only. The celebrated death's head, hanging rather like a tilted cuttle-fish bone over the decorated floor, is the only object that invites serious interpretation. By a technique that was fashionable at the time – anamorphosis, the systematically distorted projection of an optical image – an outrageous artefact has been produced.[8] The operation of impersonal mathematical laws has created an emblem of male potency from Europe's most popular emblem of death; the 'phallic structure' of cancelled manhood has been given a grotesque new physical form. And at the same time an impossible situation has been created for the viewer: the true deathliness of the image can be perceived only by sacrificing the rest of the painting's content. Only as one leaves the painting and looks down the floating cylinder does its dark import become available to the eye. For Lacan, Holbein has linked the fortunes of the phallus with those of an emerging science of subjectivity:

> All this shows that at the very heart of the period in which the subject emerged and geometral optics was an object of research, Holbein makes visible for us here something that is simply the subject as annihilated – annihilated in the form that is, strictly speaking, the imaged embodiment of the *minus-phi* of castration, which for us, centres the whole organization of the desires through the framework of the fundamental drives. (XI, 83; 88–9)

And once Lacan has allegorized Holbein's detail in this fashion everything else in the painting can be spirited away. Its conceits and enigmas, its inventive interplay of surface and edge, colour and texture, are of no particular interest once a universal key to human vision has been found. Although the painting has had its uses, and not least that of suggesting that a new Renaissance is upon us, it is no different from any other painting in the underlying structure that it reveals. All paintings are a 'trap for the gaze', just as

173

the functioning of all gazes is 'pulsatile, dazzling and spread out' (XI, 83; 89). The *objet a* may reside in the visual sphere in an unusually explicit form, but it is everywhere else too. Subjectivity is anamorphic and mortal, like sight itself.

Lacan's habit of escalating his own insights beyond their original framework suggests that the question 'can this theory have applications?' should be answered in the negative. The pressure towards generality is always intense, even in those sections of his work that look most 'applied'. Yet to express the problem in these terms is misleading, for they take no account of Lacan's own writing and speech, and of the studiously heterogeneous character that he continued to give them while he was refashioning his account of the object. The *objet a* seems on occasion to offer an absurdly smooth surface to the theoretical imagination and an air of impending tautology to everything that the theorist writes. But a practical lesson for psychoanalysis runs through Lacan's works of the 1960s and early 1970s, and this can best be understood by looking at the objectives of writing itself through the prism of the *objet a*.

The following passage occurs at a point in *Encore* where Lacan, having expounded at some length the virtues of the Borromean knot[9] as a model of intricated subjectivity, suddenly returns to the knottedness of everyday human passion:

> Why did I bring the Borromean knot into it in former times? It was to translate the formula *I ask you* – what? – *to refuse* – what? – *that which I offer you* – why? – *because it is not that* – *that*, you know what it is, it's the *objet a*. The *objet a* is no being at all. The *objet a* is the portion of emptiness that my demand presupposes, which only by being situated by means of metonymy, that is to say by pure continuity sustained from the beginning to the end of the sentence, can enable us to

imagine what desire supported by no being at all might
be like. A desire with no other substance than that
which derives from the knots themselves. (XX, 114)

What is perhaps most striking here is the way in which
Lacan's writing itself replays the interpersonal conundrum
that he is discussing. Human relationships have their inherent blind spots and anamorphic distortions, and a colloquial
formula has been found in which to encapsulate the no-win
quality that these can impart to the simplest transaction
between individuals: 'I ask you to refuse that which I offer
you because it is not that'. What I'm offering, in other
words, is neither what you really want nor what I really
want to give you. The formula, however, is not given
'straight' but in a rhythmically interrupted form: the *a*
cannot not be at work, even in descriptions of the *a*. The
point is then made again in a long sentence that refuses to
end appropriately, on the phrase 'the end of the sentence'.
Something runs through all speech that speech cannot
catch. The 'pure continuity' of desire can be preserved in
writing only by driving the propositional structure of the
sentence into a state of perpetual delinquency. Lacan is
looking for a style that will unremittingly challenge the
false optimism that all acts of predication, even the gloom-
iest, encourage. Despite the self-awareness of this writing,
however, neither the deficiencies nor the stolen glories of
the literary text are Lacan's topic. He already knows of
course that literature has its own ways of counteracting the
self-fulfilling circularity of ordinary propositional syntax,
and he has on numerous past occasions called upon texts to
show psychoanalytic speech the path towards a new semantic openness and multiplicity. In *Encore*, as in the other
volumes of the *Seminar*, we witness speech being submitted
to the ordeal of 'literarity' in order to find again its full
efficacy as speech. And his new fugitive 'object', even when

it is caught up in a sense of its own vacuity or impossibility, has an improbable positive contribution to make to this regenerative enterprise.

I say 'improbable' because Lacan's *objet a* is often gloated over as the zero point of human dignity: 'What analytic experience shows us is that, in any case, it is castration that governs desire, whether in the normal or the abnormal' (826; 323). There is an endemic tendency towards debasement in the human passions, a nostalgic impulse on the part of each individual to return to the scene of his first anxiety and his first wretchedness. And lest his reader presume to overlook his own native squalor, Lacan develops a gruesome prose poetry on the theme. Waste, refuse, detritus, faecal matter, tatters, shreds and scraps are the lot to which we are all condemned: 'It is not his rags, but the very being of man that takes up its position among the waste matter in which his first frolics occur' (582; 225). We are each of us a prodigal son and never really fit to leave the company of pigs. Yet Lacan adheres closely to Freud's teaching on the subject of the body's waste products, and reverses their value from one moment to the next. Just as, for the young child, faeces can be treated as a reward, a gift or a token of trust, so for Lacan all the unsavoury residues with which the subject is 'lined' can suddenly turn into objects of virtue. In 'Subversion of the subject' he speaks repeatedly of the 'treasure' of the signifier – that titillating foretaste of riches which comes as a gift from the Other and is not otherwise to be had.

The lesson that Lacan draws for analytic practice from the spectacle of his figment-world is plain. The object of desire, once it has been allowed to shed the fixity and wholeness that other theorists fraudulently ascribe to it, obliges the analyst to adopt a new kind of objectivity: a solid sense of professional uprightness is born of his exposure to the airy insubstantiality of all desired things. The *objet a* is the lining of subjectivity, and the double lining of the intersubjective encounter that the analytic dialogue stages. In that dialogue two desires are always in play at once, but the analyst has the responsibility to be neutral, to be neither for nor against the analysand's desire as it activates his. As he listens, he must be swept along with the other person's litter. It is only under these conditions that the analysand can discover signifying treasure in a landscape that until a moment ago seemed all loss and desolation.

The objectivity of the *objet a* has a further semi-technical implication for analytic practice, and Lacan, in explaining this in theoretical terms, again makes teasing use of the fact that only a hair's breadth separates this *a* – belonging to desire and the Symbolic order – from the *a* of the Imaginary relation. The *a* properly so called is in one sense perfectly intractable and unnourishing, and it is not easy to imagine its ever becoming a reliable ally for the therapist. Its value resides, however, in the power of refusal that it brings to bear upon the Imaginary. The analytic dialogue can never take place in a clinically clean environment of Subject–Other transactions, and the language in which each partner endlessly repositions his interlocutor adjoins and intersects another dimension that is resistant to the signifier's law. This is phantasy, in which the ego experiments with its own future. Here we may do a variety of things: imagine an ideal counterpart, or a divine figure of authority, or a utopia of fulfilled wishes; impute to the Other wishes that by a miracle chime flawlessly with our own demand; represent the Other as holding the key to our felicity, or as embodying in his or her own person the pleasure we seek. Similarly, if phantasy turns towards cruelty and death, we may imagine ourselves as the givers or receivers of a perfect pain, an exact punishment, a perpetuity of torment, or an exquisitely aimed mortal blow. Within the conditions of 'absolute non-reciprocity' (774) that govern subjectivity, that is to say, phantasy creates for us a dream of identity, symmetry and reversibility.

Lacan speaks of phantasy as a 'supple yet inextensible chain' (826; 323). It is like signification in the first of these qualities and unlike it in the second: where the one chain cannot be extended, the other cannot not be extended. In phrasing the matter like this, Lacan is again tantalizing his reader with a distinction that a moment's inattention can make invisible. The work of analysis lies in the separation of *a* from *a*, and of chain from chain. Phantasy cannot be expunged from the analytic encounter, but it can be worked with and complexified; once signification has begun, the *objet a* can emerge from among the obliging objects of the individual's inner utopia. An unwavering polemic is being pursued by Lacan in these volatile reformulations of his dialectic. He declares war, again, on analysis as a bartering of phantasies and a bolstering of the ego's defences. For 'late Lacan', analysis is an exigent art of speaking in which the vanity of human wishes is assumed from the start, and in which the mutability of the object becomes the basis for an unillusioned yet always impassioned spoken contract.

What time is it in the unconscious? Is it too early or already too late? When one event in the emotional history of the subject is thought of as causing another, is the time-lapse separating them of any consequence, or is it as empty as the gap between two consecutive logical operations? Much of what I have said so far will make questions like these seem simply irrevelant to the kind of thinking Lacan does. The 'timeless' unconscious postulated by Freud serves Lacan well in the performance of many routine tasks, and the development of a case-history can easily be thought of as a sequence of self-contained *tableaux vivants*, in each of which the various agencies of the individual mind are held in suspended animation.[10] Besides, Lacan is a campaigner for synchronicity in much of his theoretical work. He inveighs, as we have seen, against developmental models of subjectivity and the 'mythology of instinctual maturation' (263; 54), and seeks to replace them with a method of scansion that moves from one all-at-once structure to the next. The 'action of structure' takes place in logical time and not in lived time. Its explanatory power comes from the complex articulation of each synchronic state in turn, and this power will be weakened not enhanced if the theorist tries to fill in the gaps with life-historical narratives of one kind or another.

Moreover, when structures act, they are for Lacan the complete story, and analysts have no business to deck this out with supplementary tales of 'how things mostly go' or 'how things should probably be'. The notion of concatenation, to which Lacan so often resorts, does of course introduce a calibrated temporal dimension: the 'signifying chain', which subsumes the language of the unconscious and the language of ordinary speech, is by definition always on the move towards a desired future and this gives at the very least a diachronic atmosphere – a sense of individual history in the making – to Lacan's account of subjectivity. But the forward thrust of signification is often described in terms that make its temporality seem oddly smooth and characterless – 'pure' displacement, 'pure' continuity, a slippage or a passage that moves ahead with unstoppable fluency.

In talking about the time of subjectivity, and of the analytic encounter, Lacan is not, however, obliged to choose between synchronicity on the one hand and weak diachronicity on the other. From the mid-1940s he has been fascinated by problems of temporality, and as early as 'The function and field of speech' (1953) he had drawn attention to a largely neglected area of Freud's thinking on the matter. What he discovered in Freud was time skewed and syncopated by the traumatic event, and mental causality beset by an abiding paradox that seemed to set it apart from the rest of nature. The question for his later theory became 'how far do the lessons of traumatic after-shock extend?' It seemed foreign to the tenor of Freudian thought to suppose that a new time and a new system of causes came into view when pathogenic material was under discussion only to disappear again when normal mental functioning replaced it. For Lacan, as for Freud, it made much more sense to suppose that a single set of rules governed all mental events and that the pathogenic ones were a lens through which the structure of subjectivity at large could be viewed.

The crucial temporal and causal notion that Lacan isolates in the Freud corpus is *Nachträglichkeit* ('deferred action', 'retroaction'). That this notion had previously been so little discussed is in part explained by the fact that the German term and its cognates had been translated inconsistently into English and French. Where Freud himself used a single term repeatedly, his translators use a range of different terms whose affinity is far from apparent. The extraordinary force that Freud gave to the German word may be observed, Lacan says, in the 'Wolf Man' case-history (XVII, 7–122). Freud hypothesizes that his patient, having witnessed as a very young child an act of coitus between his parents, had reprocessed his memory of the event at the age of four, and then again during the analysis on which he embarked in his mid-twenties. More generally, we may suppose that the memory of such 'primal scenes' lies dormant from early childhood until puberty, when they are reinterpreted and resexualized, and may produce symptoms. In neither case is the symptom produced early on and then stored, and the action involved is not strictly speaking 'deferred': there was no action at all until the individual's resurgent sexual feeling triggered it, and action of this late-coming kind took place in the retroactive mode, as a desire-laden restructuring of the personal past. Lacan admires Freud's boldness in preferring the history of a mutant structure to the history of an event-filled private life:

> Freud demands a total objectification of proof so long as it is a question of dating the primal scene, but he no more than presupposes all the resubjectifications of the event that seem to him to be necessary to explain its effects at each turning-point where the subject restructures himself – that is, as many restructurings of the event as take place, as he puts it, *nachträglich*, at a later date. What is more, with an audacity bordering on offhandedness, he asserts that he holds it legitimate in the analysis of processes to elide the time intervals in which the event remains latent in the subject. (256; 48)[11]

Analysis itself is not of course obliged to practise a similar elision, and an elaborate sifting and sorting of the patient's biographical material may become a major preoccupation of his sessions. But beneficial therapeutic effects, when they occur, need be thought of only as a further structural transformation occurring within subjectivity and in the company, as always, of an intervening and mediating Other. When Freud's account of deferred action is rephrased by Lacan in these terms, it is clear that he is preparing the way for a general theory of psychical time.

Yet when this *nachträglich* perspective has been fully acknowledged, we have syncopation without having a paradox of particular note. Psychical time is different from 'natural' time, in the view that I have outlined so far, because the present can change the past. What is going on certainly sounds unusual. It is not, for example, the case that the individual is simply rewriting the history of

selected earlier epochs of his life, and keeping each successive version in a cumulative mental archive, for, at each
moment of rewriting, the newly produced past obliterates
its predecessors. But such operations are uncomplicated by
any sense of futurity. An entire dimension of Freud's work
redramatizes the myth of the Furies: the past is visited upon
the individual in a series of violent incursions, and his
future, if he has one, can be envisaged only as a prolongation
of these and a continuing helpless desire to lift their curse.
The retroactive mode, operating alone, produces a back-
ward-looking hope, a wish to create for oneself a past that
can be lived with. As a therapist, Freud was keenly aware
that his patients brought him their intentions, goals and
ambitions as well as their painful memories, but as a
theorist he had been reluctant to grant any causal authority
to merely possible worlds. Anticipated events had no notable influence upon the present, no pre-effects or fore-shocks
emanated from them and they did not trigger anything. When
seeking to supply psychoanalysis with its missing future
tense, Lacan went outside the Freudian tradition. In particular, he turned often to Heidegger and to the *Zukünftigkeit* or
'futurality' that he had ascribed to the Being of human beings.

Lacan, in his paper on 'Logical time' (197–213), written
in 1945 and first published in *Les Cahiers d'Art*, had
sketched a symmetrical and Janus-faced view of the subject-
in-process.[12] The subject was poised between past and
future, and his ability to anticipate, in the pressure that it
exerted upon his actions, was equal and opposite to his
ability to remember. In this paper, 'logical' time is explored
by means of a sophism in which a prison governor sets three
prisoners a puzzle in order to decide which of them to
release. But it is plain from an early stage that this tale of
competitive reasoning is offered as an allegory of any and
all subjectivity in process, and told in such a way as to
provide desires and intentions with at least a provisional

temporal map. In 'The function and field of speech' Lacan condenses the allegorical meanings of the earlier paper:

> The author of these lines has attempted to demonstrate in the logic of a sophism the temporal sources through which human action, in so far as it orders itself according to the action of the other, finds in the scansion of its hesitations the advent of its certainty; and in the decision that concludes it, this action given to that of the other – which it includes from that point on – together with its consequences deriving from the past, its meaning-to-come.
>
> In this article it is demonstrated that it is the certainty anticipated by the subject in the *'time for understanding'* which, by the haste which precipitates the *'moment of concluding'*, determines in the other the decision that makes of the subject's own movement error or truth. (287; 75)

The ordinariness of what is being described here can be readily grasped if we reclothe Lacan's logical structure in an anecdote about, say, the break-up of a relationship between lovers. In the period of impassioned calculation leading up to the definitive moment of decision, each partner occupies two positions. At the very least, the situation involves two Subjects and two Others, and each member of this quartet has a past and an intentional future: the 'time for understanding' and 'the moment of concluding' are alike in that during each of them Subject and Other on the one hand, and past and future time on the other, are indissociably interconnected. Each partner finds a course of action, and embarks on a separate future, from within an interpersonal knot. Prisoners and lovers are exciting subjects, of course, but Lacan's underlying model has no melodrama in it: an individual sitting alone and looking out of a window in silence could have incarnated the model just as well.

The elaborate syntax of these paragraphs, which makes different positions and different time-dimensions mutually implicating, already gives us a clue to the special role that language is to have in Lacan's further discussion of temporality. Language is what finally gives the model its power, its independence from anecdote, and the combined presence in speech of retrospective and anticipatory gestures produces the paradox to which I have been referring: the subject comes into being at the point of intersection between an irrecoverable past and an unattainable future; its structure is that of a ceaseless cross-stitching, in language, between what-is-no-longer-the-case and what-is-not-yet-the-case. Translating the paradox into perhaps more comfortable spatial terms, we could say that the subject is where it is because it is always elsewhere, in two other places at once; that the rights of occupancy it enjoys in respect of a given place stem from its inability to occupy that place; and that it has a home only when away from home.

Lacan has a brisk way of introducing linguistic concepts, and fragments of philological or grammatical lore, into his arguments – as if their lesson were already clear and not open to serious dispute. Retroaction may be seen at work in sentences, he reminds us, in that they achieve their final 'effect of sense' only when their last word has been given. Sentences like Winston Churchill's alleged 'This is the sort of English up with which I will not put', for example, grotesquely exaggerate a process that is everywhere in spoken language. Discourse acquires its efficacy, Lacan says, from 'the retroaction of the signifier' (839). All sentences also engage the hearer's faculty for anticipation, and many of course begin to have decided sense effects well before they close: for most hearers 'At last the weary travellers arrived at their destination', for example, will have become efficacious by the end of the fifth word. Lacan takes full note of this proleptic mechanism, but in doing so he follows a quite different linguistic route. He speaks not of sentence structure but of tense: the subject 'announces himself – he will have been – only in the future perfect' (808; 306). It is delightful to see a minor tense promoted to high office in this way. The future perfect, which is so troublesome to language-learners and seems in any case to have a rather limited warrant, emerges as the tense *par excellence* of desire and the prospective human imagination. It allows us to envisage as already complete what has not yet been fully launched, and places us already beyond the goal that we have yet to reach. Desire-in-pursuit and the subject in process have been relocated at precise points of articulation within the signifying chain.

By the time Lacan came to think of the subject's every present moment as a past futurity and a future pastness caught up together in an unstoppable signifying process, he had lost interest in the precise lessons, and the lessons in precision, that linguistics could teach. In the 1960s there were at least three ways in which linguistic structures could have been used to provide his views on temporality with stiffening. He could have been thoroughgoing in his handling either of syntax, or of tense, or of rhetoric, and drawn valuable supporting evidence for his claims from the recurrence, in each of these areas of linguistic enquiry, of common structural motifs. The contrasted rhetorical figures of *prolepsis* and *analepsis*, for example, could have been seen writing large in discourse a tension that was already written small in the structure of the sentence. But by this stage, when Lacan is formulating his most provocative statements on the empty, mobile and decentred human subject, linguistics is no longer able to offer his project support of a suitably unsettling kind. The linguistic content of Lacan's later papers is often reduced to a series of ragged shorthand messages. These allude to an existing body of theory without seeking to extend it; they suggest no coherent programme of research; and they attribute to the linguistic sciences no continuing fertility for Freudians. These sciences once had a crucial role, for it was thanks to them that psychoanalysis had been reformulated as a system of signifying law, but the defence and promulgation of that law is now too subtle a matter to be left to linguists. If the essential message of 'the unconscious structured like a language' is to be preserved, the torch must pass into other, and always other, hands. And those seeking a fuller language-based view of the subject-in-time must prepare themselves for a disappointment.

From the early 1960s, topology, and the theory of knots in particular, began to exert a special fascination on Lacan, and graphic representations of various kinds figured prominently in his writings and seminars. At an earlier stage, he had insisted that diagrams could play only a limited role – that of a summary or a mnemonic device – and warned against over-reliance on them. In 'On the possible treatment of psychosis', for example, he says of a schema that he has just been discussing at length: 'it would be better to confine this schema to the waste-bin, if, like so many others, it was to lead anyone to forget in an intuitive image the analysis on which it is based' (574; 214). And in the case of his most celebrated early diagram, the 'Schema L', he had obeyed his own rule. This is the more elaborate of the two forms in which it appears in *Ecrits*:

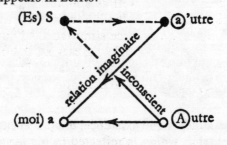

(53)

186

In commenting on this and on the simplified form

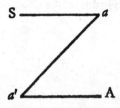

(548; 193)

Lacan reminds his reader that the 'intersubjective dialectic' represented here is a creature of language and only really accessible to those who have already followed an arduous linguistic initiation.[13] In both forms, the idea of 'subject' is being decomposed in a highly organized way. The subject is not scattered to the four winds but spread out between four interconnected points, or zones, or fields. There is no subjectivity without alterity, each diagram announces, although thinking that there might be, imagining pure selfhood on the one hand and pure reciprocity between the ego and its objects on the other, are an inextirpable feature of all subjective process. Traffic between Subject and Other always has to pass by way of the ego, or traverse the Imaginary relation between the ego and its objects. But although both versions make the same point about a quadripartite organization that can never have a kernel or a core, the second dramatizes as well as simplifies the first. The many relations – direct or indirect, reversible or irreversible – that had been shown in force simultaneously in the first diagram are reduced to a single zig-zagging lightning flash in the second. How long does the flash last? Lacan's description of the four corners gives no indication of a time axis for the subject:

> S, his ineffable, stupid existence, *a*, his objects, *a'*, his ego, that is, that which is reflected of his form in his

objects, and A, the locus from which the question of his existence may be presented to him. (549; 194)

One way of beginning to understand the temporal extension of the subject would be to set the two diagrams against each other and bring into the open the difference between simultaneity and extremely rapid motion. For Lacan, all discussion of the subject takes place under the aegis of the unconscious and cannot escape from the intermittence and rhythmicity of unconscious discourse. 'A gaping, a beating, an alternating suction' (838) is the house style of the unconscious. Its openness is that of perpetual closure; its inwardness comprises materials that will not stay inside; and its time is an always impending closing time. 'This is somewhere that will never appeal to tourists', Lacan notes in 'Position of the unconscious' (1960–64) (838). The time of subjectivity can never be pure simultaneity or pure sequence and every diagrammatic representation has to find a way of building into itself a temporal beat. The best diagram would be the one that could perfectly outmanoeuvre the conventional timelessness and two-dimensionality of the diagrammatic imagination while making a stronger kind of sense than ordinary analytic prose. Language is no longer self-evidently the best way of modelling the time-structures that language imposes.

In 'Subversion of the subject', Lacan attempted to produce a graph that would enact the alternating suction of desire and have a non-simultaneous and non-sequential time written legibly into it. The graph moves through four stages from a preliminary to a complete form, but from the first of these stages the paradox of retroaction and anticipation is set forth with audacity and wit. It is now no longer a question of choosing between two incompatible qualities, nor of letting them beat emptily against each other, but of setting down in pictorial terms the dynamic interdependence of two temporalities. Lacan's diagram attempts to show us a time-bound subjectivity that is calibrated without being chronometric – a non-linear, non-successive distribution of temporal points. The principle of *Nachträglichkeit*, on the basis of which Freud had scanned and interconnected the widely separated epochs of the individual patient's emotional history, now reappears inside every moment of human time, in the miniaturized engineering processes by which subjectivity is created and transformed:

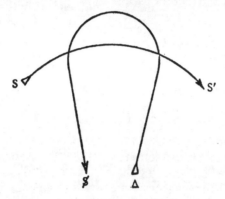

(805; 303)

The vector $\overrightarrow{S.S'}$ is that of the signifying chain, and it is unidirectional; the vector $\overrightarrow{\Delta.\$}$ is that of the desiring subject, and has two directions: it is shown here moving in reverse, but it moves forward too, by anticipation as well as retroaction.

This graph makes the more or less common-sense point that the signifying chain does not advance in an effortless and unimpeded slither of meaning, but has points of anchorage. These are the crossings between the two vectors, and Lacan refers to them as *points de capiton*. The buttoning down of the chain, that is to say, is now seen as taking place not between certain signifiers and certain signifieds but between earlier and later moments in its unfolding.[14] But

189

even while discussing the basic cell from which his subsequent and much more florid graphs are to grow, Lacan
elaborately reinterprets these crossings. Referring to the
first as A and to the second as $s(A)$, he superimposes the
Subject-Other relation on his portrayal of moment-to-
moment connections inside the chain and in so doing makes
the crossings non-commensurable again: 'Observe the
asymmetry of the one, which is a locus (a place, rather than
a space), to the other, which is a moment (a rhythm, rather
than a duration)' (806; 304). A is the place where the
'treasure of the signifier' is to be found: it is the Other
considered as the pre-existing site in which, and in relation
to which, the Subject comes into being. $s(A)$ is the Subject
thus produced, bearing the mark of the Other, hearing its
footsteps in pursuit even as it attempts to make off with the
crock of gold that the Other had guarded. Two things are
happening here as Lacan burdens and reburdens his original
graphic idea with meaning: the dialectic between Subject
and Other is being temporalized in the spasmodic mode
that it seems to necessitate, and the categories 'space' and
'time' are being brought into unproductive conflict.

The problem is that the graph, announced as a 'topology',
is not really topological enough. It does not so much
enshrine a paradox as provide an indefinitely reinterpretable
emblem or memory-aid from which paradoxes in profusion
can be made to flow. It needs to be supported by a text –
described, written about, argued or rhapsodized about – in
order to make a suitably complex kind of sense. And once
this text has been brought into existence, the original graph
begins to look undermotivated and dispensable. Drawings
of this sort are an interim measure. If the most exacting
task facing Lacanian theory is that of constructing a view of
space-time able to measure up to the Freudian unconscious
in its most problematic forms, then an existing capacity of
topology has to be more thoroughly exploited. It has to be

grasped, that is to say, as a procedure for modelling space and time continuously and interdependently. The crucial time questions asked by psychoanalysis are never, after all, the purely chronometric ones 'what time is it in the unconscious?', 'how long does a given structure last?' or 'how long does it take to travel from one structure to the next?'. The temporality of the subject becomes interesting for the analyst when it provokes questions like: 'what is it about the continuous action of a given psychical structure that produces *now* – and not at some hypothetical past or future moment – a crisis, a catastrophe, or the beginnings of a cure?' or 'how do the desultory exchanges and empty repetitions of the analytic dialogue suddenly become efficacious?'

Lacan had already made striking semi-metaphorical use of a topological notion in the closing pages of 'The function and field of speech'. There he had discussed the relation between language and death, and had asked himself what spatial schemata could be used to represent a manner of inherence that was not all inwardness, and a manner of being outside that was not all externality. A sense of death was at the root of language and the Symbolic order, but it would be to trivialize this situation to say that death was 'at their centre':

> To say that this mortal meaning reveals in speech a centre exterior to language is more than a metaphor; it manifests a structure. This structure is different from the spatialization of the circumference or of the sphere in which some people like to schematize the limits of the living being and his milieu: it corresponds rather to the relational group that symbolic logic designates topologically as an annulus.
>
> If I wished to give an intuitive representation of it, it seems that, rather than have recourse to the surface

aspect of a zone, I should call on the three-dimensional form of a torus, in so far as its peripheral exteriority and its central exteriority constitute only one single region. (320–21; 105)

The torus, in its simplest form, is a cylinder whose ends have been joined to produce a ring; its centre is always a hole, and the size, shape and position of this hole vary as the ring itself is subjected to distortion. This figure gives a precise shape to an undecidability. Death is 'inside' speech in that speech encircles it, but 'outside' it too, for as soon as speech is figured as a ring, a tubular continuum, it can no longer be centred on a point falling inside its own volume.

Lacan speaks of topology as offering analysis 'intuitive representations' at moments like this, but one could easily express the relationship between the two disciplines quite differently, and say not only that intuition was in operation long before topology entered on the scene but that topology, once installed, is in some sense an escape from it. The proposition that the torus is called upon to illustrate and enact – 'what is primordial to the birth of symbols, we find it in death' – is one of numerous overlapping and partly interchangeable formulations on death-in-language to be found in *Ecrits*, and is itself a bold 'intuitive representation'. From the triangulation of Hegel, Freud and Saussure a twilight procession of aphorisms is produced, an insistent murmur of sentences on absence and death. Against the profusion of these, and against their fuzzy-edged 'literary' character, Lacan comes to set, in his later career, the superior clarity and intelligibility of mobile three-dimensional shapes.

The Moebius strip, for example, is treated as a rhetorical figure that has become detached from language: it is a paradox, but one that is extended in space and can be passed from hand to hand in silence. To form a Moebius strip one needs simply to twist a long rectangle of paper once, before joining its ends together. This action produces a single-sided object from a double-sided one: back and front of the original rectangle are brought together in an unbroken continuity. Does this figure possess one, two or three dimensions? It is certainly striking when it is thought of as three-dimensionally extended, but its main properties can be satisfactorily illustrated in a flat drawing, and one only of these properties – single-sidedness – is topologically significant. But even if it is impossible to settle the question 'how many dimensions?', it is nevertheless plain that the real strangeness of the strip, the challenge that it issues to our ordinary sense of space, becomes apparent only when it is placed in the additional dimension of time. In passing my finger round its surface, I arrive back at my departure-point after a single trip, but on the 'wrong' side of the paper. It will require another complete trip to bring me back to the same point on the 'right' side. Here, then, is a true oddity – a manipulable figure whose spatial character is manifest only when it is thought about in time. The Lacanian unconscious 'structured like a language' has found an analogue that is not like language at all. In part, Lacan is saying simply 'the unconscious is stranger than you think and this curiosity will help you figure it out'. But he is making two further claims: that the structure of the unconscious can be understood only in terms of its temporality, and that language, which is the sole vehicle of this temporality, cannot itself complete the task.[15]

The unconscious needs a model that will be fully intelligible without being fully retrievable to the either/or style of thinking that has often been thought appropriate to it in psychoanalysis. Getting the unconscious right is not a matter of choosing between inside and out, before and after, space and time, stillness and motion, nor of discreetly intermixing these categories. What is required is a way of conceiving its inconceivability, and for this purpose the categories have to be strictly interlaced, mapped each upon each, and allowed to co-exist in an organised but unsettlable hesitation. For the later Lacan, there are, broadly speaking, two ways of doing this: by fiercely polyvalent writing, and by topological draughtsmanship. The latter enables him at moments, and against his own predictions, to look beyond language altogether and then, in a state of sublime distraction, to look back upon language and its unconscious as if from another planet.[16]

Nowhere in Lacan's later writings is this rhythm more apparent than in the seminar he gave in 1974–5 on the Real, the Symbolic and the Imaginary. The text of this seminar, which is usually referred to as *RSI* and has been published in *Ornicar?*,[17] makes extensive use of the three-link 'Borromean chain', or the 'Borromean knot' as it is more often but less accurately called. It had been clear from Lacan's earliest accounts of his triad that each of its terms had to be defined by reference to the other two,[18] but the special structural interdependence that the three orders possessed had itself been only sketchily theorized. In *RSI* the three orders are assumed to have been satisfactorily defined in advance and it is their mode of connection that now occupies centre-stage. The Borromean chain is formed from two separate links joined to each other by a third, and in such a way that if any one of the links is severed the whole thing falls apart. In a sense, Lacan's redescription of Real, Symbolic and Imaginary as concatenated in this way serves merely to give new impetus to his familiar polemic against binaristic thinking: that which is excluded from sense-making is that which makes sense hang together; no two agents or qualities or postulates can be coupled or contrasted without a mediating third. Everything that exists ex-sists – has its being in relation to that which lies outside it – and dichotomies and complementarities are no exception to the rule.

'The existent is that which turns about the consistent and creates an interval', Lacan says in a characteristic Borromean formula.[19] But there is more at stake here than an improvement in conceptual method. For the Real, the Symbolic and the Imaginary are the whole of what is, and figuring their connections is a cosmological exercise. Where others have imagined the world as a book, a library, a labyrinth, a giant serpent or a sacred ash-tree, Lacan in these topologically inspired pages imagines it as a tress, a skein, a frieze, an interlace, a consistency punctured and punctuated into existence. If it is still a signifying chain it can no longer signify anything in particular, or anything beyond its own continuance. In his introduction to *RSI*, Lacan warns his reader that much of what is to follow may seem futile or debilitated:

> This is the kind of problem that I encounter at every turn – without seeking to, it has to be said – but the very act of measuring the effects that I speak cannot avoid modulating my speech. Adding to this the tiredness of speech itself does not relieve us of the duty to report on it – on the contrary. A marginal note may be required to complete a circuit elided in the seminar, though it's not the detailed working that is 'futile' here, but, as I have stressed, the mental itself, in so far as such a thing ex-sists.[20]

The sadness here is that of one who has found the grail and not been at all impressed by it, or of one who has heard the music of the spheres and now craves silence.

In the two main areas of Lacan's later work that I have been surveying in this chapter, we find two different destinies for 'theory'. In the first case – that of the *objet a* in its perpetual flight – theory finds its furtherance by giving chase to an untrappable prey, and can easily dissolve into an endless riddling and quibbling. In the second – that of the syncopated subject-in-time – the devices that seem best able to catch the structural paradox that analytic practice reveals lead the theorist beyond the babble of theory and towards a state of rapt contemplation. Before him lie topological schemata that are at once grand, definitive and pointless. He beholds a procession of models beyond which more models in procession extend to the horizon. In both cases theory is brought to the brink of its own impossibility.

These last writings of Lacan, and the drawings with which they are interspersed, can justly be called 'adventures' in theory, I suppose. For they contain enough hazards, curiosities and reversals of fortune to make them into an extraordinary voyage in the manner of Jules Verne. But if adventures involve going abroad into a previously uncharted world then I am less sure. In a sense Lacan stays inside psychoanalysis as it had been left by Freud and erects new monitoring devices at selected points in the landscape. These devices, however, do not simply record what is going on, or put existing concepts to work in new ways. They are all of them means of defending the strangeness of Freud's work and of preserving its undecidability. Where other Freudians appoint themselves as explainers, emendators or continuators of the original theoretical texts, Lacan wants to keep on feeling their initial shock. The worst that could happen to psychoanalysis, for him, is not that it should be ignored or vilified but that it should be thought to be right, complete, consummated, self-subsistent or unanswerable. Analytic speech and analytic theory each provide the other with a necessary 'outside' – a way of refusing consistency and 'creating an interval'. And within 'theory' itself, Lacan's late models have the same sort of role: they make 'being a Freudian' into an interminable task, and an inexhaustible source of wonderment and exasperation.

Concluding Remarks

You are gazing down a steep wooded valley towards the Pacific, which is your sole horizon. A flawless vault of blue sky enfolds you, and a warm breeze brings the smell of eucalyptus to your nostrils. You reflect for a moment upon your rapture, and notice perhaps that some of the trees beneath you are bleached and broken, and that their smell has a sinister acridity in it. Your senses are working hard. It is almost as if they are doing your thinking, and ingraining their own intimation of death into the scene. In any case what is going on is so complex, and involves so many separate intensities of sight and thought and feeling, that a philosopher who tried to level it all down with a 'nothing but' would strike one, for a while at least, as a brute.

'According to our view', Schopenhauer writes in the third book of *The World as Will and Representation* (1819), 'the whole of the visible world is only the objectification, the mirror, of the will, accompanying it to knowledge of itself, and indeed, as we shall soon see, to the possibility of its salvation.'[1] In due course, Schopenhauer's 'visible world' is to be rescued and elucidated by the work of art. But when we simply open our eyes to that world, finding ourselves abandoned inside it and with no salvation yet in sight, it is one continuous flat surface, which emits and tediously repeats only one message. Our sensuous discriminations – between this blue and that, or between a living and a dead tree – have no intellectual weight. Lacan's Imaginary order is the product of a similar cancelling gesture and offers its own flat surface to the beholder's eye: the visible world is the ego's mirror, and reflected in it are the ego's dreams of identity. From the theoretical point of view, the sentience of the human organism, and the range of internal and external stimuli that it can register, are very uninteresting indeed. This does not of course mean that the world loses its variegation and its interplay of intensities. What happens in Lacan's theory is that difference is relentlessly transferred from the Imaginary to the Symbolic, from the world we see to the world we speak, from the senses to signification. Once the Symbolic has been packed with the stigmata of difference and become the seat of 'absolute non-reciprocity',[2] it is then possible for the symbolic scientist to make his somewhat condescending return journeys to the realm of sense-experience. The signifier 'opens up furrows in the real world' (550; 194), and it is thanks to the absences which are tressed and latticed into the signifying chain that the visible world becomes one of perpetual 'fading'. Your feeling that something is not quite right among the eucalyptus trees comes not from the way your senses and your reflective intelligence work but from the silent interventions of language: your organism may have all manner of intricate fade-out mechanisms built into it, but these neither produce nor affect your sense of transience. This is entirely attributable to the Symbolic in which you are trapped.

Lacan's constant stress upon the disjunctive Symbolic dimension has its moments of debilitation and of frenzied overstatement. Whether he addresses language directly, as in the major papers of the 1950s, or seeks to tease out an underlying logic for language and the unconscious, as in the later mathematicized writings, he runs the risk of answering too many questions too fast – before their interrogative force has been fully felt. And although the human subject, for Lacan, is governed by a law of intermittence, one perfectly familiar way in which this law may be experienced is removed to the margins of the picture. I am referring to the varying degrees of urgency or insistence with which language affects our lives. It is our lot as speaking creatures to rediscover muteness from time to time – in rapture, in pain, in physical violence, in the terror of death – and then to feel a lost power of speech flowing back. One may be ready to grant that these seeming suspensions of signifying law are themselves entirely in the gift of the signifier, yet still wish to have them marked off in some way as events of a special kind. A long gaze at the Pacific may be taciturn at one moment and loquacious the next. Language offers us now a retreat from sensuality, now a way of enhancing and manipulating it. Yet to these differences Lacan's theory maintains a principled indifference.

In at least two areas, however, his account of the human order as one of mobile and many-layered signification bears remarkable fruit. First, he eroticizes the language of 'theory'. At the start, I mentioned that Lacan had a lifelong quarrel with the conventional language of his discipline. Freudians other than Freud had tried to retreat from desire in the act of writing about it, and had settled for a style that advertised itself as dry, plain, clear and well-intentioned. Seeking to create for himself a style that had desire in its sinews, Lacan drew lessons from a variety of earlier writers – Plato in his mythical mood, Gracián, La Rochefoucauld, Lichtenberg, Hegel, Kierkegaard, Nietzsche and Heidegger. In each case he admired and in part imitated his distinguished predecessor's willingness to take chances with sense. Paradoxes, conceits and aphorisms were favoured as the proper instruments of experimental thought. And for Lacan things were going well not badly when a proposition collapsed under its own hyperbolic weight or was undercut by a later proposition. But writing like this was not just a matter of giving the language of psychoanalysis a new kind of brilliance and trenchancy. The psychoanalytic account of discourse could not be other than an 'erotics' and it was a matter of scruple for the analyst who became a theoretical writer to be aware of the transformations of desire that his theorizing brought about. And why drably acknowledge these, and pass to the next item of business, when the theoretical text could become a moving simulacrum of desire in movement – a carnival, a masked ball?

Lacan's writing seeks to tease and seduce. It is full of feints, subterfuges, evasions and mimicries. It unveils and re-veils its meanings from paragraph to paragraph. And even when it is crass, it is so – he would have us believe – not inadvertently but out of seigneurial disregard for the good form of the *petites gens*. Lacan is a writer of astonishing inventiveness, although this is not a tribute that he would have been particularly happy with. He thought of himself as an artist of the spoken rather than the written word, and the most famous of his seductions is still the one that he carried out upon the Parisian intelligentsia during his late lectures and seminars. The voluminous writings that he left are nevertheless an outstanding feat of literary imagination. In twentieth-century France, he is comparable only to Proust in the copiousness, the wit and the disabused intelligence with which he restages *as text* the tragicomedy of desiring human speech.

The second of the two areas that I mentioned a moment ago is that of clinical psychoanalysis itself – the work it does and the language it speaks. Lacan brings into startling new relief the fact that analyst and analysand talk, and reminds these contractually conjoined practitioners of the word that they will have to work hard if they are to understand what is going on as they confront one another. One might summarize Lacan's professional contribution by saying that he has created a new way of thinking about the transference. All analysts are in agreement that this is the central stage on which analytic therapy is performed, and many have been aware that a clinical method that is so rigorously intersubjective and dialogical offers a potentially very fertile model of intellectual enquiry to other disciplines. Lacan seeks to redescribe the special potency of the transferential encounter in terms that are fully appropriate to the wish-laden speech that it comprises: linguistic terms are to be used of linguistic materials; strict talk of rhetoric is to replace loose talk of affectivity; and when the improvisatory exchanges between analyst and analysand begin to reveal a logical structure the theorist must not shirk the task of articulating it. Practitioners who have brought this kind of scrutiny to their own procedures are the only ones who are entitled to export their models into neighbouring research territory. The Anglo-American observer whose puzzlement I evoked at the start of the last chapter will find in this set of practical recommendations the clearest possible answer to the question 'why read Lacan?': Lacan's refashioning of Freudian theory makes a new kind of sense of the 'talking cure', and provides the signifying artisans who conduct analyses, and who codify the rules and techniques laid down by the psychoanalytic guilds, with ample material for reflection.

Yet it is difficult to achieve finesse in these matters. Lacan's own work, considered as a whole, does not seem to offer a satisfactory correlation between theory and clinical practice. In particular the speculative welter of his own theoretical speech can easily drown the undistinguished locutions in which ordinary human suffering finds voice. Where for many analysts case-material acts as a necessary ballast against excessive theoretical ingenuity, for Lacan such material matters rather little, is adduced rather infrequently, and, when it does appear, finds him already hovering high above the earthbound business of the consulting room. The speech of the clinical 'case' is often dull, obtuse, inert, monotonous and repetitious, and it is one of the peculiar strengths of the Anglo-American analytic tradition to be able and willing to work patiently upon the poverty of it all, and without seeking to enrich it prematurely. Lacan, on the other hand, vaticinates at a moment's notice, and decks out therapeutic small-talk in a gorgeous apparel of figures and tropes that is, in one view of the matter, simply insulting to the patient's pain.

Lacan the logician and Lacan the mystagogue both have an alarming tendency to drift away into euphoria. And the fact that both personalities have a great deal to say about death, lack, fading, *béance*, *Spaltung* and νεῖχος does not make them any less likely to dispense a variety of false consolation. Death is endemic to the signifying chain, and the structure of the human subject is always one of catastrophe: logic says so, and polysemantic writing says so too. *Jaculation* and *jouissance* offer momentary respite from the severity of signifying law, but they too are effects of the signifier and by that well-trodden Lacanian route bring their own mortal shudder into the lives of men and women. All this is fine in so far as it draws the analyst's attention to a neglected responsibility of analytic speech – that of allowing the patient to 'signify' his death, to symbolize it (or to make sense of it and live with it, as we might say if we were bold enough to reformulate part of Lacan's message in the language of the self-help manual). But as soon as they begin to offer themselves as a complete philosophical view of death, propositions of this kind are likely to seem shallow. Let us grant for a moment that death is the ubiquitous condition of human speech, and that the only opportunity we have for saying *no* to mortality lies, fragilely, in speech itself and in the action that it may provoke. We still have a lopsided and implausible account. For we die inside the signifying chain, but outside it too. We die many times before our deaths, but we die at our deaths too and watch others dying at theirs. We die as organisms and as citizens.

Death is too complex a biological and social fact to be located pre-emptively in any one place. And although Lacan deploys a sophisticated topological imagery in order to make the point that death is both intrinsic and extrinsic to the words that speak us, he is often prepared to grant those words, and whatever lies inside them, outrageous privileges.

The immediate task that faces the followers of Lacan is that of bringing clinical cases in their full complexity and intractability back into the field of psychoanalytic enquiry. Suffering and death need to be given more weight – silently, in the Real – and freed from the consoling word-magic and matheme-magic in which Lacan came to specialize. Above all, Lacanians need to be less besotted with the Lacan legend, less given to trifling wars of succession, and much more responsive to the demythologizing intelligence that is Lacan's most remarkable legacy. Lacan is the only psychoanalyst of the twentieth century (I make no predictions for the twenty-first) whose intellectual achievement is in any way comparable to Freud's. It would be most unfortunate if the singularity of that achievement were to be obscured by the babbling of his unconditional admirers.

Chronology

1900   Freud: *The Interpretation of Dreams.*

1901   Jacques-Marie Emile Lacan born on 13 April in Paris. He is to be educated at the Collège Stanislas and at the Paris Medical Faculty.

Freud: *The Psychopathology of Everyday Life.*

1905   Freud: *Jokes and their Relation to the Unconscious, Three Essays on the Theory of Sexuality* and *Fragment of an Analysis of a Case of Hysteria* ('Dora').

1906   Saussure begins his first lecture course on general linguistics at the University of Geneva.

1909   Freud: *Analysis of a Phobia in a Five-year-old Boy* ('Little Hans') and *Notes upon a Case of Obsessional Neurosis* ('The Rat Man').

1911   Freud: *Psycho-Analytic Notes on an Autobiographical Account of a Case of Paranoia* ('the Schreber case').

1913   Saussure dies.

Freud: *Totem and Taboo.*

1914   Freud: 'On Narcissism: An Introduction'.

1915   Freud: 'The Unconscious'.

1916 Freud: *Introductory Lectures on Psycho-Analysis.*

Saussure: *Cours de linguistique générale (Course in General Linguistics).*

1918 Freud: *From the History of an Infantile Neurosis* ('The Wolf Man').

1920 Freud: *Beyond the Pleasure Principle.*

1921 Klein: 'The Development of a Child'.

1923 Freud: *The Ego and the Id.*

1925 The journal *L'Evolution psychiatrique* founded.

1926 Lacan's first co-authored publication appears in *Revue Neurologique.* The Société Psychanalytique de Paris (SPP) is founded by René Laforgue, Marie Bonaparte, Rudolph Loewenstein, Edouard Pichon and six others. Freud's *The Interpretation of Dreams* appears in French as *La Science des rêves,* translated by I. Meyerson.

1927 Lacan begins his clinical training as a psychiatrist.

Freud: *The Future of an Illusion.*

Heidegger: *Sein und Zeit (Being and Time).*

1930 Lacan's first non-collaborative publication appears in *Annales Médico-Psychologiques.*

Freud: *Civilization and its Discontents.*

1931 Winnicott: *Clinical Notes on Disorders of Childhood.*

1932 Lacan publishes his doctoral dissertation *De la psychose paranoïaque dans ses rapports avec la personnalité* (*On Paranoiac Psychosis in its Relations to the Personality*), and sends a copy to Freud – who acknowledges it by postcard.

Klein: *The Psycho-Analysis of Children*.

1933 Lacan publishes two articles in the surrealist journal *Minotaure*, and a sonnet in *Le Phare de Neuilly*. Kojève lectures on Hegel's *Phenomenology* at the Ecole des Hautes Etudes (the series is to continue until 1939).

1934 Lacan joins the SPP as a candidate member, and applies for full membership. At this time Lacan is in analysis with Rudolph Loewenstein.

1936 Lacan addresses the fourteenth Congress of the International Psychoanalytical Association in Marienbad, on the 'mirror stage' (3 August).

'Au-delà du "principe de réalité"' ('Beyond the "reality principle"').

Anna Freud: *The Ego and the Mechanisms of Defence*.

1937 Freud: 'Analysis Terminable and Interminable'.

1938 Lacan becomes a full member of the SPP and publishes his long article on the family in the *Encyclopédie Française*. Freud is driven from his home in Vienna by the Nazis and travels to London by way of Paris.

1939 During the Second World War French psychoanalysis is almost entirely suppressed by the Nazis. Lacan works in a military hospital in occupied Paris; he publishes nothing during this period. Freud dies in London (23 September), having published *Moses and Monotheism* earlier in the year. The first volume of Jean Hyppolite's translation of Hegel's *Phenomenology* appears.

1940   Freud: *An Outline of Psycho-Analysis.*

1941   Jakobson: *Child Language, Aphasia and Phonological Universals.*

1943   Sartre: *L'Etre et le néant* (*Being and Nothingness*).

1945   The SPP begins to hold meetings again. In the autumn, Lacan spends five weeks in England studying the practice of psychiatry during the war years.

'Le temps logique' ('Logical time').

Merleau-Ponty: *Phénoménologie de la perception* (*Phenomenology of Perception*).

1946   Lacan begins again to deliver professional papers. Jean Hyppolite publishes his dissertation on Hegel's *Phenomenology*.

'Propos sur la causalité psychique' ('Remarks on psychical causality').

1947   Lacan publishes a report on his English visit.

Kojève: *Introduction à la lecture de Hegel.*
Lévi-Strauss: *Les structures élémentaires de la parenté* (*The Elementary Structures of Kinship*).

1948   'L'agressivité en psychanalyse' ('Aggressivity in psychoanalysis').

1949   Lacan has a central role in planning a training programme for the SPP.

'Le stade du miroir comme formateur de la fonction du JE' ('The mirror stage as formative of the function of the I').

1950   'Introduction théorique aux fonctions de la psychanalyse en criminologie' ('A theoretical introduction to the functions of psychoanalysis in criminology').

1951   Lacan's use of 'short sessions' discussed within the SPP.

'Intervention sur le transfert' ('An intervention on the transference').

1952   The SPP establishes the Institut de Psychanalyse de Paris, with Sacha Nacht as its Director (June). Lacan replaces Nacht (December).

1953   Lacan becomes President of the SPP, and Nacht head of the Institute (January). The Institute's training programme is launched (March). Following severe internal disagreements, often involving the role and technique of Lacan, three analysts break away from the SPP to form the Société Française de Psychanalyse (SFP). Lacan resigns from the SPP and joins the SFP (June). He is informed by the International Psychoanalytical Association that his membership of that body lapses with his resignation from the SPP, the only officially recognised analytic society in France. Lacan addresses the SFP on 'Le Symbolique, l'Imaginaire et le Réel' (8 July) and delivers in Rome his 'Fonction et champ de la parole et du langage en psychanalyse' ('The function and field of speech and language in psychoanalysis') (26–7 September). In November he begins his first public seminar (on Freud's writings on technique). The series is to continue on an annual basis for twenty-seven years.

Barthes: *Le degré zéro de l'écriture* (*Writing Degree Zero*).

1954   'Introduction au commentaire de Jean Hyppolite sur la "Verneinung" de Freud' and 'Réponse au commentaire . . .' ('Introduction to Jean Hyppolite's commentary on Freud's "Negation"' and 'Reply to JH's commentary . . .'). Seminar I (1953–4): *Les écrits techniques de Freud* (*Freud's Papers on Technique*).

1955 'Variantes de la cure-type' ('Variants of the typical treatment').
'Le Séminaire sur "La lettre volée"' ('Seminar on "The Purloined Letter"').
'La chose freudienne ou sens du retour à Freud en psychanalyse' ('The Freudian thing, or the direction of a return to Freud in psychoanalysis').
Seminar II (1954–5): *Le moi dans la théorie de Freud et dans la technique de la psychanalyse* (*The Ego in Freud's Theory and in the Technique of Psychoanalysis*).

1956 Lacan translates Heidegger's 'Logos' for *La Psychanalyse*.

'Situation de la psychanalyse et formation du psychanalyste en 1956' ('The situation of psychoanalysis and the formation of the analyst in 1956').
Seminar III (1955–6): *Les psychoses* (*The Psychoses*).

Jakobson and Halle: *Fundamentals of Language*.

1957 'La psychanalyse et son enseignement' ('Psychoanalysis and its teaching').
'L'instance de la lettre dans l'inconscient ou la raison depuis Freud' ('The agency of the letter in the unconscious or reason since Freud').
'D'une question préliminaire à tout traitement possible de la psychose' ('On a question preliminary to any possible treatment of psychosis').
Seminar IV (1956–7): *La relation d'objet et les structures freudiennes* (*Object relations and Freudian structures*).

Klein: *Envy and Gratitude*.
Winnicott: *The Child and the Family* and *The Child and the Outside World*.
Chomsky: *Syntactic Structures*.

1958 'Jeunesse de Gide ou la lettre et le désir' ('Gide's youth or the letter and desire').
'Die Bedeutung des Phallus' ('The meaning of the phallus').
'La direction de la cure et les principes de son pouvoir'

('The direction of the treatment and the principles of its power').

'Remarque sur le rapport de Daniel Lagache: "Psychanalyse et structure de la personnalité"' ('A remark on Daniel Lagache's report: "Psychoanalysis and the Structure of Personality"').

Seminar V (1957–8): *Les formations de l'inconscient (The Formations of the Unconscious).*

1959   The SFP requests affiliation to the IPA.

'A la mémoire d'Ernest Jones: sur sa théorie du symbolisme' ('In memory of Ernest Jones: on his Theory of Symbolism').

Seminar VI (1958–9): *Le désir et son interprétation (Desire and its Interpretation).*

1960   'Propos directifs pour un congrès sur la sexualité féminine' ('Guiding remarks for a congress on feminine sexuality').

'Subversion du sujet et dialectique du désir dans l'inconscient freudien' ('The subversion of the subject and the dialectic of desire in the Freudian unconscious').

'Position de l'inconscient' ('Position of the unconscious').

Seminar VII (1959–60): *L'éthique de la psychanalyse (The Ethics of Psychoanalysis).*

1961   SFP granted Study Group status by the IPA; full recognition cannot be granted until Lacan is phased out of its training programme.

Seminar VIII (1960–61): *Le Transfert (The Transference).*

Foucault: *Histoire de la folie (Madness and Civilization).*

1962   'Kant avec Sade' ('Kant with Sade').

Seminar IX (1961–2): *L'Identification (Identification).*

1963   Lacan appointed part-time lecturer at the Ecole Pratique des Hautes Etudes, and editor of the *Champ freudien* series at Editions du Seuil; he resigns from the SFP.

Seminar X (1962–3): *L'Angoisse (Anxiety).*

1964 Lacan founds the Ecole Freudienne de Paris (EFP).

'Du "Trieb" de Freud et du désir du psychanalyste' ('On Freud's "Trieb" [Drive] and the desire of the psychoanalyst').
Seminar XI (1964): *Les quatre concepts fondamentaux de la psychanalyse* (*The Four Fundamental Concepts of Psychoanalysis*).

Barthes: *Eléments de sémiologie* (*Elements of Semiology*).
Althusser: 'Freud et Lacan'.

1965 The SFP is dissolved.

'Hommage fait à Marguerite Duras, du ravissement de Lol V. Stein' ('Homage to Marguerite Duras, on the rapture of Lol V. Stein').
'La science et la vérité' ('Science and Truth').
Seminar XII (1964–5): *Problèmes cruciaux pour la psychanalyse* (*Crucial Problems for Psychoanalysis*).

Althusser and Balibar: *Lire le Capital* (*Reading Capital*).
Chomsky: *Aspects of a Theory of Syntax*.

1966 Lacan publishes *Ecrits*, his selected papers, to which seven new pieces (prefaces or afterwords) are added; he addresses a colloquium at Johns Hopkins University, Baltimore.

Seminar XIII (1965–6): *L'objet de la psychanalyse* (*The Object of Psychoanalysis*).

Foucault: *Les mots et les choses* (*The Order of Things*).

1967 The EFP introduces its own training programme.

Seminar XIV (1966–7): *La logique du fantasme* (*The Logic of Phantasy*).

Laplanche and Pontalis: *Vocabulaire de la psychanalyse* (*The Language of Psycho-Analysis*).
Derrida: *L'écriture et la différence* (*Writing and Difference*), *La voix et le phénomène* (*Speech and Phenomena*), *De la grammatologie* (*Of Grammatology*).

1968   The review *Scilicet* is launched by the EFP. Lacan expresses
       support for the student movement during the 'May events'.
       A Department of Psychoanalysis is opened at the
       University of Vincennes by followers of Lacan.

       Seminar XV (1967–8): *L'acte psychanalytique* (*The
       Psychoanalytic Act*).

1969   Seminar XVI (1968–9): *D'un Autre à l'autre* (*From one
       Other to the other*).

1970   Seminar XVII (1969–70): *L'envers de la psychanalyse* (*The
       Hidden Face of Psychoanalysis*).

       Barthes: *S/Z*.

1971   Seminar XVIII (1970–71): *D'un discours qui ne serait pas
       du semblant* (*On a Discourse that wouldn't be
       Appearance*).

1972   Seminar XIX (1971–2): . . . . *Ou pire* (. . . *Or worse*).

       Deleuze and Guattari: *L'Anti-Œdipe* (*Anti-Oedipus*).

1973   Seminar XX (1972–3): *Encore* (*Again*).

1974   The Vincennes department becomes 'Le Champ freudien'
       with Lacan as scientific director and Jacques-Alain Miller
       as president.

       Seminar XXI (1973–4): *Les non-dupes errent* (*The Non-
       dupes Wander/The Names of the Father*).

1975   Lacan lectures at Yale and MIT.

       Seminar XXII (1974–5): *RSI* (*Real, Symbolic, Imaginary*).

1976   Seminar XXIII (1975–6): *Le sinthome* (*The Sinthome*).

       Foucault: *Histoire de la sexualité I* (*History of Sexuality I*).

1977   Seminar XXIV (1976–7): *L'insu que sait de l'une bévue s'aile à mourre* (*One knew that it was a mistaken moon on wings of love*)

1978   Seminar XXV (1977–8): *Le moment de conclure* (*The Moment for Concluding*).

1979   Seminar XXVI (1978–9): *La topologie et le temps* (*Topology and Time*).

1980   Lacan dissolves the EFP (amid protests) and creates La Cause freudienne; attends an international conference in Caracas.

Seminar XXVII (1980): *Dissolution* (*Dissolution*).

1981   Lacan dies on 9 September.

Notes

CHAPTER ONE

1. Page numbers appearing without other indication in my main text refer to *Ecrits* (Seuil, 1966). Wherever possible, translations have been taken from Alan Sheridan's *Ecrits. A Selection* (Tavistock Publications/Norton, 1977); occasionally, I have modified Sheridan's generally excellent renderings. Where two page numbers are given, the first refers to the French edition and the second to the English. In cases where a single page number appears the paper concerned is not included in *Ecrits. A Selection* and the translation is my own.

2. My quotations from Freud are taken from *The Standard Edition of the Complete Psychological Works* (translated from the German under the general editorship of James Strachey, 24 vols, Hogarth Press and Institute of Psycho-Analysis, 1953–74). References to volume number and page are given in my main text.

3. *Les complexes familiaux dans la formation de l'individu. Essai d'analyse d'une fonction en psychologie*, Navarin, 1984. This work has yet to appear in English translation. Lacan's article originally appeared in the eighth volume of the *Encyclopédie Française*, Larousse, 1938.

4. For a brief comparative discussion of 'instinct' and 'complex' as analytic terms, see 'Beyond the "reality principle"' (1936), *Ecrits*, 88–89. Laplanche and Pontalis define 'complex' as an 'organized group of ideas and memories of great affective force which are either partly or totally unconscious. Complexes are constituted on the basis of the interpersonal relationships of childhood history; they may serve to structure all levels of the psyche: emotions, attitudes, adapted behaviour' (*The Language of Psycho-Analysis*, 72).

5. 'The intrusion complex represents the experience that the primitive subject has, for the most part when he sees one or several of his counterparts share domestic relations with him – in other words when he realises he has siblings' (*Family Complexes*, 35–36).

6. For a fuller account of this concept, see below 92–4.

7. Lacan's objections to the phrase 'human sciences' are summarized in 'Science and truth' (*Ecrits*, 855–77; see in particular 859). On the 'conjectural sciences', see XI, 44; 43.

8. Lacan wrote in 'The function and field of speech' (1953): 'It is in the *name of the father* that we must recognise the support of the

symbolic function which, from the dawn of history, has identified his person with the figure of the law' (278; 67).

9. For a fuller discussion of Freud's *Nachträglichkeit* ('retroaction'), see below 180–90.

10. On Freud's switch from a dyadic to a triadic mental topography, see below 88–90; on the concept 'signifying chain', see below 66ff.

11. Lacan reached this view of the analytic process at an early stage in his career. For a detailed 'phenomenological description of the psychoanalytic experience', see 'Beyond the "reality principle"' (1936), *Ecrits*, 82–84.

12. References to the published volumes of Lacan's *Seminar* will be given in my main text, in the form: volume number + page. Where two page numbers are given, the first refers to the French original and the second to the English translation. (The individual volumes are listed, together with translation details, on pp. 223–4 below.) Where only one page reference is given, the volume concerned has not yet appeared in English and the translation is mine. Jacques-Alain Miller, in his *Entretien sur le Séminaire*, describes his editorial role in preparing the transcripts for publication and discusses the senses in which he may be considered the 'co-author' of the published volumes.

CHAPTER TWO

1. Lacan's paper was recorded as having been delivered – under the title 'The Looking-Glass Phase' – in *The International Journal of Psycho-Analysis* (Vol. 18, Part I, January 1937, 78). For further details, see Dor, *Bibliographie des travaux de Jacques Lacan*, 42. A printed version of the paper did not appear until 1949, although brief summaries had already been given in 'Remarks on psychical causality' (1946; pub. 1950) and 'Aggressivity in psychoanalysis' (1948).

2. The fullest intellectual biography of the early Lacan is to be found in the second volume of Elisabeth Roudinesco's *La Bataille de cent ans. Histoire de la psychanalyse en France* (see in particular 116–61). David Macey's *Lacan in Contexts* also provides a wealth of background information.

3. This characteristic statement occurs in 'Remarks on psychical causality' (*Ecrits*, 151–93).

4. The relevant dates are to be found in n.1 above.

5. Winnicott's remarks are to be found in 'Mirror-role of Mother and Family in Child Development' (1967) (*Playing and Reality*, 130–38) and Trilling's on p. 25 of *Sincerity and Authenticity*.

6. Lacan's descriptions of the *corps morcelé* are likely to have been influenced by Hans Bellmer's photographic sequence *Dolls*, which appeared in *Minotaure* in 1936. On the complex historical and iconographical background to imagery of this kind, see Rosalind Krauss's essay 'Corpus Delicti' (in *L'Amour fou. Photography and Surrealism*, ed. R. Krauss and J. Livingston, 57–100). For Freud on Hoffmann's *The Sandman*, and the

mechanical dolls that figure prominently in the tale, see 'The "Uncanny"' (1919), XVII, 219–52.

7. Lacan discusses Freud's use of Empedocles in 'The function and field of speech' (318–20; 102–4).

8. *The Presocratic Philosophers*, ed. G.S. Kirk and J.E. Raven, 336.

9. For Freud's use of the term *imago*, which was introduced by Jung in 1911, see XI, 181, XII, 100, 102 and Laplanche and Pontalis, *The Language of Psycho-Analysis*, 211.

10. For a brief sketch of Freud's (infrequent) use of the phrase 'primary identification', see Laplanche and Pontalis, *The Language of Psycho-Analysis*, 336–37.

11. On the matter of narcissism, 'early' and 'late' Freud are separated by no more than a few years. For although the second model was to be fully stated only in *Group Psychology and the Analysis of the Ego* (1921) (XVIII, 130–31) and *The Ego and the Id* (1923) (XIX, 30), its essentials were already present in the *Introductory Lectures* of 1916–17 (XVI, 416).

12. Paranoia: 'Chronic psychosis characterized by more or less systematized delusion, with a predominance of ideas of reference but with no weakening of the intellect and, generally speaking, no tendency towards deterioration' (Laplanche and Pontalis, *The Language of Psycho-Analysis*, 296).

13. *The Unspeakable Confessions of Salvador Dali*, 140–41. On the relationship between Lacan and Dalí, see Roudinesco, *Histoire de la psychanalyse en France*, II, 125–7.

14. *Unspeakable Confessions*, 143.

15. Melanie Klein's 'Some Theoretical Conclusions regarding the Emotional Life of the Infant' (1952) describes succinctly the genesis and the interplay of the 'paranoid-schizoid' and 'depressive' positions (*Envy and Gratitude and Other Works*, 1946–63, 61–93). On the development of Klein's ideas, see Hanna Segal, *Klein* (1979) and *The Selected Melanie Klein*, ed. Juliet Mitchell (1986).

16. Transference: 'For psycho-analysis, a process of actualization of unconscious wishes. Transference uses specific objects and operates in the framework of a specific relationship established with these objects. Its context *par excellence* is the analytic situation. In the transference, infantile prototypes re-emerge and are experienced with a strong sense of immediacy. As a rule what psycho-analysts mean by the unqualified use of the term 'transference' is *transference during treatment*. Classically, the transference is acknowledged to be the terrain on which all basic problems of a given analysis play themselves out: the establishment, modalities, interpretation and resolution of the transference are in fact what defines the treatment' (Laplanche and Pontalis, *The Language of Psycho-Analysis*, 455). Lacan's 'four fundamental concepts', as discussed in volume XI of the *Seminar* (1964), are the unconscious, repetition, the transference and the drive.

CHAPTER THREE

1. See *Ornicar?*, No. 24, Autumn 1981, 37. This article by Jacques-Alain Miller ('Encyclopédie', 35–44) is a reprint, on the occasion of Lacan's death, of a brief intellectual biography written for the *Encyclopedia Universalis* in 1979.

2. A detailed 'institutional history' of Lacanian psychoanalysis is to be found in Elisabeth Roudinesco's *Histoire de la psychanalyse en France* (on the 1953 expulsion, see II, 236 ff.). Briefer accounts in English are provided by Sherry Turkle, *Psychoanalytic Politics* (1979) and David Macey, *Lacan in Contexts* (1988). For a combined historical and theoretical account of Lacan's 'short sessions' and related matters of training and technique, see Moustapha Safouan, *Jacques Lacan et la question de la formation des analystes* (1983).

3. Condensation: 'One of the essential modes of the functioning of the unconscious processes: a sole idea represents several associative chains at whose point of intersection it is located'. Displacement: 'The fact that an idea's emphasis, interest or intensity is liable to be detached from it and to pass on to other ideas, which were originally of little intensity but which are related to the first idea by a chain of associations' (Laplanche and Pontalis, *The Language of Psycho-Analysis*, 82, 121). Freud's first detailed account of these mechanisms is to be found in *The Interpretation of Dreams* (IV, 279–309).

4. Lacan's most optimistic account of Freudian exegesis is to be found in his celebrated paragraphs on the unconscious as 'that chapter of my history that is marked by a blank or occupied by a falsehood' (259; 50); these paragraphs are also an ingenious résumé of Freud's characteristic archaeological and 'writerly' metaphors.

5. This seminal work was first published, by Charles Bally and Albert Sechehaye, in 1916. Their edition was based on notes taken during the lecture courses delivered by Saussure at the University of Geneva in 1906–7, 1908–9 and 1910–11.

6. These concepts are listed on p. 216 above (n. 16).

7. Lacan's stress on the signifier *as system* places him at a far remove from Saussure, for whom the system of language resided in *langue* (the underlying linguistic code) as distinct from *parole* (the utilization of the code in speech); *langue* could be thought of as the overall 'system' of signs, but signs lost their systemic character as soon as either of their components (signifier or signified) was considered in isolation.

8. Lacan's debt, fully acknowledged in 'The agency of the letter' (495; 176), is to the second part of *Fundamentals of Language* (1956), co-written by Jakobson and Morris Halle. This part, 'Two Aspects of Language and Two Types of Aphasic Disturbances', has often been reprinted – most recently in Jakobson's *Language in Literature*, ed. Krystyna Pomorska and Stephen Rudy, 95–114.

9. The indispensable work on Freud's indebtedness to the linguistic sciences is John Forrester's *Language and the Origins of Psychoanalysis* (1980).

10. For definitions of these terms, see above 217, n. 3.

11. Jakobson himself, from whom the terms *metaphor* and *metonymy* were borrowed, had proposed a quite different pattern of equivalence between his terms and Freud's: 'displacement' and 'condensation' were both metonymic, whereas 'identification' and 'symbolism' were metaphoric (see *Language in Literature*, 113).

12. For example, in an account of the symptom quoted above on p. 55, and in his various descriptions of analytic therapy as the 'restoration' of lost orders of meaning (see p. 217 n. 4 above).

13. Lacan's main discussion of the *points de capiton* is in the section of *The Psychoses* referred to earlier in the paragraph, but see also *Ecrits* 503; 154.

14. Lacan's criticism of Freud on this matter is of course aimed at only one tendency of his thinking. Freud on the one hand adhered to a 'Cartesian' model of the ego – and campaigned on its behalf – and on the other hand provided the single most impressive critique of that model that modern European culture possesses. And his critique had to do with the dividedness of all human subjects, and not, as Lacan reminds us, with 'more or less curious cases of split personality' (523; 171).

15. Lacan makes repeated use of this topographical metaphor (see 548; 193 for a straightforward instance) borrowed from Freud, who had borrowed it from G.T. Fechner. For Freud's *anderer Schauplatz*, see *The Interpretation of Dreams* (IV, 48 and V, 535–6) and the *Introductory Lectures* (XV, 90).

16. The unconscious is *not* the primordial, Lacan insists, for 'what it knows about the elementary is no more than the elements of the signifier' (522; 170); in other words, even as primordiality is being taken away from one cherished analytic notion it is being re-ascribed to another: the signifier.

CHAPTER FOUR

1. Freud's first model was itself triadic in the sense that it distinguished three systems – unconscious, preconscious and conscious – but he customarily treated the 'preconscious-conscious' as a continuum, sharply divided from the unconscious. For a detailed history of Freud's switch from the first to the second 'topography', see Laplanche and Pontalis, *The Language of Psycho-Analysis*, 449–53.

2. On the emergence of the three orders, see David Macey, *Lacan in Contexts*, 228–29.

3. Lacan develops this contrast clearly in Chapter XVII of *Freud's Papers on Technique* (I, 233–44; 208–19).

4. 'Fetishism: the Symbolic, the Imaginary and the Real' (1956), 274.

5. On the narrative structure of the *Phenomenology*, see M.H. Abrams, *Natural Supernaturalism*, 225–37.

6. For Hegel's main discussions of the *schöne Seele*, see the *Phenomenology of Spirit* (1807), trans. A.V. Miller, 221–28, 397–409; for Lacan's re-use of the concept, see *Ecrits*, 172–75, 292 (Sheridan: 80) etc.

7. This passage, not included in Mehlman's translation (*French Freud*, 38–72), is in part a commentary on Lacan's 'Schema L', which is reproduced and discussed on p. 186 below.

8. Object-relation: 'Term enjoying a very wide currency in present-day psycho-analysis as a designation for the subject's mode of relation to his world; this relation is the entire complex outcome of a particular organization of the personality, of an apprehension of objects that is to some extent or other phantasied, and of certain special types of defence. We may speak of the object-relationships of a specific subject, but also of *types* of object-relationship by reference either to points in development (e.g., an oral object-relationship) or else to psychopathology (e.g., a melancholic object-relationship)' (Laplanche and Pontalis, *The Language of Psycho-Analysis*, 277–78). Lacan's usual reference, when he speaks of object-relations theorists, is to Melanie Klein and her followers. On the psychoanalytic conception of 'the object', see below 163ff.

9. *Basic Works of Aristotle*, ed. Richard McKeon, 246. For Lacan's proposed translation of the terms,

see also *Ecrits*, 39 (*French Freud*, 70–71).

10. *De la psychose paranoïaque dans ses rapports avec la personnalité* (*On Paranoiac Psychosis in its Relations to the Personality*) was first published by Le François in 1932 and republished by Seuil in 1975.

11. On Lacan's adaptation of Edouard Pichon's adaptation of this juridical term, see Roudinesco, *Histoire de la psychanalyse en France*, I, 315–16 and II, 127.

12. *Phenomenology of Spirit*, trans. A.V. Miller, 27.

CHAPTER FIVE

1. Freud writes of the phallic phase in a footnote added in 1924 to the *Three Essays* (1905): 'This phase, which already deserves to be described as genital, presents a sexual object and some degree of convergence of the sexual impulses upon that object; but it is differentiated from the final organization of sexual maturity in one essential respect. For it knows only one kind of genital: the male one' (VII, 199–200).

2. Freud's most exhaustive account of the castration complex, and its centrality to psychoanalytic thought, is to be found in *Inhibitions, Symptoms and Anxiety* (1926) (XX, 87–156).

3. On the history of this debate, see Juliet Mitchell and Jacqueline Rose's indispensable *Feminine Sexuality* (1982).

4. On this quality and its opposite – the 'adhesiveness' of libido – see

Laplanche and Pontalis, *The Language of Psycho-Analysis*, 319, 12–13.

5. Freud's discussion of *Ichspaltung* is to be found mainly in 'Fetishism' (XXI, 152–57), 'Splitting of the Ego in the Process of Defence' (XXIII, 275–78) and *An Outline of Psycho-Analysis* (XXIII, 144–207).

6. On Freud, Lacan and the Presocratics, see above 28–9.

7. Page numbers preceded by 'MR' refer to Juliet Mitchell and Jacqueline Rose's *Feminine Sexuality*. This work contains translations of 'The meaning of the phallus', 'Guiding remarks for a congress on feminine sexuality', sections of Seminar XX (*Encore*) and other contributions by Lacan and his co-workers to the discussion of feminine sexuality.

8. For Klein's equation of breast and penis, see *Envy and Gratitude and Other Works* (1946–63), 79, 199, etc.

9. 'El Desdichado', usually printed as the first of Nerval's *Les Chimères*, contains the line 'Modulant tour à tour sur la lyre d'Orphée'.

10. For a brief guide to Freud's views on bisexuality, see the editorial footnote on XIX, 33 (*The Ego and the Id*).

11. Robert T. Petersson, in his *The Art of Ecstasy. Saint Teresa, Bernini and Crashaw* (1970) quotes the relevant passage from Teresa's *Life* (p. 40) and the whole of Crashaw's 'A Hymn to the Name and Honour of the Admirable Saint Teresa', and provides a copious photographic and descriptive account of the Cornaro chapel.

12. This article has been reprinted as an addendum to *De la psychose paranoïaque*, Seuil, 1975, 389–98.

13. Catherine Clément, in her *Vies et légendes de Jacques Lacan* (1981), retraces this feminine lineage in Lacan's work (see in particular pp. 217–27). Lacan's 'Hommage fait à Marguerite Duras, du ravissement de Lol V. Stein' appeared in 1965.

14. Evenly suspended attention: 'Manner in which, according to Freud, the analyst should listen to the analysand: he must give no special, *a priori* importance to any aspect of the subject's discourse; this implies that he should allow his own unconscious activity to operate as freely as possible and suspend the motives which usually direct his attention. This technical recommendation to the analyst complements the rule of free association laid down for the subject being analysed' (Laplanche and Pontalis, *The Language of Psycho-Analysis*, 43).

CHAPTER SIX

1. Lacan's clinical work is studied by Stuart Schneiderman in his *Returning to Freud. Clinical Psychoanalysis in the School of Lacan* (1980), which collects case-material from a variety of Lacanian analysts including Lacan; Rosine Lefort's *Naissance de l'Autre* (1980) contains two detailed case-studies conducted within a Lacanian perspective.

2. See below, pp. 200–3.

3. *Partialtrieb* (component instinct or drive): 'Term designating the

most fundamental elements that psycho-analysis is able to identify in breaking down sexuality. Each such element is specified by a source (e.g. oral instinct, anal instinct) and by an aim (e.g. scopophilic instinct, instinct to master). The qualification 'component' does not simply mean that these instincts are individual types within the class of the sexual instincts – it is to be taken above all in a developmental and structural sense: the component instincts function independently to begin with, tending to fuse together in the various libidinal organizations' (Laplanche and Pontalis, *The Language of Psycho-Analysis*, 74).

4. Freud introduced this term in 1920 (in *Beyond the Pleasure Principle*) and continued to use it for the remainder of his career (see XVIII, 38–41, etc.).

5. See, for example, *The Ego in Freud's Theory and in the Technique of Psychoanalysis* (II, 370; 321).

6. *Working Space*, 6–9.

7. John Rowlands reviews current knowledge of the historical content and context of the painting in his *Holbein: the Paintings of Hans Holbein the Younger* (1985), 85–87.

8. On the techniques involved, see Jurgis Baltrušaitis, *Anamorphic Art* (1969).

9. The analytic uses of the Borromean knot are discussed below, pp. 194–5.

10. On the 'timelessness' of the Freudian unconscious, see 'The Unconscious' (1915) (XIV, 187).

John Forrester reviews Lacan's extensions of the Freudian account of temporality in his 'Dead on time' (*The Seductions of Psychoanalysis*, 168–218).

11. A notable instance of the 'audacity' that Lacan mentions is to be found in a long footnote to the 'Wolf Man' case-history (XVII, 45); this note also contains Freud's longest general description of 'deferred action' in action.

12. In the mirror stage paper itself, which dates from the same period, Lacan not only sketches a complex temporality for the subject but places a special stress upon the anticipatory mode: 'This development is experienced as a temporal dialectic that decisively projects as history the formation of the individual. The *mirror stage* is a drama whose internal thrust is precipitated from insufficiency to anticipation . . .' (97; 4).

13. Lacan's commentary on the fuller form of this diagram is quoted on pp. 100–1 above.

14. On the *points de capiton*, see above p. 74 and p. 218, n. 13. The temporal dimension of this metaphor is already sketched in *Les psychoses* (III, 303–4).

15. Lacan often discusses the Moebius strip during these years: see, for example, *The Four Fundamental Concepts* (XI, 143; 156 and 213; 235). On the mathematical background, see Jeanne Granon-Lafont's invaluable *La topologie ordinaire de Jacques Lacan* (1985).

16. In one of Lacan's most extraordinary late papers –

'L'Etourdit' (*Scilicet*, 4 (1973),
5–52) – he reviews the whole of his
own (and Freud's) achievement
from the vantage point of topology.

17. *RSI* is to be found in four
consecutive issues of *Ornicar?*
(1975, Nos 2–5).

18. Lacan's earlier formulations on
the R–S–I triad are reviewed in
Chapter IV above.

19. *Ornicar?*, 1975, No. 3, 102.

20. *Ornicar?*, 1975, No. 2, 88. This
passage is also to be found in J.
Granon-Lafont's *La topologie . . .*,
142.

CONCLUDING REMARKS

1. *The World as Will and
Representation*, trans. E.F.J. Payne,
Vol. I, 266.

2. See above, p. 178.

Bibliography

Lacan: Principal Publications

The fullest guide so far published to Lacan's writings is Joël Dor's *Bibliographie des travaux de Jacques Lacan* (Paris: InterEditions, 1983). For the reader of Lacan in English, David Macey's *Lacan in Contexts* (London and New York: Verso, 1988) is particularly helpful. Below are listed all the writings by Lacan to which I have referred above, together with a number of suggestions for further reading. Unless otherwise stated, the place of publication for all works in French is Paris.

Les complexes familiaux dans la formation de l'individu. Essai d'analyse d'une fonction en psychologie (Navarin: 1984) [reprints 'La Famille', *Encyclopédie française* (Larousse), VIII, 1938].

De la psychose paranoïaque dans ses rapports avec la personnalité (1932), followed by *Premiers écrits sur la paranoïa* (Seuil, 1975).

'Desire and the Interpretation of Desire in *Hamlet*', *Yale French Studies*, 55/6, 1977, 11–52 [a part-translation of Seminar VI by James Hulbert].

Ecrits (Seuil, 1966).

Ecrits. A Selection, trans. Alan Sheridan (London and New York: Tavistock Publications/Norton, 1977).

'L'Etourdit', *Scilicet*, No. 4, 1973, 5–52.

The Ego in Freud's Theory and in the Technique of Psychoanalysis (*The Seminar*, Book II), ed. Jacques-Alain Miller, trans. Sylvana Tomaselli, notes by John Forrester (New York: Norton; Cambridge: Cambridge University Press, 1988).

'Fetishism: the Symbolic, the Imaginary and the Real' (with W. Granoff), in *Perversions: Psychodynamics and Therapy* (New York: Random House, 1956).

The Four Fundamental Concepts of Psycho-Analysis (*The*

Seminar, Book XI), ed. Jacques-Alain Miller, trans. Alan Sheridan (London: Hogarth Press and Institute of Psycho-Analysis, 1977).

Freud's Papers on Technique (*The Seminar*, Book I), ed. Jacques-Alain Miller, trans. with notes by John Forrester (New York: Norton; Cambridge: Cambridge University Press, 1988).

'Hommage fait à Marguerite Duras du ravissement de Lol V. Stein', *Cahiers Renaud-Barrault*, No. 52, 1965, 7–15.

Le Séminaire, 27 annual series, 1953–80, of which the following have been published:

I: *Les écrits techniques de Freud* (Seuil, 1975).

II: *Le moi dans la théorie de Freud et dans la technique de la psychanalyse* (Seuil, 1978).

III: *Les psychoses* (Seuil, 1981).

VI: *Le désir et son interprétation* (*Ornicar?*, 1981–83, Nos. 24–27, in part).

VII: *L'éthique de la psychanalyse* (Seuil, 1986).

XI: *Les quatre concepts fondamentaux de la psychanalyse* (Seuil, 1973).

XX: *Encore* (Seuil, 1975).

XXII: *RSI* (*Ornicar?*, 1975, Nos. 2–5).

XXIII: *Le sinthome* (*Ornicar?*, 1976–77, Nos. 6–11).

XXIV: *L'insu que sait de l'une bévue s'aile à mourre* (*Ornicar?*, 1977–79, Nos. 12–18).

XXV: *Le moment de conclure* (*Ornicar?*, 1979, No. 19, in part).

XXVII: *Dissolution* (*Ornicar?*, 1980–81, Nos 20–23).

Télévision (Seuil, 1973).

'Seminar on "The Purloined Letter"', *Yale French Studies*, 48, 1972, 38–72 [a translation by Jeffrey Mehlman of *Ecrits*, 11–41].

'Of Structure as an Inmixing of an Otherness Prerequisite to Any Subject Whatever', in *The Structuralist Controversy*, ed. Richard Macksey and Eugenio Donato (Baltimore and London: Johns Hopkins University Press, 1970, 186–200).

Lacan: Selected Reading

Below are listed works devoted solely or principally to Lacan. Books containing chapters or sections on Lacan are to be found in the final part of this bibliography.

Benvenuto, Bice and Kennedy, Roger, *The Works of Jacques Lacan. An Introduction* (London: Free Association Books, 1986).

Brennan, Teresa, *History after Lacan* (London and New York: Routledge, 1991).

Clément, Catherine, *Vies et légendes de Jacques Lacan* (Grasset, 1981) [tr. A. Goldhammer (New York: Columbia University Press, 1983)].

Davis, Robert Con (ed.), *Lacan and Narration. The Psychoanalytic Difference in Narrative Theory* (Baltimore and London: Johns Hopkins University Press, 1983).

Dor, Joël, *Bibliographie des travaux de Jacques Lacan* (Paris: InterEditions, 1983).

Dor, Joël, *Introduction à la lecture de Lacan*, I: *L'inconscient structuré comme un langage* (Denoël: 1985).

Fages, Jean-Baptiste, *Comprendre Jacques Lacan* (Privat: 1971).

Felman, Shoshana, *Jacques Lacan and the Adventure of Insight. Psychoanalysis in Contemporary Culture* (Cambridge, Mass. and London: Harvard University Press, 1987).

Gallop, Jane, *Reading Lacan* (Ithaca and London: Cornell University Press, 1985).

Granon-Lafont, Jeanne, *La topologie ordinaire de Jacques Lacan* (Point Hors Ligne, 1985).

Grosz, Elizabeth, *Jacques Lacan. A Feminist Introduction* (London and New York: Routledge, 1990).

Jameson, Fredric, 'Imaginary and Symbolic in Lacan: Marxism, Psychoanalytic Criticism, and the Problem of the Subject', *Yale French Studies*, 55/56, 1977 (*Literature and Psychoanalysis*), 338–95.

Julien, P., *Le retour à Freud de Jacques Lacan* (Littoral, 1985).

Juranville, Alain, *Lacan et la philosophie* (Presses universitaires de France, 1984).

Kerrigan, William and Smith, Joseph H., *Interpreting Lacan*, Psychiatry and the Humanities, 6, (New Haven and London: Yale University Press, 1983).

Kremer-Marietti, Angèle, *Lacan ou la rhétorique de l'inconscient* (Aubier Montaigne, 1978).

Lemaire, Anika, *Jacques Lacan* (1970) (Brussels: Pierre Mardaga,

1977) [trans. David Macey (London: Routledge and Kegan Paul, 1977)].

MacCannell, Juliet Flower, *Figuring Lacan. Criticism and the Cultural Unconscious* (Beckenham: Croom Helm, 1986).

Macey, David, *Lacan in Contexts* (London and New York: Verso, 1988).

Marini, Marcelle, *Jacques Lacan* (Pierre Belfond, 1986).

Mehlman, Jeffrey (ed.), *French Freud. Structural Studies in Psychoanalysis* (*Yale French Studies*, 48, 1972).

Miller, Jacques-Alain, 'Encyclopédie' [a brief intellectual biography of Lacan], *Ornicar?*, 1981, No. 21, 35–44.

Miller, Jacques-Alain, *Entretien sur le Séminaire*, avec François Ansermet (Navarin, 1985).

Mitchell, Juliet and Rose, Jacqueline (eds), *Feminine Sexuality. Jacques Lacan and the 'Ecole freudienne'* (Macmillan, 1982).

Muller, John P. and Richardson, William J., *Lacan and Language. A Reader's Guide to 'Ecrits'* (New York: International Universities Press, 1982).

Ogilvie, Bertrand, *Lacan: la formation du concept de sujet (1932–49)* (Presses universitaires de France, 1987).

Palmier, Jean-Michel, *Lacan* (Jean-Pierre Delarge, 1972).

Perrier, François, *Voyages extraordinaires en Translacanie* (Lieu commun, 1985).

Ragland-Sullivan, Ellie, *Jacques Lacan and the Philosophy of Psychoanalysis* (Croom Helm and the University of Illinois Press, 1986).

Roustang, François, *Lacan: de l'équivoque à l'impasse* (Minuit, 1986).

Safouan, Moustapha, *Jacques Lacan et la question de la formation des analystes* (Seuil, 1983).

Schneiderman, Stuart, *Jacques Lacan. The Death of an Intellectual Hero* (Cambridge, Mass. and London: Harvard University Press, 1983).

Schneiderman, Stuart (editor and translator), *Returning to Freud. Clinical Psychoanalysis in the School of Lacan* (New Haven and London: Yale University Press, 1980).

Sichère, Bernard, *Le moment lacanien* (Grasset, 1983).

Stanton, Martin, *Outside the Dream. Lacan and French Styles of Psychoanalysis* (London: Routledge and Kegan Paul, 1983).

Turkle, Sherry, *Psychoanalytic Politics. Freud's French Revolution* (Burnett Books/André Deutsch, 1979).

Wilden, Anthony, ed., *The Language of the Self. The Function of Language in Psychoanalysis* ['Fonction et champ' by Jacques Lacan. Translated with notes and commentary by A.W.] (Baltimore and London: Johns Hopkins Univesity Press, 1968).

Other Works

Abrams, M.H., *Natural Supernaturalism. Tradition and Revolution in Romantic Literature* (New York and London: Norton, 1971).

Althusser, Louis, *Positions* ['Freud et Lacan', 9–34] (Editions sociales, 1976).

Aristotle, *Basic Works of Aristotle*, ed. Richard McKeon (New York: Random House, 1941).

Baltrušaitis, Jurgis, *Anamorphic Art* (1969), trans. W.J. Strachan (New York: Harry N. Abrams, 1977).

Benveniste, Emile, *Problèmes de linguistique générale* [1] (Gallimard, 1966) [on psychoanalysis and language, 75–87].

Bersani, Leo, *The Culture of Redemption* (Cambridge, Mass. and London: Harvard University Press, 1990).

Bersani, Leo, *The Freudian Body. Psychoanalysis and Art* (New York: Columbia University Press, 1986).

Bettelheim, Bruno, *Freud and Man's Soul* (London, Chatto and Windus/Hogarth Press, 1983).

Bowie, Malcolm, *Freud, Proust and Lacan. Theory as Fiction* (Cambridge and New York: Cambridge University Press, 1987).

Brennan, Teresa (ed.), *Between Feminism and Psychoanalysis* (London and New York: Routledge, 1989).

Dali, Salvador, *The Unspeakable Confessions of Salvador Dali*, as told to André Parinaud, trans. Harold J. Salemson (London: W.H. Allen, 1976).

Deleuze, Gilles and Guattari, Félix, *L'Anti-Œdipe* (*Capitalisme et schizophrénie*, I) (Minuit, 1972).

Deleuze, Gilles and Guattari, Félix, *Mille Plateaux* (*Capitalisme et schizophrénie*, II) (Minuit, 1980).

Derrida, Jacques, *L'Ecriture et la différence* (Seuil, 1967).

227

Derrida, Jacques, *La Carte postale, de Socrate à Freud et au-delà*, (Aubier-Flammarion, 1980) ['Le Facteur de la vérité' (on Lacan), 441–524].

Donato, Eugenio and Macksey, Richard (eds), *The Structuralist Controversy* (Baltimore and London: Johns Hopkins University Press, 1970).

Eagleton, Terry, *The Ideology of the Aesthetic* (Oxford and Cambridge, Mass.: Blackwell, 1990).

Ecrire la psychanalyse, Nouvelle revue de psychanalyse [Gallimard], No. 16, Autumn 1977.

Forrester, John, *Language and the Origins of Psychoanalysis* (London: Macmillan, 1980).

Forrester, John, *The Seductions of Psychoanalysis. On Freud, Lacan and Derrida* (Cambridge and New York: Cambridge University Press, 1990).

Foucault, Michel, *Histoire de la sexualité* (Gallimard. I: *La volonté de savoir*, 1976; II: *L'usage des plaisirs*, 1984; III: *Le souci de soi*, 1984).

Francion, Nicolas (ed.), *Almanach de la dissolution* (Navarin, 1986) [On the dissolution of the Ecole freudienne de Paris].

Freud, Sigmund, *Gesammelte Werke*, edited by Anna Freud and others, 18 vols (London: Imago, 1940–52 [Vols 1–17] and Frankfurt am Main: Fischer Verlag, 1968 [Vol. 18]).

Freud, Sigmund, *The Standard Edition of the Complete Psychological Works*, translated from the German under the general editorship of James Strachey, 24 vols (Hogarth Press and Institute of Psycho-Analysis, 1953–74).

Gallop, Jane, *Feminism and Psychoanalysis. The Daughter's Seduction* (London: Macmillan, 1982).

Green, André, *Un œil en trop. Le complexe d'Œdipe dans la tragédie* (Minuit, 1969).

Hartman, Geoffrey H. (ed.), *Psychoanalysis and the Question of the Text* (1978) (Baltimore and London: Johns Hopkins University Press, 1985).

Hegel, G.W.F., *Phenomenology of Spirit*, trans. A.V. Miller, with Analysis of the Text and Foreword by J.N. Findlay (Oxford: Clarendon Press, 1977).

Hegel, G.W.F., *La Phénoménologie de l'Esprit*. Traduction de Jean Hyppolite, 2 vols (Aubier Montaigne, 1939–41).

Hyppolite, Jean, *Genèse et Structure de la 'Phénoménologie de l'Esprit' de Hegel* (Aubier Montaigne, 1946).

Irigaray, Luce, *Ce sexe qui n'en est pas un* (Minuit, 1977).

Jakobson, Roman, *Language in Literature*, ed. Krystyna Pomorska and Stephen Rudy (Cambridge, Mass. and London: Harvard University Press, 1987).

Jakobson, Roman and Halle, Morris, *Fundamentals of Language* (The Hague: Mouton, 1956).

Johnson, Barbara, *The Critical Difference. Essays in the Contemporary Rhetoric of Reading* (Baltimore and London: Johns Hopkins University Press, 1980).

Kirk, G.S. and Raven, J.E., *The Presocratic Philosophers. A Critical History with a Selection of Texts* (London and New York: Cambridge University Press, 1957).

Klein, Melanie, *Envy and Gratitude and Other Works, 1946–63* (London: Hogarth Press and Institute of Psycho-Analysis, 1980).

Klein, Melanie, *The Selected Melanie Klein*, ed. Juliet Mitchell (Harmondsworth: Penguin, 1986).

Kojève, Alexandre, *Introduction à la lecture de Hegel* (Gallimard, 1947).

Krauss, Rosalind and Livingston, Jane (eds), *L'Amour fou. Photography and Surrealism* (New York and London: Abbeville Press/Arts Council, 1985, 1986).

Lacoue-Labarthe, Philippe and Nancy, Jean-Luc, *Le Titre de la lettre* (Galilée, 1973).

Laplanche, Jean and Pontalis, J.-B., *Vocabulaire de la psychanalyse* (Presses universitaires de France, 1967) [trans. Donald Nicholson-Smith as *The Language of Psycho-Analysis* (London: Hogarth Press and Institute of Psycho-Analysis, 1973)].

Leclaire, Serge and Laplanche, Jean, 'L'Inconscient. Une étude psychanalytique', in *L'Inconscient* (Desclée de Brouwer, 1966), 95–130 and 170–7 [trans. Patrick Coleman in *French Freud*, ed. Mehlman, 118–75].

Lefort, Rosine (with Robert Lefort), *Naissance de l'Autre. Deux psychanalyses: Nadia (13 mois) et Marie-Françoise (30 mois)* (Seuil, 1980).

Lévi-Strauss, Claude, *Les structures élémentaires de la parenté* (1947) (The Hague: Mouton, 1967).

Mannoni, Maud, *La théorie comme fiction. Freud, Groddeck, Winnicott, Lacan* (Seuil, 1979).

Mitchell, Juliet, *Psychoanalysis and Feminism* (Harmondsworth: Penguin, 1975).

Mounin, Georges, *Introduction à la sémiologie* (Minuit, 1970) [on Lacan, pp. 181–8].

Petersson, Robert T., *The Art of Ecstasy. Teresa, Bernini, and Crashaw* (London: Routledge and Kegan Paul, 1970).

Roudinesco, Elisabeth, *Pour une politique de la psychanalyse* (Maspero, 1977).

Roudinesco, Elisabeth, *La Bataille de cent ans. Histoire de la psychanalyse en France, Vol. I: 1885–1939* (Ramsay, 1982); *Vol. II: 1925–1985* (Seuil, 1986).

Rowlands, John, *Holbein: The Paintings of Hans Holbein the Younger* (Oxford: Phaidon, 1985).

Rycroft, Charles, *A Critical Dictionary of Psychoanalysis* (Harmondsworth: Penguin Books, 1972).

Saussure, Ferdinand de, *Cours de linguistique générale* (1916), ed. Tullio de Mauro (Payot, 1978) [trans. Wade Baskin (London: Fontana, 1974)].

Schopenhauer, Arthur, *The World as Will and Representation* (1819), trans. E.F.J. Payne (two volumes) (New York: Dover, 1969).

Segal, Hanna, *Klein* (London: Fontana Press, 1979).

Stella, Frank, *Working Space* (Cambridge, Mass. and London: Harvard University Press, 1986).

Timpanaro, Sebastiano, 'Freud's "Roman Phobia"', *New Left Review*, 147, September–October, 1984, 4–31.

Trilling, Lionel, *Sincerity and Authenticity* (London: Oxford University Press, 1972).

Wilden, Anthony, *System and Structure. Essays in Communication and Exchange* (London: Tavistock Publications, 1972).

Winnicott, D.W., *Playing and Reality* (1971) (Harmondsworth: Penguin Books, 1974).

Wright, Elizabeth, *Psychoanalytic Criticism. Theory in Practice* (London and New York: Methuen, 1984).

Lacan's *Ecrits* in French and English

The following complete list of the papers collected in *Ecrits* will enable the reader to identify the source of all my quotations from that work. The page numbers appearing in the left-hand column below refer to the original French text, and those on the right to the nine papers that comprise Alan Sheridan's *Ecrits: A Selection*. Translation details for the seminar on Poe's 'The Purloined Letter' and the 'Guiding remarks for a congress on feminine sexuality' are to be found on p. 224 and p. 220 n. 7 above.

Lacan

Lacan

Index